Tawfiq al Hakim
playwright of Egypt

Richard Long

Ithaca Press London 1979

To Dr Peter J Clark –

with gratitude and affection

Copyright © Richard Long

First published in 1979 by
Ithaca Press   13 Southwark Street   London SE 1

ISBN   0   903729   35   0

Printed in England by
Anchor Press Ltd and bound by
Wm Brendon and Sons Ltd
both of Tiptree Essex

TABLE OF CONTENTS

Preface	iii
List of Long Plays under Discussion	vii

Part One: 1   The Path to Fame

1 The Melting Pot	1
2 Paris	11
3 The Law and Arab Literature's Greatest Year	20
4 'Shahrazad' and the Debacle of 'The Cavemen'	30

  2   Neglect before Revolution

1 Political Skirmishes	39
2 The View from the Ivory Tower	48
3 In Step with the Masses	57

  3   Honour in his own Country

1 Coming to Terms	64
2 Speaking to the World	76

  4   Irrationalism and Troilus and Cressida

1 Experimentation and Consolidation	85
2 Under Two Presidents - Disenchantment and Recovery	99

Part Two: The Major Themes

1 The Human Reality: Time and Place	118
2 Woman - enigma, idol and rival	132
3 1 Egypt under the Pashawat	146
2 The Deception of the Revolution	153
Egypt, the World and the Bomb	164

Part Three: Background and Assessment   178

Appendices

1 The Egyptian Prose Theatre before Tawfiq al Hakim	202
2 The Plays of Tawfiq al Hakim	208
3 a Foreign Editions of Al Hakim Plays	212
b Production outside the Arab World	216
Further Reading: a Books and Articles	217
b Journals, etc.	222
Index	223

Preface

Though I was an undergraduate student of Arabic at Cambridge until 1961, this book did not have its beginnings until the next year when, browsing in the library of McGill University's Institute of Islamic Studies, I came quite by accident upon a play entitled 'Journey into the Future' by an Egyptian author called Tawfiq al Hakim. In my ignorance, I had not believed that Arabic was capable of transmitting contemporary thought, and the clarity and power of the language of this technology-based drama were a revelation which impelled me - an already committed 'Arabist' - to abandon then and there the early and medieval Arabic in which I had had my grounding in favour of the modern language.

My conversion did not, however, lead to much during the subsequent five years, most of which I spent in Baghdad, though I did begin to collect volumes by and about Al Hakim and other contemporary Arab men of letters in an unconcentrated kind of way. Not until the end of 1967 did the idea occur to me of making him a serious object of study, and it would probably have come to nothing had I had any inkling of the size of his output. To complete the text which follows took over seven years of my spare time, during which Al Hakim was, on the whole, an unbegrudged companion. His prolific pen was not the only factor causing delay, however. Most of the writing was done in difficult places, blessed with unpleasant climates and remote from reliable suppliers of Arabic source-materials. More relevantly, convinced of the quality of Al Hakim and other modern authors, I continually interrupted it to do articles about him, translate some of his plays and undertake more general work in the fields of contemporary Arabic and its literature. I do not regret any of this, for it elicited a gratifying response from a neglected audience.

I have incurred many debts. The Army, by sending me on an exercise to Libya during National Service, made it inevitable that I would study Arabic afterwards at Cambridge, where I was encouraged by Dr D. M. Dunlop, now at Columbia University. To McGill I owe thanks for putting twentieth-century Arabic in my path. More to the point, I am grateful for the opportunities I have had to discover for myself that modern Arabic and its literature (and Al Hakim in particular) are marketable commodities. They were afforded me by Professor Elie Kedourie, editor of <u>Middle Eastern Studies</u>, Mr John Sturrock of the <u>Times Literary Supplement</u> (and its former editor, Mr Arthur Crook), Mr Michael Binyon, at one time with the <u>Times Educational Supplement</u>, Mr Alan Gilchrist of Longman's Arab World Division, Miss Elsie Ferguson of the BBC's Further Education (Radio) Department and Mr Dan Gillon, erstwhile editor of <u>New Middle East</u>. Facilities generously made available to me at St Catharine's College, Cambridge, by Mr A. A. L. Caesar, who was my tutor, and at the University's Department of Oriental Studies and Middle East Centre libraries, by Professor R. B. Serjeant, greatly aided me.

The book which has emerged from this kindness and experimentation is not a work of literary criticism but an attempt - the first in any language - to describe Al Hakim's life and the whole of his writing together. It offers observations, in differing degrees of detail, on 32 of his 33 long plays, the major component of his huge oeuvre, and on his recurrent themes; because the plays are unknown in the United Kingdom, and because few even of the Arab critics get beyond 'The Cavemen', 'Shahrazad', 'Praksa', 'Pigmalyun', and 'Solomon the Wise', I have felt it necessary to present synopses without which no introduction to the Arab world's greatest modern author would, sadly, be of much value to a non-specialist reader. It aims to prepare students of Arabic, who are disproportionately few in the UK, to expect to find merit in contemporary Arabic literature, where British Oriental Studies do not readily admit that it exists. It seeks to interest and inform other categories of scholars, such as the compilers of encyclopaedias of world writing who at the moment either overlook or travesty Al Hakim. It has no pretensions to be of service to potential producers.

There is a surprisingly modest amount of source-material on Al Hakim in languages other than Arabic, and disturbingly little in English. My major sources are Arabic, most of them deficient, in relation to an endeavour of the present kind, in that they usually do not advertise their dates of publication. Al Hakim's own works do not, and make him needlessly difficult to chronicle. Perhaps out of deviousness, he has permitted the issuing of versions of his books which, as a rule, differ more or less from their originals (and all of which I cannot claim to have mastered); as a consequence he has prompted such serious thoughts as that the 'Soft Hands' we have is not the one applauded by President Abd an Nasir. His publisher is apparently apathetic where increasing his sales or telling the world of his achievements are concerned. Partly for this reason, Appendices 2 and 3 are rather sketchy (Al Hakim has been consistently performed on stage, radio and television throughout the Arab world, but the records are anything but complete and I have not tried to chart them), but nonetheless I considered it worth giving such information as they do contain.

In order not to deter the lay reader (it is mainly for him that I have written), I have rarely used Tawfiq al Hakim's full name, normally confining myself to the unorthodox, but not disrespectful, Hakim instead. (When part of a quotation, he appears in a variety of other guises, the retention of which accords with my policy of not altering other people's transliterations even when - Anouar Abd al-Malek is an instance - I disagree with them). Similarly, I have only Arabized Isis, Oedipus, Solomon, and other familiar figures when introducing them and not been as conscientious as I might have wished over my own transliterating. Except in quotations, I have nowhere indicated stress, vowel length, the letter ^{c}ain when initial and (apart from in Allah) the final silent ha'. I have shown final ^{c}ain (as ^{c}) and hamza (') only when I felt that it would be inappropriate to adhere to the Hawley principle.* I fear that I have not been consistent either. No distinction has been drawn between the two hs, ts, etc., of Arabic, but one has been essayed between dialectal variations of pronunciation, so that Egyptian _gim_ and Levantine _jim_, for example, both occur in the text.

Though the basic background sources of the first five chapters have not been listed and support, throughout, has not been mustered for every separate point made (unless of special interest or controversial

---

* D. F. Hawley, The Trucial States (Allen and Unwin, London, 1970) p 11: 'I have omitted as many Hamzas and ^{c}Ains as I possibly could without confusion, since a text is considerably easier for the general reader without them.'

nature), there is a regrettably large number of references. They contain almost nothing which more properly belongs to the text and need not detain those who wish only to acquire a fair idea of what I have to say without checking the accuracy of my statements. When I have had a choice of sources, as has frequently been the case, I have generally noted the most accessible one; only those which are not fully catalogued in the Further Reading list are comprehensively described in the references. Quotations from 'A Sparrow from the East' are from its most complete version, the Winder translation whose title I have not adopted.

The definitive survey of those aspects of Al Hakim which I have tried to cover here remains to be made. This one is undoubtedly imperfect, for it would be an impossibility for even a full-time Al Hakim specialist, resident in Egypt, to keep up with the whole of the ceaseless periodical, and especially daily, material by and about him. (The closure in 1970-1 of the most valuable keys to it, the journals Magallat al Magalla and Al Masrah, left an enormous gap which has yet to be filled and was further widened by the disastrous effect on Al Adib of the Lebanese civil war.) It also recounts a number of happenings for which it indicates no cause and raises several questions to which it does not supply answers. Al Hakim, whom I have tried but failed to meet, could provide clarification. It is lamentable that he should have had to wait until now before having a book in English devoted to him. It is sincerely hoped that this study of the last of the first great modern Egyptians (Taha Husayn and Mahmud Taymur died in 1973) will do something to make up for lost time. Tawfiq al Hakim is still active, and I trust will continue for years to be, if only as "the respected Al Ahram columnist" of British newspaper reports.

Richard Long
Abu Dhabi, October 1977

List of Long Plays under Discussion with publication dates and in approximate order of writing

Modern Woman	1952
The Cavemen	1933
Shahrazad	1934
Expulsion from Eden	1937
The Suicide's Secret	1937
A Life is Wrecked	1937
A Bullet in the Heart	1937
Praksa, or The Difficult Business of Ruling	1939-60
The Angel's Prayer	1941
Pigmalyun	1942
Solomon the Wise	1943
King Oedipus	1949
The Peaceful Nest	1950
The Thief	1950
Rejuvenation	1950
Soft Hands	1954
Her Majesty	1956
Isis	1955
The Deal	1956
Death Game	1957-64
The Thorns of Peace	1957
Journey into the Future	1957
The Sultan's Delemma	1960
The Tree Climber	1962
Food for Every Mouth	1963
A Hunting Trip	1964
A Train Journey	1964
Shams an Nahar	1965
The Dilemma	1966
Fate of a Cockroach	1966
The Anxiety Bank	1967
This Comic World	1971

PART ONE

1 The Path to Fame

1 The Melting Pot

> ... I knew there was a treasure-
> house in the world of literature ...
> which they were hiding from our
> eager eyes.
> (From the Ivory Tower)

The life of Tawfiq al Hakim is fairly well documented in outline, the framework being mainly provided by the autobiographies, the novels (which he vainly denies are of use for biographical purposes)[1] and works like The Literary Art. Mystery, however, clouds many details, some important. The critics, who have signally failed to produce a conscientious account of his life and writing, normally differ over dates, and Hakim, who has otherwise put a great deal of himself into his books, has done little to help them to achieve accuracy: Life's Prison, the most valuable of his pieces of autobiography, has hardly a date in it. Frequent resort to speculation is inevitable.

The date of birth of this immensely prolific playwright, short-story writer, essayist and novelist was for long in doubt, but may now be accepted with some confidence as 9 October 1898.[2] The place was never in dispute. He was born in the house of his mother's elder sister in Alexandria. His father, Isma^{c}il al Hakim, could not be present because of the exigencies of his legal duties in As Santa, where medical services were rudimentary in comparison with those available in Egypt's second city. In his absence, his wife called their son Husayn Tawfiq Isma^{c}il

Ahmad al Hakim,[3] which he did not like (he had wanted the boy named Zuhayr, after the Jahili poet Zuhayr b Abi Silmi,[4] but had to wait until the birth of his second son and last child before he could have his way) and determined to have legally changed. He did not do so. Though Hakim does not use three of his names, Husayn Tawfiq al Hakim is occasionally to be found.[5]

Isma^{c}il, the middle-class son of an Azharite who chose to live in the rif, or countryside, and owned land there,[6] had an estate of 300 acres near Damanhur[7] which the family used as its base. He held a position of some weight in the regional judiciary, had earned the honorific of Bey and, prior to his marriage at least, had been a man of considerable cultural stature, worthy to be mentioned by Aziz Abaza,[8] the prominent verse dramatist, as a poet, albeit a bad one. His wife, Asma al Bustami,[9] the daughter of an Ottoman army officer, caused Turkish blood to flow in the veins of her sons, as it did or does in those of other major Egyptian writers such as Qasim Amin, Ahmad Shawqi, Mahmud Taymur and Yahya Haqqi. She was extremely conscious of her descent from the Turkish rulers of Egypt and took care always to emphasize her difference from, and her belief in her superiority to, the Egyptians among whom she lived. Being of strong and stormy character (when she was a girl her contemporaries invariably submitted to her leadership, and she married against her widowed mother's wishes), she succeeded to a large extent in forcing her weaker husband to sever his links with the peasant circles in which he had been accustomed to move[10] and made no secret of her contempt for the fallahun who worked for him. A factor in her success was her husband's anxiety to be regarded as a member of the Turkified ruling class. His marriage certainly brought him kudos from his former social equals.[11]

The domestic atmosphere was unhappy. Tawfiq was much attached both to his father, whom he never knew as the man he once had been and with whom he had little intimate conversation, and to his father's peasant kinsmen. His mother did everything she could to sabotage these relationships in the main succeeding. To his great distress, she forbade her son to associate with his chosen friends and tried to instil in him hatred of the British overlords of Egypt. Though she seems to have devoted much time to talking to him, he loathed her and all her ways, which are crushingly described in <u>The Soul's Return</u>, and spared no effort to thwart her ambition to bring him up as a little Turkish aristocrat who dressed differently from his contemporaries, flaunted his comparative wealth and was to be addressed only as Tawfiq Bey. His mother obviously loved him but was unable to express her feelings in a form acceptable to her son. At an early age the seeds of his misogyny were sown.

The state of affairs at home greatly affected the boy, who grew up unable to communicate with a preoccupied and heavy-handed father and a misguidedly over-possessive mother. He resisted all their plans for him, spent as much time as he could by himself, became reserved and secretive, and lived on his imagination. His mental faculties developed early, and his concern for intellectual matters, the first of which were drawing and music (both of which, although his mother was fond of them,[12] he gave up because of parental ridicule),[13] displayed the remarkable precocity which has characterized many phases of his career. External influences, some of them parentally introduced, directed it towards literature and the theatre. One was the Araguz (the Turkish Karagöz, the oriental equivalent of the Punch and Judy show), his childhood delight in which he has described in The Literary Art.[14] Another was the appearance in Dusuq, where the family was at the time, of a troupe which performed the plays of Shaykh Salama Higazi and to whose production of an adaptation of Romeo and Juliet Tawfiq was reluctantly taken by his father. Not the least of them was the reading aloud to him by his mother, when she was recuperating after a long illness, of Arab stories and European tales translated into Arabic; it would be surprising if she did not also tell him Turkish stories and thus contribute something to The Cavemen, Pigmalyun and The Tree Climber. Credit is due, but lacking, to her for inspiring her son to try to read for himself, which he succeeded in learning to do before going to school.

At the age of six according to The Soul's Return, in his eighth or ninth year as stated in Life's Prison, Tawfiq became an active participant in art. (The first estimate seems, from other evidence, to be the correct one.) The longest of the 53 chapters of The Soul's Return chronicles the step, which followed the arrival of an all-female touring musical company called Al Awalim in the Alexandria area. Though it was not regarded as being wholly respectable,[15] Tawfiq contrived to attach himself to it and to establish a close relationship with its 30 year old leader, Labiba Shakhla[c], who was sympathetic towards the boy. She was a wit who sang, played the ud and, when occasion required, belly-danced. She allowed him to join in the activities of the troupe. He sang with the ladies at wedding parties, helped them to carry their props around, and worshipped her. His mother also came to approve of Labiba after the company had performed at a family celebration and, forgetting her inhibitions about mixing with lower-class persons, invited her to become a regular summer visitor to the house in Damanhur. She several times resided there for long periods and brought some cheer into the life of Tawfiq's infirm grandmother.

The effect of this early encounter with Al Awalim on the boy's future is incalculable but was obviously great. It undoubtedly confirmed him in his instincts towards the theatre and helped to shape the pattern of his juvenilia. It gave him his happiest pre-school days, which were devoid of contact with the children of his own age with whom he longed to consort.

His educational career in Egypt was noteworthy on account of his repetition of the first year of each of its three stages. His primary schooling was rendered unsatisfactory by the constant removals from one place to another entailed by his father's legal functions, but he was never able to tell his parents of his difficulties for fear of their wrath and of his father's hand or stick. By his clumsy methods Isma^{c}il, who set impossibly ambitious standards, managed to put him off poetry in his early school years, and off swimming for life. Hakim attended many primary schools of varying quality, doing well in some but finding himself struggling in others. At home, however, he read as widely as circumstances from time to time allowed, and the information which - unknown to his father - he acquired in secret and under strainful conditions (usually by the light of a candle under his bed) probably helped him to pass his primary certificate - the stage at which most of his comrades ended their education - from Damanhur infant school. Thus far he had enjoyed himself, being able to express his personality at school as he was impotent to do at home. Maintaining his links with Labiba Shakhla^c's troupe, he proceeded to secondary school, taking two years - spent in two different institutions in Alexandria - to earn promotion to the second form. He then moved, in 1915, to the Muhammad Ali Secondary School in Cairo. Contrary to what has been said by the commentators, the reason for the transfer is clear: two of his paternal uncles came from Cairo to stay, discovered that he was weak at mathematics, of which subject one of them was a teacher, and suggested that he should go to live with them in order the better to prepare for his secondary certificate. His mother and father were both pleased by the proposal and agreed that his childhood, which had been miserable whenever he had not been away from home, should end at this point.

The household in the Sayyida Zaynab quarter in Cairo consisted of three of Isma^{c}il's brothers, one of his sisters and a male servant.

Tawfiq's mother despised them all. It is strange, therefore, that she should have consented to her son boarding with them. He found the arrangement greatly to his liking and revelled in his translation from the restraint and tensions of home to the free and easy atmosphere which prevailed in his relatives' house, where he shared a bedroom with the uncles and the servant and pulled his full weight. He remained with them until halfway through his time as an undergraduate and then rented a small villa where his brother Zuhayr - a dancing enthusiast and playboy with a serious side, who later furthered his agricultural studies in Toulouse and whose character he envied - joined him to complete his schooling.

Tawfiq did not enjoy his secondary education which, despite his general neglect of his studies, was completed in 1921 when he had already attained the advanced age of 22. It was seriously interrupted by the uprising of 1919 and its lengthy aftermath. His bakaluriyya (baccalaureat) must have been of above-average merit for, according to some sources, it provoked a contest with his parents about the higher academic discipline he should pursue. He had taken no part in prescribed extra-mural activities but, having decided that writing was to be his metier,[16] concentrated entirely on literary matters. He did not mix much and was regarded by his fellows, who respected him, as an intellectual. His teachers gave him individual attention, but he was impressed by neither their abilities or methods:

> '... School did everything to make literature distasteful to me and to make me afraid of language. It set before me the most loathsome (from the points of view of meaning and thought) of Arabic books, the most difficult in language and composition, and the least suitable for introducing a budding spirit to the beauty of creation. School taught me to hate Arabic poetry ...
> '... I remember that English literature inspired me to write a short play when I was at secondary school. I took it proudly to the teacher of Arabic literature, only to be rewarded by a contemptuous lack of interest. But, in fairness, I must record that a brave master one day risked introducing us to verses ... of Al Abbas b al Ahnaf ... From that day I knew there was a treasure-house in the world of literature and poetry which they were hiding from our eager eyes.'[17]

If Hakim regarded his secondary schooling as of little direct utility, the years in Cairo during which he underwent the bulk of it afforded him valuable formative experience in three distinct extra-curricular areas. His second traumatic encounter with the opposite sex is narrated in detail in The Soul's Return. He fell in love with the beautiful daughter of the retired doctor who lived next door. In the novel he calls her Saniyya. He was to teach her to sing (he apparently had a fine voice) while her formal role was to instruct him in the piano. For a short time the relationship appeared to develop romantically well. Then Tawfiq had, unwillingly, to go home to Damanhur for a ten-day school break. He returned after five, impelled by a letter from his aunt which he believed Saniyya had written, and already worn down by his mother's unbearable behaviour towards her husband's employees. But he not only found that Saniyya (to whom it was only a game) was not his correspondent but that the aunt had delivered the coup de grace by accusing her of being a slut. There was soon to be some justification for the use of this term but, before it was adduced, Tawfiq made a desperate effort to persuade the girl to allow them to continue where he believed they had left off. It failed pitifully, and he departed from their last meeting having deposited with her a mass of poetry and prose he had penned in praise of her. He sank into depression, both mental and physical, from which he was superficially rescued only by his keen, if undistinguished, participation in the stirring events of the following year. All the critics agree that the Saniyya episode gave him a shock from which he has never completely recovered.

He took part in political activities for the first time in his life when he became an anti-British activist during the revolution which followed the exiling of Sa^{c}ad Zaghul to Malta in March 1919. He chose as his contribution the composition of patriotic songs (sometimes both music and words), some of which gained popular currency. For his pains he was arrested on a conspiracy charge and interned with his uncles, in the Cairo citadel; thanks to his father's efforts they were soon transferred to the citadel's hospital. His imprisonment was brief and sounds to have been far from uncomfortable, and he was soon back with his parents in the introspective condition which was the invariable concomitant of proximity to them.

Finally during this phase, in which he reports that he had the greatest difficulty in obtaining playscripts to read, he gave evidence of his growing commitment to the theatre as his chosen medium of artistic expression. While at the Muhammad Ali Secondary School he wrote a number of plays for Al Awalim suitable for conversion into musicals, and in 1918 or 1919 composed the first of his post-adolescence pieces. Called

The Burdensome Guest (Ad Dayf ath Thaqil), it was an attack on the British occupiers of his country. A Cairo theatre accepted it[18] but did not stage it because it did not get past the British censor.[19]

Encouragement came from play-going whenever time and money permitted. Particularly important was his presence at productions by Georges Abyad, whom he considered the pioneer of tragedy in Egypt and greatly admired, of translated works such as Oedipus Rex, Othello and Hamlet and, to a much lesser extent, by Abd ar Rahman Rushdi of translated melodramas. He formed a youthful troupe of three which established a small, but sometimes well-attended, theatre at one of its member's homes and for which he both wrote and produced plays.

In 1921 he entered the Law School of what became in 1925 the Egyptian (now Cairo) University. This was against his own wishes to further his studies at the College of Arts but in deference to the determination of his father that he should train for a legal career. Little has emerged about the four years he spent as an undergraduate beyond allegations that some of the Englishmen who taught him were inadequately qualified and - notably a Mr Melville - used to arrive for lectures in a drunken condition, and the fact that he was a student of no particular talent, had to repeat the first year, allowed his studies to be much disrupted by writing plays and attending rehearsals, and obtained his lisans (licentiate) in 1925.[20] (In the same year Yahya Haqqi, the critic and writer of short stories who was born in 1905, also graduated from the Law School and Muhammad Mandur [1907-65], 'the greatest critic our modern literature has known'[21] and an austere commentator on Hakim's work, enrolled.) The university, like school, possessed few texts of plays, but he nevertheless stepped up his dramatic output during his time there, writing the remainder of his pre-Paris juvenilia: Aminusa, a musical inspired by De Musset, which was handed over unfinished to a fellow student to do what he liked with in 1922;[22] Modern Woman (Al Mar'a al Gadida, 1923); The Bridegroom (Al Aris, an adaptation from the French, 1924); Solomon's Ring (Khatim Sulayman, 1924, a 'comic opera'[23] modified from the French in conjunction with Mustafa Mumtaz and supplied with music by a pupil of Ahmad Abu Khalil al Qabbani,[24] Kamil al Khal^{c}i[25], whose fee was £E 30 - the renowned Sayyid Darwish had asked for £E 600);[26] and The Suitor (Al Khatib, 1924). He completed most of Ali Baba, an operetta (1925). None of these was printed at the time, but the original Act Two of the second,[27] the whole of it as published - much altered[28] - in 1952, and Act Four of the last,[29] which was finished in France,[30] have been preserved. Modern Woman, as we now have it, is an unremarkable approach to the subject of women's emancipation which concentrates not so much on the rights and wrongs of the campaign to abolish the veil as on attempting to discredit female claims that friendship between the sexes is possible and not necessarily an excuse for immorality. This long play, well written in the colloquial, is not unworthy of its author[31] and is perhaps a late comment on the treatise of the same name published in 1901 by Qasim Amin. In it Hakim shows himself to be a proponent of love. The extant act of Ali Baba, also in the colloquial, is unambitiously amusing; Mandur has miscalculated in stating it to be Hakim's third drama. For the rest, the titles of the plays about which we have no knowledge give the clue to two of his major future preoccupations - legend, and the relations between the sexes. Adham may be right in saying that his incentive to write during this period came more and more from the increasing attention drawn to the theatre by plays of Farah Antun, Muhammad Lutfi Gum^{c}a, Ibrahim Ramzi and Muhammad Taymur which he undoubtedly saw. He is also probably correct in remarking that Hakim would have published his early plays at a later date if they had contained 'anything much in the way of art', a view shared by Abd as Subur.

It is not clear when Hakim ceased to be an active collaborator with Al Awalim. It seems likely, however, that The Burdensome Guest was originally intended for them and that the five later works (not including Aminusa) were all directed towards the Akasha company, a troupe with some national stature managed by the hard-dealing Zaki Bey Akasha in its headquarters in the Uzbakiyya Gardens in Cairo. The company, whose productions gave music and song a prominent place[32] despite the poor quality of its singers, performed The Suitor,[33] Solomon's Ring [34] and The Bridegroom - for which Hakim was paid £E 20 - in 1924, and Modern Woman (without success)[35] and Ali Baba in 1926 while their author was in Paris. In a reference to his pre-Paris writing Hakim describes it scathingly as having been 'after the fashion current at that time', and elsewhere he says that he did not really begin to leave adaptation behind until after his return from Europe. Nevertheless the products of this period were, according to Abd as Subur, more popular with audiences than his later works, and Landau says[36] that the Akasha company put them on at a number of theatres and that they are still performed by new or amateur groups. Rizzitano[37] is in agreement with this latter statement which, if true, would suggest that the task of collecting texts of the unpublished plays[38] is not an insuperable one. They, and his regular attendance at theatrical performances, made Hakim well known in Cairo stage circles, a fact he concealed from his parents by having himself professionally styled Husayn Tawfiq, under which name he contributed a number of articles to the magazine At Tamthil (The Dramatic Art).[39]

To judge from the flimsy documentation, he had to date made his mark by drawing selective inspiration from the melting-pot of the contemporary Egyptian stage and not by bringing to the light of day much that was original. Already, however, he seems to have been writing only in prose and had certainly decided that the farce was not for him. Otherwise he had followed the other two major trends of the times by dipping into the classics (Ali Baba) and co-operating closely with the musicians. There appears to be no reason to suppose that he could not have continued to base himself on the methods of Abyad and Wahbi for another decade and eventually been able to command higher fees for his work. He was already an established author, Zaki Akasha was anxious to produce him and, in all, he had made a promising beginning. But for Paris he might easily have earned for himself a mention in histories of modern Arabic literature without deviating from paths already well signposted.

REFERENCES

1 Dawara 2, p 34
2 Mallakh, pp 5, 102, 163, Naqqash, p 55, TAY, p 164. Cf SD, p 111
3 Mallakh, p 168
4 Ibid, p 165
5 Eg on the scroll presented to him with his qiladat al gumhuriyya in 1958 and in Who's Who in the Arab World?, 1971-2, Beirut, p 1248
6 LA, p 275
7 K. Schoonover, MW 45, 1, p 27
8 In Dawara 2, p 153
9 Mallakh, p 193, where her photograph appears
10 Naqqash, p 61
11 Ibid, loc cit
12 Mallakh, p 170
13 LL, p 198
14 pp 42-7. See also TF, p 17
15 K. A. Vasileva, in an appendix to The Sultan's Dilemma, p 212. Hakim in Al Ahram, 13 August 1971

16 LL, loc cit
17 FTIT, pp 110-2, LIB, pp 132-6
18 Naqqash, p 56
19 Ibid, p 55, Papadopoulo, pp 226-7
20 Mandur 2, p 9, and Papadopoulo, p 222, incorrectly have 1924
21 Dawara 2, pp 171-2
22 Cf TF, pp 18-19
23 See playbill in Mallakh, p 173
24 Najm, p 121
25 On whom, see TF, pp 28-32
26 LA, p 50
27 In Ra^{c}i, pp 168-95
28 Ibid, p 11
29 In ibid, pp 196-208
30 Ibid, p 22
31 Shukri, pp 22 and 95, disagrees
32 Ra^{c}i, in UNESCO, p 88
33 Papadopoulo, p 227
34 Dawara 1, p 258
35 Ra^{c}i, p 10
36 p 101
37 In OM 23, p 256
38 Dawara 1, loc cit, has appealed for the scripts of Hakim's juvenilia to be surrendered by the groups possessing them, for the sake of the history of the theatre
39 See those reproduced in LA, pp 168-71 and 172-4

Hakim boarding the boat to France

2 Paris

If Taha Husayn was at heart an educator and Haykal a politician, Tawfiq al Hakim was the one writer who was essentially an artist comparable to the familiar French prototype.
(Nadav Safran)

The game was up when Zaki Akasha brought one of Hakim's plays to Alexandria and the true identity of Husayn Tawfiq was betrayed to his parents. Although they did not approve, his father seems to have taken the revelation calmly. Hakim having, to his great surprise, obtained his lisans (he was third from bottom on the pass list), the question now became where, non-theatrically speaking (a dramatic career was unthinkable), he should go from there. Isma^{c}il had his own unpalatable ideas, but nonetheless opted to put the matter into the hands of Ahmad Lutfi as Sayyid (1872-1963), who had been a contemporary and friend of his at the Law School.

Lufti as Sayyid, one of the most imposing figures in modern Egyptian thought, spent a number of years after graduation in the government legal service before emerging as a founding member of the People's Party (1907) and the editor of its mouthpiece Al Garida. With the appointment of Sir Eldon Gorst as British Agent and Consul-General and the coming of the First World War, the party and the newspaper went into decline, and in 1915 As Sayyid was appointed Director of the National Library. He was a member of Sa'ad Zaghlul's political circle in the period which preceded the events of 1919, and joined the Wafd party. When he quickly fell out with Zaghlul, he occupied himself for two decades in the Egyptian University, which he had helped to establish, first as Professor of Philosophy and then as Rector. He became, and remained until his death, the first president (the second was Taha Husayn) of what is now the (Cairo) Arabic Language Academy, and later attained ministerial rank. His significance in the short term for Hakim and his great influence on twentieth-century Arabic letters stemmed from the fact that his political philosophy caused him to adopt, and to be the chief spokesman of, the modernist school of literary thinking, and that, at this time at any rate, he was wholeheartedly in favour of close cultural contact with the West and especially with France. Isma'il naturally wished his son to take up the law and had, indeed, already selected a chamber for him to practise in, but his famous old friend said that the answer was for Hakim to proceed - as he himself had not - to Europe.

The advice was taken, even though it spoiled his mother's plans for a rich marriage, partly because his parents believed that thus they would shield their son from the evil world of the theatre. It is not clear why Paris was picked, though this was where Lutfi as Sayyid would have recommended. Nor is it evident how Hakim, unconsciously emulating the example of Taha Husayn, who had worked closely with As Sayyid for a long time, gained entry to the Sorbonne. It is certain, however, that Isma'il and his wife had no conception of the mistake they were making, as they would have seen it, in allowing their son to be let loose in the intellectual capital of the world. Nor did they appreciate how deep already was his attachment to art, or how little genuine interest he had in the law, which before him Muhammad Husayn Haykal (1889-1956) and Muhammad Taymur (1892-1921) had studied in France. (The former, a relative and student of As Sayyid, wrote his pioneering novel Zaynab there.) In his turn Hakim was to be followed to the Sorbonne by Muhammad Mandur.

On arrival at the College des Lois in the autumn of 1925, the still introverted Hakim broke all but completely with the law. He undertook no organized academic programme, attending only lecture-courses on subjects which attracted him[1] (including a good many on art and one given by James Joyce on the history of English poetry), and eventually failed to obtain the doctorate he had ostensibly set out for: 'My nature [was] made to fly in space, not to fall into the chains of doctorates and limited university knowledge.' Finding himself in an unimagined world of infinite culture ('Paris ... was an open book, the Book of the Higher Life')[2] he threw himself into Western art, which in turn fostered his own. He filled his three-year sojourn with an astonishing amount of reading, seeing, writing, thinking and living, unrelieved by holidays. French posed no problems for him since it had been the chief language of his Law School course. Suitably enough, while disapproving of the godlessness of Europe, he turned into a bohemian, in order perhaps to show that he felt himself, as a 'sparrow from the East', to be different from most of his fellow-students - 'I do not dress like the rest and I do not smoke because smoking is a habit much in evidence. Perhaps I would smoke if the rest gave up.' He seems to have led a lonely life: his only regular visitor, in his remote first digs at least, was Husayn Fawzi, who in 1925 began five years of research in oceanography.[3]

He read on average 100 pages a day, making, like Hemingway, periodic visits to Sylvia Beach's bookshop in order to restock. The breadth of his reading may be judged from the mention in A Sparrow from the East of Anacreon, Plato, Umar-e Khayyam, Hafiz, Poe, Maeterlinck, Gide, Valery and Cocteau; in Life in Bud of Homer, Aeschylus, Sophocles, Euripides, Aristotle, Cervantes, Lope de Vega, Calderon de la Barca, Moliere, Goethe, Ibsen, Nietszche, Rimbaud, Wilde, Blasco Ibanez, Joyce and Huxley; and in Abd as Subur of De Musset. His major initial foray, perhaps undertaken as a result of his respect for Abyad, was into Aeschylus, Sophocles, Euripides and Aristophanes, whom he deemed the sources of the true drama and the ancestors of Europe's flourishing theatre - the tragedies composed for which, however, he saw as corruptions of those of the masters - and for whom he conceived a deep admiration. He likewise rated Russian and French literature highly but summed up the English authors he devoured as 'adventurist', 'in the widest, most beautiful and most noble sense'. They epitomised 'the literature of roaming the seas', as against the French 'literature of rest'. Their adventurism was displayed in Raleigh, Defoe, Scott and Stevenson (marine); Dickens and Galsworthy (social); Shakespeare and Byron (human and psychological); Macaulay and Carlyle (historical); and Wells and Shaw (intellectual). This sweeping and inadequate judgement, made by an almost entirely self-tutored student whose only guides were the views he had picked up in his own country and in the heady world of his paradise of learning - which, it should be noted, afforded him playscripts in abundance for the first time in his experience - should not be too harshly dismissed. There is, indeed, some vague insight in it, and the fact remains that he has not been uninfluenced by English literature. He much enjoyed Shaw at this time and granted qualified approval to <u>Ulysses</u> and <u>Point Counter Point</u>. (He 'knew' English by the age of 15[4] and read the latter at least in the original.)

He was astonished to find that, in Europe, unstaged plays were considered, 'between the covers of a book', to be art. He says that before he left for France no Arab dramatist had sought that label for his unperformed work and that thus a rift had developed unchecked between the theatre and 'literature'. The idea of publishing plays, or expecting them to be the object of serious critical regard before they had been produced, did not occur even to Ahmad Shawqi. Arab letters would not have countenanced such even from him.[5] In Hakim's opinion[6] the diametrically opposed European attitude, which he believed Egypt could come to adopt, arose out of Europe's inheritance of the Greek theatrical legacy. He claimed later and with justice that <u>The Cavemen</u>, <u>Shahrazad</u> and <u>Pigmalyun</u> were not written to be acted and that he had given up aiming at the theatre very early - possibly during his Paris period.[7]

He did not, however, spend a large proportion of the time he devoted in Paris to the European examples of his favourite genre brooding over playscripts in his lodgings. On the contrary, having noted with satisfaction a phenomenon not met with before, he focussed his energies on the live stage, frequenting the theatres and the Opera, revelling in Pirandello, by whom he was dazzled,[8] Ibsen and Shaw, and delighting in the poetry of the Folies Bergeres and the Moulin Rouge.[9]

He considered it 'a catastrophe that I should be ignorant of any single one of the arts, or of any branch of knowledge.'[10] He describes himself as 'Reading and reading until I had read everything. I left myself uninformed about nothing of the history of intellectual activity. I drank deep of the literature, philosophy and arts of all the nations.' The same went for the sciences, for music and, of course, for art. It is on the face of its surprising that, with Arab music as his background, he should have so quickly taken to, and fallen in love with, that of the West. But he was no great devotee of the oriental kind,[11] and Beethoven particularly, Stravinsky, Mozart, Schumann, Schubert, Richard Strauss and Wagner outdistanced it, in his judgement, by so much that it became of almost no concern to him. The scale of his concert-going was formidable. His favourite composer (Beethoven), whom Stravinsky later replaced in his affections, had a significant impact on him both at this time and during his subsequent career. His attachment to the art he found available in Paris is shown by his claim that, at one period of his stay at least, he spent the whole of every Sunday in the Louvre.

His determined pursuit of every accessible aspect of European culture led him almost inevitably to another traumatic confrontation with Woman. This time she took the form of Emma Durand, a girl employed in the booking-office of the Odeon - where, unknown to him, Zaki Tulaymat was a directly contemporary student.[12] The episode, which lasted only two weeks, occurred very soon after his arrival in France. It is idealised in his autobiographical novel A Sparrow from the East, in which Emma is disguised as Suzy Dupont (and the author as Muhsin), and lifted him out of the depressed condition he had carried with him from Egypt. It also forced him momentarily to lay aside his survey of his artistic surroundings, which - absurdly - rankled with him for many years and crops up in a number of the plays of his early maturity. He went back to his theatre and music, but not, it would appear, to his former psychological state, when the relationship ended. It had a limited literary usefulness in that it provoked him to write a playlet in French entitled Devant Son Guichet. Dedicated to Emma and dated 1926, it consists mainly of a lively duologue between Muhsin and Suzy. Though probably composed after Emma had rejected him for another,[13] it is, like the related portions of A Sparrow from the East, entirely free of bitterness of tone. It was first published, later, in a journal called Magallati (edited by Ahmad as Sawi Muhammad, who translated it into Arabic) in which Expulsion from Eden, A Bullet in the Heart and at least two more of his plays made their initial appearance in print.

He was amazed by the freedom enjoyed by European women but, despite his family's warnings, readily[14] took advantage of it in further affairs, like that he had with Sacha Schwarz. She is probably the Rim referred to in The Temple Dancer, and their squalid three month cohabitation is recounted in much the longest letter in Life in Bud.[15] In this case at least Hakim got his own back on Woman, treating Sacha most unkindly after ceasing to love her as soon as she had given herself to him. He would seem eventually to have made a total sacrifice of Venus to Apollo.

He completed Ali Baba in France and, in addition to Devant son Guichet, penned a slim collection of poems (1926-7, but not published until 1964) and two other books. (A third, The Dream - Al Hulm - receives a mention, but no details are known of it; another, to have been a three-volume work on the history, theories and problems of art, was torn up after 50 pages, to his eventual regret.) The first was Al Awalim, a story of some charm and skill. As its name implies, it was written in honour of the troupe which nurtured his childhood inclinations towards the theatre; as was appropriate, the dialogues of which it is mostly made up are in extreme colloquial. It was finished in June 1927, and had been designed to form only part of a larger book which came out in 1934 as The Artists; it was subsequently included in the second edition of The Temple Dancer. Of far greater import than the totality of his other writing was The Soul's Return, an autobiographical novel of well over 500 pages which also was completed in 1927.[16] It is not evident whether or not he composed the whole of it in Paris or had embarked upon it before leaving Egypt. According to Shukri, it was initially in French and only later put into Arabic. This would have been a mammoth undertaking, but one of which the remarkably industrious Hakim was by no means incapable. In support of the claim is the fact that it was not published for six years; against are Hakim's declaration in Life's Prison that he withheld it for a long time in order to construct an even larger work around it[17] and his statement, in a 1934 letter to Taha Husayn,[18] that 'I have spent the years revising what I write before I publish it ...' The Soul's Return only narrowly escaped destruction at his hands for, realizing that he could not cope with it and his book on art simultaneously, he came close to jettisoning it because of the insecure status of the novel form in Arabic,[19] which had made Haykal too fearful to admit his authorship of Zaynab.[20] Having decided not to, Hakim proceeded consciously to found the Arab novel.[21]

While he was writing in France, he was hurt by the scornful tone of Egyptian newspaper revewis of plays of his being staged in Cairo. They and the examples of Pirandello and the rest, perhaps helped persuade him to abandon 'the easy art' of his juvenilia, with its 'facile, guaranteed success' with the public, if not with the critics. He did not, however, finish a play in Paris apart from Ali Baba and Devant Son Guichet, though he laboured on The Cavemen.

It was not without a struggle that he was able to reconcile the lessons of his past with the feast set before him in Paris. Convinced of the need, superficially by no means accomplished, to preserve his eastern spirit from the materialism and lax attitudes of Europe ('Under the hot breath of modern culture my own faith is trembling like a fragile petal'),[22] he managed at the same time to avoid taking up an extreme stance as between East and West. He contrived intellectually to balance the corruption, as he saw it, of the East by the West and the potential of the latter for the universal good.[23] It was extraordinary that he should have been able to do so in view of his early rejection by the West as represented by Emma Durand. His position is defined in Muhsin's conversations, in A Sparrow from the East, with Ivanovitch, the Soviet emigre with starry-eyed ideas about the purity of the East, to whom Hakim elsewhere [24] acknowledges his debt. It enabled him to construct a bridge between himself and European culture across which he has since frequently passed and which, broadly speaking, was of the kind advocated by As Sayyid and Tagore - one of his idols - for the freeing of their countries from the Western yoke.[25] (There are no grounds seriously to suppose that, then or later, Hakim saw his as serving this purpose.) He felt the necessity for another bridge, becoming a passionate believer in the interdependence of the various arts: 'I realized that there was no way of understanding an art-form other than through knowledge of the rest of the arts.' He cites Beethoven's friendship with Goethe, explains how an apposite accompanying filmstrip helped him finally to understand Stravinsky's 'Rite of Spring' and regrets that the strong and helpful collaboration between the different arts of the days of Kitab al Aghani was absent from the modern Arab world. (This was his sentence of death on the operetta as, with the assistance of various composers, he had practised it in Egypt. It foreshadowed his speedy abandonment of the philosophy of interdependence which he passed on to Nagib Mahfuz.)[26]

Life in Bud and, to a lesser degree, A Sparrow from the East record the minutiae of his life in these momentous years for him and for Arabic literature. The former is a collection of letters of highly, and often nauseating and ponderous, intellectual content, written to Andre, the friend with whose parents he lodged at one period during his Paris days. None of them is fully dated; the first few were written in Paris, the large majority after his return to Egypt. They were originally in French, but he translated them into Arabic in 1937-8 and they were published in 1943. The salient theme of the two books is the as yet unrevealed impact of Europe (he calls it 'my true contact with civilization'), both classical and modern ('I cannot say with the "revolutionaries", "Away with the old," for the old is ... new for me'), on the drama of a born writer - one who, before he had mastered his new environment and although he was not destined to be a novelist of wide international repute, had already set up in The Soul's Return one of the landmarks of the Arab novel. Another is the effect on him of living in the Christian world, which was to influence his writing in unusual and largely unremarked fashion.

The phase came to an end in mid-1928 when he was found wanting by the examiners, whom, too late, he had striven hard and worriedly to please. He did well in the History of Ideology and Economic Doctrine (from Aristotle to Marx), Political Economy, and Industrial Law, and only fell down on Finance. This, however, was enough. He bolstered himself with the thoughts that his study of the prescribed texts had been nothing to him beside the rest of his reading and that his personality was not one suited to examinations, but was overcome with apprehension lest his failure meant 'the great disaster' whose 'hour I have so often anticipated with dismay and consternation'. It did, and he left 'beloved Paris' for 'my desert' on the evening of 24 May 1928, after receiving communications from his father ordering him home, threatening him with condign punishment if he used for other purposes the money sent him for the journey, stating that a legal post awaited him, and making it plain that he would not be permitted to attempt to live by his pen. The recession in Egyptian letters soon brought appreciation of one reason for this condition, which he accepted with unwilling and temporary understanding. His last communication from Paris to Andre, announcing his departure, was, typically, half taken up with thoughts on contemporary music and on two performances of Hamlet. He would have liked another two years in Paris.

REFERENCES

1 Details in LIB, p 50
2 IST, p 134
3 I. A. Ibrahim,'Isma^{C}il Mazhar and Husayn Fawzi: two Muslim "Radical" Westernisers', MES 9, 1, pp 35-41
4 The Soul's Return 2, p 51
5 Preface to King Oedipus, p 12
6 Ibid, pp 13-14
7 Preface to Pigmalyun
8 Farag, p 79
9 LA, p 38
10 Ibid, p 60. Cf the eponymous short story The Devil's Pact
11 LIB, p 174. Cf the later Justice and Art, p 94
12 Landau, p 92
13 Cf Mallakh, p 192, who believes that Hakim wrote it the night before his first approach to Emma and handed it to her when he made his initial demarche

14 Mallakh, p 186
15 Mallakh's account, in pp 143-154, differs somewhat in detail
16 Naqqash, p 56
17 See also Tarabishi, p 186
18 Husayn, p 116
19 Mallakh, p 135
20 Ibid, loc cit
21 Ibid, p 136
22 IST, p 125, LA, pp 125-6, 270-1. Cf Taymur, p 47
23 Taha Husayn, who in theory went further by detecting no basic difference between the Egyptian and European minds (eg in Chapter 6 of Mustaqbal ath Thaqafa fi Misr), in practice did the same
24 In LIB, pp 25, 68
25 See Naqqash, pp 14-16, 18, 28
26 Dawara 2, p 272

3 The Law and Arab Literature's Greatest Year

> I am not sure it would be considered quite decorous for me as a Clerk of Session to write novels.
> (Sir Walter Scott)

> ... there is but one book in Arabic, and that the Arabian Nights.
> (Ronald Storrs, Orientations)

Hakim's first letter to Andre from Alexandria, where he discovered that no job had after all been reserved for him, was desolate. The second was no more cheerful: 'I am living in an intellectual climate - if Egypt has anything you could call such - which someone like me cannot live in;' his former friends had nothing to offer to lift his sense of complete isolation. The third letter reiterated these sentiments: 'I'm tired of everything and everybody and I have no faith that a country like Egypt will in the foreseeable future acquire an intellectual life. There is no life in Egypt for those who live for thought.' The prospect of a post in the law was oppressing him and he was in a mood to 'smash' his future and everything else as well. The fifth letter emphasized his feeling that he had become an anomaly: 'I am in one valley, everyone else is in another. They look at me and say, "He's either stupid or a genius." I never remember people making any (other) judgements about me ... One group, among them my father, says I'm stupid; another, among them my mother, says I'm a genius.' (His father, according to Aziz Abaza,[1] was most scathing at this time about the play-writing aspirations of 'this worthless youth'.) Halfway through Life in Bud he is still disoriented, complaining that he is unable to indulge in friendships, let alone love. Later still he speaks of himself as being out of his time and says that the cultured people in Egypt may be counted on the fingers of two hands. The number of professional theatre companies, he calculated inexactly, had fallen to nil, that of Zaki Akasha among others having gone bankrupt and ceased operations. 'The theatre in Egypt ... had died,' killed by the reverberations of the slump and by 'the wrangling of the political parties [which] had distracted minds from art and its practitioners.'[2] Only amateur groups were available to produce the plays he was to complete in the next five or six years, since Wahbi and Ar Rihani were not likely to be attracted by his new style.

It took some time for his legal service to begin, and then it was only in the form of a pre-appointment apprenticeship to the office of the public prosecutor of Alexandria. After some months in this he was not selected for establishment in the legal corps. He meanwhile persevered with his writing, in French (though it cannot have been for long) according to Abd as Subur, and set himself to study the literature of his own people. With regard to the theatre, he came to the conclusion, not unexpectedly, that, consisting as it did of only two elements (tears and laughter), it required a third - the cultural, such as he had witnessed in Paris.

Mandur criticizes him during this waiting period for failing to make close contact with the Egyptian people. If he did not do so this was hardly a matter for censure, given his unwilling return to an imperfectly-remembered homeland and his uncertain job situation within a sphere of work for which he had long before lost all appetite. In any case, he was rounding off The Cavemen; he had had four versions in draft, and the final one was begun and completed in Egypt in 1928.[3] It is vital to note that he wrote of it, to Andre, at this time that

> 'it is neither contemporary nor historical, and not even a true play ... Perhaps it is neither more nor less than an artistic work based on dialogue - a literary dialogue for reading only. It has never occurred to me to offer it for production. The expression "play-acting" (tashkhis) which exposed me to abuse at the time of my first literary efforts [a reference presumably to the critiques which had reached him in Paris] continues to ring in my ears ... My present purpose is to give dialogue a genuine

> literary worth so that it may be read on the basis that it is literature and thought ... (The work) is not one of significance. I do not regard it as out-shining my earlier manuscripts to any degree.'

This statement, which demonstrates his intention to emulate the European way of doing things, is the unanswerable last word in the artificial debate, to break out later, as to whether or not The Cavemen and others of his plays were designed for production. It is, though no further comment was necessary, backed up by Ar Ra^{c}i,[4] who says that Hakim decided to opt for publication rather than the stage when, on his return from France, he realized what a poor state the theatre was in. This is, of course, correct, performance at some time under the right circumstances by no means being excluded:

> '... No writer gets it into his head to write a play for reading only, without imagining it staged, however difficult this might be. Even one who publishes a play first is really aiming to stage it in the reader's mind while its production in the theatre remains difficult for some reason.'[5]

In 1929 Hakim finished Expulsion from Eden (Al Khurug min al Ginna), the first of a series of dramas which The Cavemen was to precede into print. Originally called A Woman's Inspiration (Al Mulhima), it harks back to the Emma Durand episode and is, despite its sentimentality, worthwhile. Its third and final act in particular is full of autobiographical allusion. A full-scale work, it has not been performed at national level in Egypt, but has been seen in Syria[6] since 1959 and, in the mid-1960s, made into a bad film;* it has not been translated, as it deserves to be. Post Mortem (Ba^{c}ad al Mawt), a polished and witty comedy in literary Arabic whose story-line is extremely slight, was finished in the same year. It is an exercise in misogyny, whereas its predecessor was a statement of non-comprehension of the female psyche.

In 1930 Hakim's official horizons widened when he was established and appointed second-in-command to the public prosecutor in Tanta, a post from which he was later transferred to be effectively head both of the public prosecutorship and of the law court of Dusuq, a small town of some importance. He was appalled to find that the law only brooked dis-

---

* Sa^{c}ad ad Din Tawfik, pp 142-3, Tarabishi, p 90. Mallakh, p 222, credits Hakim with eight films, among them 'Expulsion from Eden', 'A Bullet in the Heart', 'A Rural Deputy's Diary', 'The Sacred Bond', and 'Soft Hands'. 'The Wedding Night' is another.

cussion of 'shop' matters in off-duty conversation and that his career would be jeopardized if his connection with the theatre came to light - not that he viewed the law in the long term as a career, but merely as a temporary means of keeping the wolf from the door. He hated Dusuq and needlessly feared lest his time-consuming official duties snuff out his inspiration for good. In fact they provided him with plenty of material for use in his second best novel, A Rural Deputy's Diary, which he completed in Tanta in 1933, and later in Justice and Art, and afforded him the leisure - though, if The Diary is to be believed, it must have been leisure reclaimed from sleep - to finish three more long plays. During the same period he had to parry determined attempts by his family to marry him off.

The first of the plays, written in 1930, was A Life is Wrecked (Hayatun Tahattamat), the best of those ante-dating the publication of The Cavemen. Set in the rif, its rural background undoubtedly owes much to Hakim's experience at the time but, though Shahin, the character who is undone, is a lawyer in Tanta, the autobiographically derivative material is of no significance. In the colloquial, it concerns a man who goes off the rails when his wife leaves him for another and kills himself at the end with a revolver belonging to his usurper. There is much that is good in it: the masterly realism of the scenes in which Shahin is arrested by a nightwatchman when bent on vengeance and in which his endeavour disastrously fails; the humour and dramatic incident; and the almost cathartic effect of Shahin's plight and consequent suicide. The play's sequel, the one-act The Piper (Az Zammar, written in the same year), reintroduces many of the same characters without being in any way noteworthy.

A Bullet in the Heart (Rasasatun fi' l Qalb) has enjoyed greater favour. Also in the colloquial, it was completed in 1931 and was written specifically for an amateur company, The Drama Supporters' Club (Gam^{c}iyyat Ansar at Tamthil), with the object of persuading it to move away from the Kishkish Bey type of performance. The Club did not produce it, but Hakim later recast it as a scenario for a film (1944)[7] in which Muhammad Abd al Wahhab, supported by Ali al Kassar, took the chief role and which led to an exchange of words in the press between Hakim and Ahmad as Sawi Muhammad.[8] It is the only long play written before The Cavemen came out to have been published by itself. Ali ar Ra^{c}i thinks highly of it and believes that Hakim's dramatic progress was held up because, owing to a dispute over who should have the well-drawn part of Nagib, it was not staged at the time of its completion.[9]

As far as the non-Egyptian audience is concerned, however, the non-production in 1931 or, indeed, at any time of this naive, guileless comedy is of no consequence at all, for in the previous year Hakim had written Shahrazad.[10]

Though it did not realize it then, and perhaps never has, modern Arabic literature had its greatest year in 1933 when Hakim published The Cavemen (May) and The Soul's Return (December). The Cavemen (Ahl al Kahf), his finest play, whose shape was modelled on that of Beethoven's Fifth Symphony with its movements played by mistake in reverse order,[11] was first circulated in a limited edition, the bulk of which was distributed among writers - the top of the list being Husayn Fawzi - men of letters and prominent contributors to newspapers and magazines. They acclaimed it and Hakim, till then remembered only for Modern Woman and Ali Baba,[12] was overnight hailed as the foremost Arab dramatist. The newspaper Al Balagh, the daily organ of the Wafd, spoke of its resemblance to Maeterlinck, and Taha Husayn, who was for the moment in the wilderness, 'was almost beside himself with joy'.[13] He discussed the play at some length in an article in the newspaper Ar Risala,[14] saying that it was

> 'a significant event not ... in contemporary Arab literature only but ... in Arab literature as a whole. I say this without reserve and hesitation and I say this rejoicing in it and delighted at it. What lover of Arab literature would not rejoice and be delighted when he can say, confident in what he is saying, that a new genre has come into being..., that a new door has been opened to writers and that they have become capable of carrying (the genre) further and proceeding with it to lengths and heights we did not believe they could conceive of yet?
> 'Yes, this story is a significant event marking a new age in Arab literature ... I have no hesitation in saying that it is the first story created in Arab literature which can be called a real play and which could be said to have enriched Arabic literature ... , enhanced the importance of Arabic literature and enabled it to stand firm against modern and ancient foreign literature ... those foreigners who are interested in Arabic literature will read it in utter amazement ... and, further, ... foreign critics who love true literature will, if it is translated for them, be able to read it, find great pleasure in it, find fruitful enjoyment in it and praise it with the favour they reserve for the skilful play which the great writers

of Europe compose ... I confess that I am unreservedly and illimitably astonished by the writer's mastery ... you must read it. No Arab literary intellectual must be ignorant of this unprecedented literary work ... Tawfiq al Hakim has made a new departure in Arabic literature; there can be no doubt about this.'

Husayn's review includes some account of the play, almost all of it in the same euphoric spirit as that of the foregoing quotation. His analysis is limited but acute, and points in it, one important, the other less so, particularly need mentioning. The first is his chiding of Hakim for two faults - for 'shocking errors in language' and 'ugly mistakes, some of which violate the essence of the language ... in grammar and morphology,' which he begs him to correct before allowing a reprint to be made;* and, interestingly, for disregarding the rights of spectators by making the work over-long in places, so that it is suitable for reading but not for acting. In this connection he adds that 'I am extremely anxious that this play should be acted.' The less basic point is that the doyen of Arab critics sometimes adopts a tone which is offensively patronising. Having said that The Cavemen, despite his glowing praise of it, has not done 'all that I wish for the drama in ... Arabic literature', he later adds, with regard to the grammatical errors he alleges that Hakim has perpetrated, 'I should be happy to take over from him the (task of) correction if he wished.' Hakim's indignation at this was not voiced at the time, and neither was his rejection of Husayn's lionising of him. They were soon exchanging letters in Ar Risala[15] on recondite literary topics.

Husayn's advice about the language of The Cavemen was ignored. The play, whose publication had probably been delayed until Hakim could see his way out of the law, by continual revision and - perhaps - while its author waited in case a company arose which might be capable of doing it justice,[16] was a few months later made available to a wider readership. Its publication was a source of great pleasure to Hakim, who still regarded Egypt as culturally inert, 'a sleeping land covered in pebbles'[17] and to portray whose feelings of disorientation is perhaps one of the play's many symbolic aims. In his preface to King Oedipus he prides himself upon

---

* This point perhaps sheds some advance light on a confusing remark by Luwis Awad (in Ostle, p 185) to the effect that Husayn, and the political parties, attacked Hakim as a debaser of Arabic in his use of the colloquial in dialogues in A Bullet in the Heart, The Soul's Return, etc, and caused him to abandon it and adhere to the classical while seeking a middle way.

the acknowledgement of men of letters that The Cavemen 'was of the genus "Arabic literature", acted or not. Thus was accomplished my aim ... that Arabic literature should come to accept drama off the stage. The West has similarly accepted it. Stetkevych[18] celebrates it as constituting the first effective fusion of classical Arabic and dramatic action. Barbour said of it,[19] 'Though written as a play this piece has probably hardly sufficient action to succeed in the theatre. It breaks, however, entirely new ground in modern Arabic literature. The story is delicately conceived, imaginative, and the language impregnated with a gentle satire which makes it very attractive to read.' Gaston Wiet, in an introduction to the 1940 French version, describes it as 'un drame d'une fine psychologie'. Landau detects in its supernatural air - in Mandur's words, 'the bewitching poetic atmosphere which pervades the whole play' - a resemblance to Maeterlinck and speaks in praise of the philosophical dramas, and of The Cavemen, which he is unlikely to have seen, in particular:

> 'Le decor fantastique, le deroulement extraordinaire de quelques-unes de ses pieces comme Les Gens de la Caverne, sont des plus attachants; et pourtant, aussi etrange que cela paraisse, cette suite d'evenements irreels emporte notre conviction, car la vitalite de l'auteur leur donne un relief saisissant. On relira sans cesse, avec le meme plaisir, ses reflections sur la solitude du chien etranger dans la ville, perdu au milieu des autres chiens qui flairent en lui quelque chose de louche et de mysterieux ...'[20]

Rubinacci, who translated the play into Italian, also surmises, in his introduction, that Maeterlinck was The Cavemen's 'modello ispiratore'. Federico Corriente Cordoba, prefacing his Spanish version, rates its author as 'magnifico observador, agudo critico ... exacto en su magnifica comprension de la realidad y espiritu de Egipto.'

Like so many masterpieces, The Cavemen has several levels of meaning. It is a gripping story in which peaks of dramatic tension - as when the shepherd, trying to proffer Decian coins, is brought cruelly up against the fact that something has gone badly wrong with his world, or when the three fugitives, having fled to the cave a second time, become convinced that the new Tarsus is not a dream by the realization that their clothes are of non-Decian style - contrast movingly with plains of illusory calm. Above all it is a timeless study of time and reality and, in the second place, of the power of truth.

The Soul's Return (Awdat ar Ruh), with Haykal's Zaynab (1914), Husayn's Al Ayyam (1926), Muhammad Farid Abu Hadid's Ibnat al Mamluk (1926) and Ibrahim Abd al Qadir al Mazini's Ibrahim al Katib (1931) to compete with, is by general consent the first real novel in Arabic. Adham and Shukri, in whose opinion it is Hakim's greatest work, see it as marking the birth of that of Egypt. Abd as Subur, who concurs, considers that it moved the Arabic novel 'enormous strides along the correct path', bringing it into line, by its thought, artistic structure, language and method, with the best that Europe had to offer and being capable of inspiring Arab readers as Manfaluti had never done. Anouar Abd al-Malek regards it as the first Arab sociological novel.[21] Heyworth-Dunne,[22] anachronistically, rates it 'one of the best studies of Egyptian social and political life during the early years of the revolution under Zaghlul Pasha' and commends 'the flexibility of Tawfiq al Hakim's style, and the ease with which he expresses his thoughts ...' Cowan, writing very much later,[23] sums the book up as 'the first attempt by a real artist in words to portray the lives of the Cairene lower-middle classes and their sudden awakening to national consciousness after the revolution of 1919;' he adds that the novel - unlike Zaynab, for all its fame - 'had an incalculable influence on other writers',[24] among them Nagib Mahfuz in Shukri's opinion. Fathi Ridwan still remembers 'how we acclaimed (its) appearance and considered it a new page in our literary life.'[25] Cowan also deems it 'a true expression of the national awakening'. In corroboration, Mandur says that it sounded the advance for the Egyptian nation, and Naqqash, who unconvincingly claims that Saniyya symbolizes Egypt, maintains[26] that it was a by-product of Lutfi as Sayyid's Egyptian National Movement.

The Soul's Return came out in Russian translation in 1935 and in French in 1937. It was greeted with much interest by the press of French-speaking Europe: 'Everything about this novel enchants us;' '... it is tremendously enjoyable reading;' '... a delicate satire comparable to (that) of Voltaire in Candide ... Its great charm entices the reader along to the end of the book.'[27] Hakim will not, at the time, have entirely relished the comparison with Voltaire.

This writer finds it hard to understand how The Soul's Return, in spite of its undoubted accent on the peasantry as being the builders of the Egypt of the future, could have had any great effect on the political reawakening of the Egyptian people. The novel is, apart from a short autobiographical passage set in the rif, the story of Hakim's life with his uncles and aunt in Cairo and of the impact upon them of

Saniyya, and only in the last two chapters does the pro-Zaghlul uprising enter the plot. This is, as Yahya Haqqi agrees,[28] out of tune with the rest of the book, which is noteworthy for its skilful construction, consummate development, live characterization, wit and wisdom, and may certainly be spoken of along with the best European novels of the 1930s. But there can be no doubt of its influence. Gamal Abd an Nasir read it in 1934-5 while still at secondary school and it made the most powerful impression on him of all the many books, from many countries, which had come his way;[29] Luwis Awad insists[30] that it had a potent morale-boosting impact on his generation: 'Among we youth of the '30s there was not one who doubted that it [accurately pointed] our way to the revival of our national holy war against the English;' and Kamal al Mallakh has described[31] the uplifting effect which, together with The Cavemen and Shahrazad, it had on him in his early years. Hakim denies strongly[32] that its aims were exclusively autobiographical.

Though the first real play and the first real novel in Arabic, astonishingly, had issued from one pen, seven months apart in the same year, their author was not to find himself suddenly basking in glory and literary ease. He still had no settled career, the stage had not tried him. The track was to continue ill-defined, difficult and steep, and he probably would not have understood had it been otherwise.

REFERENCES

1   In Dawara 2, p 153
2   This reading of events is reiterated in IST, pp 139-41, and LA, pp 139-40
3   Preface to King Oedipus. In the introduction to his translation of the play, Rubinacci speaks of almeno sei versions being extant
4   In UNESCO, p 89
5   Hakim to Farag, p 185
6   UNESCO, p 144
7   Muhammad Aziza, in UNESCO, p 100, who regards it as a good example of a bad filmed play. Sa^{c}ad ad Din Tawfiq, pp 60, 155 considers it the twentieth best film made in Egypt
8   Mallakh, p 27

9   Ra^{c}i, pp 37, 39
10 Postscript to Isis
11 Hakim in Al Ahram, 29 November 1968
12 Barbour, in BSOS 8, p 1009
13 Naqqash, p 48
14 Reproduced in Husayn, pp 85-90
15 Reproduced in IST, pp 54-87, and Husayn, pp 91-101
16 Preface to King Oedipus
17 IST, p 70 (letter to Taha Husayn)
18 In Ostle, p 159
19 In BSOS 8, p 1010
20 Landau, p 128
21 Anouar Abd al-Malek, Anthologie de la Litterature Arabe contemporaine: les Essais, p 420
22 In MEJ 2, 3, p 316
23 In Vatikiotis, p 172
24 For another British opinion, see the f.n. to Adham, pp 229-31, in which Hakim is accounted the first Egyptian novelist and The Soul's Return the best Egyptian novel.
25 In Dawara 2, p 249
26 Naqqash, pp 8, 20, 87, 89-91
27 See pp 4-8 of the latest hardback edition. For other views, see AR, p 91
28 Fagr al Qissa al Misriyya, p 134
29 Awad 1
30 Ibid
31 p 18
32 In AR, pp 90-2

4 'Shahrazad' and the Debacle of 'The Cavemen'

> ... (<u>Shahrazad</u>) must be played on the French stage with taste and understanding so that the beauty and depth of the poetry be not lost. (Lugne-Poë)

> At the outset of Shaw's theatrical career the best newspaper critic in London said Shaw's pieces were NOT PLAYS ... (Eric Bentley)

> - If (<u>The Cavemen</u>) is not great, what is a great play? - <u>The Cavemen</u> is a thing which was dead and buried years ago. (An exchange between an admirer and Hakim in <u>The Devil's Pact</u>)

In the year after the new dawn Hakim brought out a collection called <u>The Artists</u> (<u>Ahl al Fann</u>) which was made up of <u>The Piper</u>, <u>Al Awalim</u> and a short story entitled <u>The Poet</u> (<u>Ash Sha^cir</u>, written in 1933). It was dedicated to Labiba Shakhla^c, thinly disguised as 'Al Usta Hamida al Iskandaraniyya, the first person to teach me the word art'. Infinitely more weighty was <u>Shahrazad</u>, which was published in the same year. The most difficult of his plays, unforgettable above all for an atmosphere of mystery which takes us back to that which less appropriately enwrapped

Ali Baba, it portrays for us his ideal woman, but does more than that. In The Sultan of Darkness he attempts to explain its symbolism. Firstly,[1] he declares Shahrazad to be a personification of nature; her slave is darkness, the wazir is the heart and King Shahriyar is the intellect, and 'Their movement around Shahrazad is the movement of all mankind around nature.' (Adham,[2] on the other hand, sees Shahrazad as life and the other characters as Hakim in various of his aspects.) Secondly,[3] he says that he was writing 'the tragedy of (the) doubt about the (possibility of) human progress continuing in a straight line.' This affirmation comes after a long disquisition on the Greek contribution to modern civilization, the principal element in which he believes to have been its grafting of doubt onto the thinking it had inherited. Shahrazad was intended to raise question-marks over the progress the Queen had been able to achieve vis-a-vis her husband, and over the advancement and improvement of mankind as a whole. Has Shahrazad succeeded, by converting Shahriyar from an irresponsible animal into a man of reflection, in ensuring that he and his successors will keep to the wiser path and remain impervious to the decivilising attractions of darkness and the heart? There is, deliberately, considerable doubt about this, and about its symbolic extension, by the end of the play, which Hakim has labelled an 'idealistic allegory'.[4]

Shahrazad had other functions as well. One, according to him, was to be his major investigation of the theme of 'place' and reality, another to act as 'a mediator between the popular and official spheres [of Arabic literature], the wall standing between which I was trying to break down' - by which he meant, in brief, that the play was written to be acceptable both to those uninitiated into this kind of drama and to professional arbiters who had acknowledged The Cavemen to be 'literature' even though it had not been performed. The latter were again convinced, but there is no evidence that the former were in any way conscious that Shahrazad even existed. Nonetheless, he claimed that 'this wall has finally been demolished since the entry of Shahrazad.'[5]

From the official side, Taha Husayn's review[6] was as enthusiastic as, and less carping than, that he had devoted to The Cavemen. The play was still nothing like 'the ideal', but it was a second example of a new genre 'the like of (which) the whole of our Arab literature has not known', and both its language and length were acceptable. It was, however, patently not actable because ordinary audiences would not understand a 'Platonist dialogue' and because there were no suitable Egyptian interpreters for it. Only in his last paragraph did Husayn recommend more care and polishing, still more attention to language, more application, reflection, study and learning, and more reading of philosophy. On this occasion Hakim took serious offence, objecting particularly - and consistently, since the fact that he had again made publication his initial choice of medium had by no means ruled out production under propitious circumstances - to the charge of non-actability. The ensuing quarrel between the blind critic and Arab literature's new discovery developed rapidly and is narrated in Part Three of this book.

In his account Muhammad Mandur takes Shahrazad away from the centre of the stage and declares that the theme is whether or not a human being can live by and for the intellect, devoting himself to knowledge and ignoring the calls of the body and the heart, symbolized respectively by the slave and the wazir.[7] (Adham,[8] in a non-biographical interpretation, judges these two to be two facets of Shahriyar himself in the time when he loved Shahrazad.) Mandur's view overlooks a number of obvious features of the play - the facts, for example, that Shahrazad herself is highly intelligent and rational and that her husband has become not a positive thinker but an introspective sceptic riven by ill-founded jealousy - but it has the general support of Hakim.[9] Najm[10] is indisputably right in rating Shahrazad as 'one of the most glorious' plays in Arabic literature, and even Mandur conceded that, of the plays in Arabic on the Shahrazad theme (by Aziz Abaza, Ali Ahmad Bakathir, etc.), Hakim's was the most meaningful, intellectually inspired and atmospheric.[11] Kritzeck, introducing a translated scene from the play,[12] comments that it 'shows how far the Arab theatre came, in a relatively short time, from rudimentary theatrical forms to highly sophisticated drama.'[13]

The first translation made of Shahrazad, a work much influenced by music of the type of Stravinsky's 'The Firebird'[14] and by Hakim's dabbling in philosophy,[15] was into French in 1936. Georges Lecomte wrote a preface to it in which he said, among much else that was extremely favourable, that the play had not 'ceased somewhat to amaze our Cartesian minds while completely captivating them'; Lugne-Poë appended a word of endorsement, and it was his name that Hakim took in vain in looking back on Shahrazad in the preface to Pigmalyun. Reiterating that the former had (correctly, given the failure of The Cavemen) been composed with no thought of a possible production, he goes on to express his certainty that under the right conditions it could be successfully performed and to pile further enigma on its enigmatic nature:

'[Lugne-Poë] knows the difficulties of this kind of work. The whole problem lies in projecting the poetry and philosophy in the

theatre as they project themselves in print. This is what he himself did with the plays of Ibsen (he was the first to present them to the French) and with Oscar Wilde's Salome (he was the first to produce it for the world) ... Unfortunately for me, old age has reduced this great artist and long ago cut him off from the theatre. Would he have produced Shahrazad if he had read it at the height of his artistic energy? Who knows? Perhaps he would. Would that he had. That would have been glory indeed.
'But even better would be the joy of seeing those bewildered concepts, high-flown expressions and characters with one foot on the ground and the other in the sky established in the frame - any frame - of taste and comprehension.'

For the crime of publishing The Cavemen, Hakim was asked in 1934, much to his father's chagrin, to resign from the Legal Corps,[16] in which he seems to have done well[17] despite absent-mindedness. In retrospect he could think of it as 'a theatre and acting and spectators'.[18] He left the rif, which he loathed,[19] to become Head of the Ministry of Education's Investigation Bureau (qalam at tahqiqat), a quasi-legal post which offered him greater stability and freedom than had the law proper. In the following year he made a demoralising comeback in the theatre, when The Cavemen was staged. By the 1930s Egyptian audiences were used to the spectacle of tragedies emanating from abroad, but found the Arabic equivalent of a Greek or French tragedy (which Hakim, in his preface to Fate of a Cockroach, maintains that it is)[20] too demanding for them with its lofty language ('language philosophique et tres recherchee'),[21] somewhat remote incidents and characterization and, above all, lack of physical action. Hakim's purpose had been to 'write an Egyptian tragedy on an Egyptian foundation' - a foundation he believed to be in essence a conflict between Man on the one hand and time or place on the other - and this was too much for audiences who had had two years in which to read The Cavemen but had probably not done so, and who had not been weaned away from their uncritical fervour for Ar Rihani. The play received the signal honour of being chosen as the opening production of the first official Egyptian troupe, the National Company (Al Firqa al Qawmiyya), which was founded in 1935 on the recommendation of a Ministry of Education board of enquiry which included Taha Husayn.[22] Its enjoyment of a government subsidy indicated that for the authorities the stage was at last worthy of recognition and support.[23] Khalil Mutran, who later commissioned a Comedie Francaise report on the state of the drama in Egypt,[24] was appointed Director of the Company, a position he occupied until 1942. The Company got off to a bad start. Those few people who came to see The Cavemen at the Opera did not appreciate it and some of them fell asleep. Its failure was so resounding that only four works by Hakim were produced in Egypt in the next twenty-one years. 'What a loss for the theatre!' Farag exclaims.[25]

Hakim realized that a Cairene audience required a different approach from that which he had seen to be de rigueur for the dinner-jacketed spectators of Paris, and he regretted that he had allowed The Cavemen to be sprung on an unselected Egyptian audience. His distinction between the play in book form and the staged work was vindicated, for few of those who had enjoyed reading The Cavemen felt inclined, unaware of any connection between 'literature' and the theatre, to watch it performed, as they stayed away from the plays of 'the less brilliant Mahmud Taymur' and Ali Ahmad Bakathir.[26] The outcry provoked by The Cavemen among playwrights (Ar Rihani, and unsuccessful dramatists of the traditional schools), critics and politicians,[27] who considered it a dangerous and blasphemous insult to the established norms of the stage, had the unfortunate effect of creating a lobby which, then and afterwards[28] (after it had been followed by The Merchant of Venice, Antigone and King Lear), sought to pillory it and its author and to halt the operations of the Company. It helped to usher in an era of stagnation in Egyptian culture which kept its successors off the boards and lasted until the revolution.[29] Abd as Subur states that the debate about it as a piece of theatre - and similarly about Shahrazad - was still heated in 1965. Thus, Ar Ra^{c}i's opinion of it remains not very high ('piece non depourvue de qualites litteraires'),[30] while Ghali Shukri regards it as 'the first real Egyptian tragedy' if not 'the first genuinely Egyptian play'. It was, however, to be well received when produced in Italian at a Palermo Congress on Mediterranean Affairs in the 1950s.[31] As a book, which has been translated into French, Italian, Japanese and Spanish and, in part, into English, a survey published in 1952[32] showed it to be Hakim's most popular.

There is no question that the failure of The Cavemen on the stage caused Hakim great unhappiness. He wrote to Zaki Tulaymat, who had produced it, to protest at the way (which he could perhaps have influenced if he had tried) he had handled it[33] and then, rather after the manner of Yamlikha, Marnush and Mishilinya or, alternatively, Strindberg, fled the live theatre. Wrongly, Ar Ra^{c}i[34] and Mandur do not take seriously his insistence that its performance was not in his mind when he wrote it and that accordingly he did not call it a play. He says that he was surprised and apprehensive when it began to be mentioned in connection with the inauguration of the National Company, was over-persuaded, and allowed the idea to come to fruition. It is, nonetheless, extraordinary, though in character, that he claims to have attended none of the rehearsals and to have come on the last night only because he had been misled into believing that it had been a success. He found what he says he had feared, 'that this work is completely unsuitable for acting' or, at least, that it was not actable before Egyptian audiences. Habitually moved by the spectacle of everyday emotions - love, jealousy, hate, etc., - 'what are they to think when they are confronted by a struggle between Man and time, Man and place or Man and his personality?' He departed from the theatre, convinced that, under the circumstances, the audience's reaction was correct, determined to have nothing more to do with the National Company and bewailing the facts that there was no troupe to do justice to <u>The Cavemen</u> and break in Egyptian audiences gently to his unprecedented work[35] ('This kind of story needs a special production in a special theatre') and that Lugne-Poe, whose Theatre de l'Oeuvre had closed in 1929, was no longer active.

It was Hakim's misfortune at this time, and to a great extent it still is, that like his cavemen he was, after Paris, dealing with a society which could not understand him. With his radically altered style he was immeasurably far ahead of his dramatist colleagues and of the playgoers they were accustomed to attract. Nothing like <u>The Cavemen</u> had been seen before, and he was aiming far too high:

> 'My object ... was to inject the element of tragedy into an Arab Islamic subject - tragedy in the ancient Greek sense, which I had inherited, of a struggle between Man and hidden, supernatural forces. I deliberately did not use Greek legends as a source, but the Qur'an.[36] My aim was not simply to extract a story from the Noble Book and set it in a dramatic framework, but to look at our Islamic legends with the eye of Greek tragedy and bring about a fusion of the two mentalities and the two literatures.'

He maintained that he had succeeded on both counts.[37] Whether or not this were so, the play, which struck the Egyptian theatre at the least propitious moment, caused it to plunge even deeper into its crisis of confidence.[38]

An interesting aspect of <u>The Cavemen</u> on which there has been no worthwhile comment is its basis in Christianity. The fugitives in the cave of Ar Raqim are Christians, Christ figures prominently in their

36 Tawfiq al Hakim

conversations, and Tarsus, pagan at the time of their flight, has become Christian long before their first reawakening. All this is in spite of the fact that Hakim's primary inspiration was the Qur'an. (Subsidiary influences were the Book of the Dead, the Torah, the four Gospels, 'ancient Egypt',[39] the miracle story of a group of early Christians who fled the oppression of the pagan Emperor Decius (249-51) and awoke in their cave in the reign of the Christian Emperor Theodorus II (408-50),[40] and a number of secondary sources listed by Adham.)[41] Writing in Al Ahram on 13 August 1971, Hakim said that, given that Egypt had progressed from paganism to Islam via Christianity, 'it was no coincidence that ... I should have written The Cavemen in a Christian context ...' The truth is rather that, as is demonstrated by the Christianity of many of his short stories and the frequent references to Biblical and Christian material which pepper his work as a whole, Hakim's character and his Paris sojourn disposed him to regard Islam and Christianity as almost equally valid versions of the religious truth.[42] His fervent attachment to the former only serves to heighten the significance of his concern with the latter.

There can be little doubt that The Cavemen is a play which, not only in relation to the Arab theatre of its day (in terms of which it is a miracle), may properly be called great. It is deplorable that British audiences and readers have not been given the chance to evaluate it - as, with differing degrees of adequacy, they have five others of the long plays - in a translated version, for it will stand comparison with the very best. Hakim's huge oeuvre is marked by much unevenness, but his finest plays are without serious flaw. Leaving Shahrazad aside, what causes The Cavemen to outshine those mentioned so far - misogynistic dramas of purely Egyptian social interest and of no comparable weight in the main - is its universal rather than local theme, its single-minded exploration of that theme and its sustainedly affecting atmosphere. Its only defects are three over-long monologues, one of which concludes the first act, and two lengthy expositions of the Japanese legend of Hiroshima, which is introduced as a precedent for the rebirth of the cavemen. Mandur may well be right in saying of The Cavemen that what Hakim had seen of the European drama in Paris provoked him to rise above national social and political issues, and subjects he knew the public would relish, to concentrate on universal topics. This theory, however, leaves Expulsion from Eden, superficially more complex than The Cavemen, and its sisters inadequately accounted for. The fact of the matter must be that, before his first great play, Hakim was a born dramatist who did not know his potential or imagine that, through broadening his vision while seeking inspiration in the literature of his own people, he could emulate Ibsen and Pirandello by writing about themes which were the concern of all men. It was his tragedy that Arab playwrights had not been in a position to do the same kind of thing before and did not attempt to follow his example, and that the adverse reactions of his colleagues in the theatre and of his audiences should have forced him alternately to lower and raise his sights throughout the rest of his career. Even now, The Cavemen has not been subjected to the attentions of critics who have succeeded in explaining and appreciating it satisfactorily, as a book let alone as a play. As to its suitability in the latter role, Fathi Ridwan, in a comment which utterly damns the stage of the time, has said,[43] '... We did not consider Tawfiq al Hakim to be a writer for the theatre then, despite his publication of numerous plays, for if we had done so we would have been devaluing him.' Unlike Chekhov's The Seagull, which failed at first for reasons similar to those which destroyed The Cavemen, Hakim's most sublime play has never been vouchsafed a 'special production', and a masterpiece has thus been allowed to be almost totally neglected.

REFERENCES

1   p 21
2   p 123
3   SD, p 35
4   Preface to The Tree Climber
5   Ibid
6   Husayn, pp 102-6
7   Mandur 2, pp 58, 62
8   pp 120-1
9   AR, p 19
10 p 367
11 Mandur 2, p 63
12 Herbert Howarth and Ibrahim Shukrallah in Images from the Arab World, London, 1944
13 James Kritzeck (ed), Anthology of Islamic Literature from the Rise of Islam to Modern Times, Pelican, London, 1964, p 97
14 Preface to The Tree Climber

38 Tawfiq al Hakim

15 LA, pp 97, 99
16 Papadopoulo, pp 230-1
17 MDS, p 119
18 Justice and Art, pp 134-6
19 AHD, p 52
20 Farag, p 87, supports him
21 Nada Tomiche, in UNESCO, p 118, f.n. 2
22 Mandur 1, p 47
23 Ra^{c}i, in UNESCO, p 88
24 Mandur 1, loc cit
25 p 80
26 Ra^{c}i, in UNESCO, p 89
27 LP, p 225
28 Farag, loc cit
29 Galal al Ashari, in MAG, May 1971, p 45
30 In UNESCO, p 88
31 LL, pp 90-5, TAY, p 61
32 Kermit Schoonover, 'A Survey of the best modern Arabic books', in MW 42, 1, pp 48-55
33 Ra^{c}i, p 32
34 Cf Chapter 3, reference 4, where an earlier, contradictory view is indicated
35 Farag, p 80
36 Verses 9-26 of Sura 18
37 Preface to King Oedipus, pp 39-40
38 Dawara 1, pp 294-5
39 LIB, p 178
40 Mandur 2, p 41
41 Cf Gibbon, The Decline and Fall of the Roman Empire, Chapter 33, and Cable and French, The Gobi Desert, pp 205-6, for two of the alternative accounts of the legend
42 Taha Husayn is even more neutral. See Mustaqbal ath Thaqafa fi Misr, Chapter 5
43 In Dawara 2, p 250

Part I : Chapter II   Neglect before Revolution

1 Political Skirmishes

> It is better for a writer to die of hunger than to sell his soul to the devil called Power.
> (In the Spotlight of Thought)

The controversy sparked off by The Cavemen, with which the National Company had not been dissatisfied, would have been inflamed if Shahrazad had been staged. The Company thought, however, that its next season [1936-7] should be opened by a drama to be written by Taha Husayn. 'But it appears that Dr Taha suggested that I collaborate with him in writing it. The Director of the Company welcomed this [idea] ... The thing apparently became serious, but I was otherwise preoccupied. I had already gone to Paris and fallen ill there.' This was in the summer of 1936, in the May of which year Hakim's father had died of typhoid. (His mother was still alive in 1973.)[1] He was advised in Paris to seek a change of air, remembered a Swiss mountain resort recommended by Taha Husayn as a place where they might meet up, and made his way there to convalesce with the friend with whom he was on close terms again, if not for long. As they were enjoying themselves in literary tasks and in fishing, a 'nice' letter arrived from Khalil Mutran asking how they were getting on with their play on Al Mutanabbi, who Hakim had not been told was to be its subject. The dramatist and his mentor, who was in fact working on a book on the great classical poet, could not give up their relaxation for the sake of such a project, and Hakim stalled in his reply. Believing that his correspondent had completed the major part of a drama about Harun ar Rashid, he proposed that the script be sent to them so that they might help him to finish it in time for the impending season. The offer, which smacks of that made to him by Husayn in the matter of the alleged grammatical lapses in The Cavemen, came to nothing, for Mutran had not even begun the job.[2]

The spectacle of the two famous authors playing truant is an engaging one. In Hakim's case at least, however, it was not mere frivolity. The subject of Al Mutanabbi did not appeal, he was recuperating and he and Husayn were, at the latter's prompting,[3] composing together a novel which was an instance of collaboration unique in modern Egyptian letters.[4] Above all, the National Company's efforts over The Cavemen made it inevitable that he would not be much attracted by proposals emanating from them. The joint work was The Enchanted Palace (Al Qasr al Mashur), which, completed 'during a week or two',[5] was published in the same year. It is a charming and amusing, if rather esoteric, fantasy which embroils its authors, who penned the chapters alternately in this game of intellectual 'Consequences', with Shahrazad without requiring either to fall into any traps of the kind set for many of the protagonists of a number of Hakim's most important plays. It is no doubt Husayn's sudden enthusiasm for the theme, provoked by Shahrazad,[6] which decided Hakim to ignore the Mutanabbi idea with such finality. As very much the senior partner, Husayn has the last word in the novel, which is dedicated to his wife, by having Hakim brought to trial. During the course of the hearing he is made to admit that his authorship is as yet imperfect, and the charge that he is still inexperienced - in reality difficult to sustain in the face of the evidence of The Cavemen and Shahrazad - is upheld by the judge. Over twenty years later Husayn was still unrepentant about the latter: '... he wrote this story but he can't explain it.'[7]

After recovering from his illness Hakim went to the Salzburg Festival, where he saw Dr Faustus on a puppet stage and Faust directed by 'the then greatest living producer, Max Reinhardt';[8] marvelled at Toscanini (he described him and Reinhardt as 'giants of art never equalled');[9] and revelled in Gluck's Orfeo ed Euridice and in the rest of the ballet presented. He returned home via Paris, where he held negotiations with publishers which were probably connected with the French editions of Shahrazad and The Soul's Return.

In the February of this same year the third play of his maturity had appeared. Muhammad is an enormous work, divided into ninety-five scenes apportioned among a prologue, three acts and an epilogue. It falls outside the scope of this book except insofar as it is worthy of remark that its author's vision of the Prophet is of a man involved in human society - 'a classical Greek hero' -[10] rather than in a special relationship with Allah; that to write a play, if such it can be called, about the Prophet was a bold undertaking;[11] and that its size and the vast amount of labour which went into it well exemplify Hakim's phenomenal industry. In his comments on it[12] Landau abandons critical judgement by saying, ' ... ce n'est ni dans le drame, ni dans la comedie que le talent de al-Hakim se manifeste pleinement, mais dans le genre historique romance.'

In 1937 Hakim had two publications. One was entitled Plays of Tawfiq al Hakim (Masrahiyyat Tawfiq al Hakim), a collection which, in two parts, put into durable print (for, with one exception, the first time) Expulsion from Eden, Post Mortem, A Life is Wrecked, The Piper, A Bullet in the Heart, Devant son Guichet in its Arabic version (Amama Shubbak at Tazakir) and two new one-acters: The River of Madness (Nahr al Gunun), a striking playlet which anticipated Ionesco's Rhinoceros by nearly a quarter of a century; and The Gentle Sex (Ginsuna al Latif),[13] a fatuous anti-feminist snippet. At least the first, fifth, sixth and seventh of these had featured earlier in Magallati. The preface to Pigmalyun clearly implies that, in contradistinction to The Cavemen, Shahrazad and Pigmalyun itself, the eight were designed to be acted. Ironically enough, the three great ones all have been, while only Post Mortem and The Gentle Sex of the collection have. The latter was performed at an Egyptian Women's Union function in 1935, thus showing that Hakim's idiosyncratic views on equal rights were already thought worth exhibiting, and the former as the curtain-raiser to its 1937/8 season by the despised National Company,[14] which retitled it The Suicide's Secret (Sirr al Muntahira), which it will hereafter be called. It did moderately well at the Opera, but none of the critics has felt that the re-establishment of contact between Hakim and the Company calls for special notice; neither has Hakim, who may not, of course, have been consulted about the production. There is certainly no further sign of a working relationship having been inaugurated.

The second publication in 1937 was A Rural Deputy's Diary (Yawmiyyat Na'ib fi'l Aryaf), Hakim's second-best novel and most translated work. It purports to be his diary during a twelve-day period of his second legal posting and is a slight, enjoyable ramble round the corrupt judicial circuit of the rif. Arresting and fluent, it has appeared in English, French, German, Hebrew, Romanian, Russian, Spanish and Swedish versions, has been made into a film in Egypt[15] and has been much praised. Philip Woodruff[16] describes it as 'impressive' and a tale which 'grips one from start to finish'; Vernet[17] reckons it the first Arab novel with no debt to the West. Apparently in contradiction, the translator of the second Spanish edition (1955) compares it with the Generation of '98 type of novel, but goes on to call it 'una obra maestra' and to wax lyrical about the excellence of its language. Mandur[18] regards it, with Justice and Art and some of Hakim's (autobiographical) fiction, as a better piece of social criticism than any drama he published before 1952. There may be validity in this view if Praksa is not accounted 'social criticism' and the short plays of 1950 are debarred from the category because of their slightness - but Mandur was nothing if not an ideologist who, believing that culture had to be realistic, could hardly have been expected to approve of most of what Hakim wrote before the Revolution. The Diary was certainly intended to be reformist,[19] and it paved the way to the setting-up of a Ministry of Social Affairs.[20] With the Arab public at large it is very popular.[21] Far less ambitious than The Soul's Return (one critic[22] adjudges both as deserving 'a high place in modern world literature'), it has no doubt been translated far more than its predecessor on account of the readier appreciability of its subject-matter, its straightforwardness, attractive plot and lack of philosophical subtlety, and its comparative brevity. To translate The Soul's Return (as Hakim may have done) is a giant task, and this has denied most of the world a splendid, universal novel which may be read over and over again with enjoyment and by the side of which the Diary quickly palls.

1938 maintained the reformist impetus. It was a year of essays and prose works on political, social, religious, cultural and autobiographical themes: The Tree of Ruling (Shagarat al Hukm); The Devil's Pact (Ahd ash Shaytan), whose title refers to the Devil of Art about whose persecutions Hakim has frequently complained; In the Spotlight of Thought (Tahta Shams al Fikr), a book of philosophical letters and articles dating from 1933 which has been expanded in later printings; and the novels A Sparrow from the East (Usfur min ash Sharq) and King of the Parasites, or The History of the Life of a Stomach, the latter being episodes, drawn after classical Arab models, from the career of a fictitious sponger and miser called Ash^{c}ab, after whom it was renamed when it was subsequently revised. The first of these volumes contained a number of short satirical plays; the second included two, one of which - 'Twixt Dream and Reality (Bayna'l Hulm wa'l Haqiqa) - was the precursor of Pigmalyun. The Tree of Ruling derided the king, the politicians and the political methods of the times, and passages[23] of In the Spotlight of Thought violently and recklessly attacked democracy as organized, for the rich and against the poor in Egypt and called for the banning of the tarbush, in protest against the wearing of which Hakim took to sporting his celebrated parties - for he had castigated them all - down upon him, a civil servant. The Tree of Ruling said that only a 'blessed revolution' could save the country. The reaction of Muhammad Mahmud's Liberal Constitutional Party was to call for Hakim's removal from his post.[25] It is extraordinary that the extreme official antagonism towards him which as the atmosphere cooled took the settled form of labelling him a communist, which he was not, should have cost him only a fortnight's pay. He had become, however, too substantial a figure to be treated cavalierly and protested, in the face of this punishment, that it was the prerogative of every citizen and author, even if a servant of the state, to publicise corruption and abuses of the political system.

He spent the August of 1938 in the Alps, lonely and railing against art in general and Ibn Abd Rabbihi's Al Iqd al Farid in particular.[26] It was probably, but not certainly, after his return that his reputation in official circles suffered further through his apparent involvement in the Sanhuri case. He and Dr Abd ar Raziq as Sanhuri, a professor at the Law School (and later a holder of the deanship there and of the post of Under Secretary of the Ministry of Education), were poised to launch a scheme which had as its object the improvement of students at the University through their greater familiarization with the lives of Ramsis II, Umar b al Khattab, etc., when As Sanhuri was found guilty, to Hakim's consternation, of seeking to turn the same students into political activists and expelled from the University. Hakim's part in the affair was not scrutinized,[27] but no doubt some conclusions were drawn. He was not, however, ready to leave his chosen arena, and was next found in combat with the Shaykh of Al Azhar who, after A Rural Deputy's Diary had become a secondary school set text, complained to his superiors in the Ministry of Education about its bitter comments on shari'a law officers.[28] In turn Hakim directed articles against the Shaykh which accused him of interference with the freedom of thought; he was questioned by the Egyptian upper house and told to retract by his Minister, which he refused to do and left this battlefield also unscathed.[29]

It comes as no surprise that a 14 year absence from from the Egyptian stage began in 1938, after his one-act play of no worth, A Journalistic Incident (Hadithun Suhufi), had been presented at the Women's Union. (No significance attaches to the venue.) It is no contradiction that, in November, he formally proposed the establishment of a Ministry of

Social Affairs[30] and that, set up with great rapidity, it opened its doors in the following year with its creator as Director of its Social Guidance Board. Perhaps the authorities thought to shackle an embarrassing reformist maverick with the trappings of official respectability. If they did, they were disappointed, at least at first, for he frequently annoyed them by his writing. There were many threats of disciplining, transfer and dismissal, and another fortnight's wages were lost[31] but, thanks to support among the intelligentsia, not least from Taha Husayn and the newspapers which did the initial printing of offending articles - which subsequently formed the backbone of his essay collections - no draconian measures were taken against him, not even when he greeted an incoming Mustafa an Nahhas government with an article in Al Ahram which called the electoral system 'pseudo'.[32] The smear of communism, however, was given so much ammunition by his next play that he found things becoming uncomfortable and had to adopt for a time the outward appearance of a dutiful servant of the country.

In 1939, as a follow-up to The Tree of Ruling and in reaction to the loud outcry against it, he published Praksa, or the Difficult Business of Ruling (Praksa, aw Mushkilat al Hukm). It is one of his best plays and contains many ingredients, such as the wit and ribald humour of Act Two, which combine to make it of wide potential appeal. Primarily an exercise in political arguments, it turns the knife in the wound and flaunts its author's scorn for his party detractors. He was not so confident of his invulnerability, however, as to feel able to bring out the whole six act work at this time. The three acts which were issued in the year in which the Second World War began (the remaining three were printed in 1960), and which are complete in themselves, were nevertheless quite enough to endanger him further. Praksa I, as it is convenient to identify them, does much more than paint 'an accurate picture of the corruption of parliamentary life by superb artistic means ... ', as Sami al Kayyali opined.[33] It is not as limited as this, though Al Kayyali was no doubt correct when he added that, by publishing the play, Hakim had made clear where he stood to his own satisfaction 'in the face of those who would not understand that his sound criticisms were those of a writer seeking reform for reform's sake and not something for himself.' The major theme of his earliest full-length political drama is, as its sub-title indicates, government - who it should be done by, how it should be done. The play touches, at the beginning, on the rule of the whole (male) population of Athens, takes us through a feminist uprising against it to the assumption of complete power by the women's leader,

Praksa, and concludes with a military dictator holding sway. With it, we are back to the highroad of Hakim's classically-inspired work, which connects The Cavemen with Isis (1955), but now the superstructure is very different from both the former and from Shahrazad. The starting-point this time is The Ecclesiazusae of Aristophanes, to whom, in a dedication, Hakim makes obeissance: 'To Aristophanes, lord of Greek comedy, I submit my crime, craving his forgiveness.' It is doubtful whether Aristophanes would have felt an apology to be necessary, though he would perhaps have appreciated the preface, in which Hakim further devalues himself. He exhorts us to read the original before embarking on Praksa I - a course which would seem to be neither essential nor enlightening - and continues: 'Merely participating with Aristophanes in one of his stories revealed to my eye what the experience of writing 15 [sic] plays did not, taught me what I had not learned of the secrets of this difficult art and demonstrated to me characteristics and faults (in my work) which it would not have been easy for me to detect. I beg forgiveness for my inadequacy, but who can measure up to Aristophanes?' All this rings falsely coming from the author of The Cavemen and Shahrazad and was probably an elaborate attempt to pull the wool over the eyes of the authorities and convince them that, all appearances to the contrary, Praksa I was merely a bit of fun devoid of political motivation. The attempt failed.

Hakim has always been a highly impressionable, but at the same time extremely selective, writer. It is at first glance, however, puzzling that his third foray into the classics should have led him to Aristophanes, but even more so is the fact that he should have been spurred on to compose a play as good as Praksa I when starting off from one as middling as the slim Ecclediazusae, which has always been the lowest rated of its author's comedies. Mandur makes this point rather nicely by saying that it 'is not considered to be ... among Aristophanes's outstanding plays' and by continuing that 'when he wrote it his years were advanced'.[34] Hakim states in the preface to King Oedipus that he saw in Praxagora a character whom he could modify in such a way as to make her a vehicle for the ideas he was eager to set down on paper at the time and that, as in the later cases of Shaw's Pygmalion and Sophocles's Oedipus, it was only the outer shell of the character that he needed. This does not help very much, and it would remain strange that such minimal inspiration as he required should have been drawn from Praxagora, with her all-embracing and ludicrous communism, and from The Ecclesiazusae, with its total lack of character development, had not Taha Husayn placed the why and wherefore on record.[35] Praksa I arose, he says, out of a series of discussions, held 'these days [when] the intellect is on trial', in a conclave of literary men 'provoked by the ordeal of Ustaz Tawfiq al Hakim' which The Tree of Ruling had brought upon him. Their conversations led the participants to contrast the freedom of opinion of ancient Athens with the lack of it in Egypt, to talk about Aristophanes and his Ecclesiazusae in particular and to ponder the vogue in Europe of updated Greek plays such as those of Giraudoux and Cocteau. The consensus had decided that Egyptian authors should take an artistic and political risk and attempt to compose this kind of drama when Hakim turned up one day at the salon with Praksa I in his hand. Husayn lauds him for his authorship of the first Greek-type comedy in Arabic and hopes that others will follow his lead without having first to undergo tribulations like his. He agrees with him that Praksa I does not come up to Aristophanes, in part because he is 'forbidden by the constraints of our new life and by the constraints on our tastes and our moeurs to utilise the verbal and artistic freedom which the Greek poet used. In addition he is forbidden by the regulations of our social and legal administration to expose himself to [charges of] communism or anything approaching it ... Literature in fetters is not comparable with free literature.'

Having launched his defiant riposte, which of course invoked the very accusations Husayn supposed it impossible to attract in the conditions of the times, Hakim retired from the public fray and steered clear of controversy - soon losing his communist reputation - until the last years of the decaying monarchy.

REFERENCES

1 Mallakh, p 157
2 Hakim in Al Ahram, 6 August 1971
3 Mallakh, p 282
4 Ibid, p 260
5 Husayn, in his part of the preface to the 1957 Kitab al Hilal edition
6 Cachia, p 196
7 Husayn, loc cit
8 Hakim, loc cit. More details are in LA, p 48
9 Ibid, loc cit

10 Safran, p 214
11 Subur 2, p 29
12 P 126. Cf M.M. Badawi, The Journal of Arabic Literature 2 (1971), pp 166-9: 'a chronicle play, Brechtian in a bad sense'.
13 Originally called Girls of my Country (Banatu Biladi): Rizzitano, in OM 23, p 265, f.n. 3
14 Adham, p 184, Farag, p 80. (Rizzitano, in OM 23, p 262, f.n. 7, says that the Company performed the play on several occasions but is presumably referring to a run of a number of performances). See also the preface to Pigmalyun.
15 In 1969, the scenario being by Farag: Sa^{c}ad ad Din Tawfiq, p 175
16 In MEJ 2, 4, p 479. For a translated view from The Spectator, see AR, p 92
17 Literatura Arabe, p 190
18 Mandur 2, p 32
19 IST, pp 99-100. In AR, p 104, Hakim says that most leading politicians read it but that it had no direct effect on conditions in the rif.
20 Hiwar 15, p 44
21 Makarius, Anthologie, p 134
22 K.A. Vasileva, in Soviet Literature, February 1957
23 Eg. pp 118, 136
24 AR, pp 27, 84, ARD, p 54, which give interesting background details
25 ARD, p 84
26 Mallakh, p 46
27 AW, pp 24-5
28 Rizzitano, in OM 23, p 256, f.n.
29 ARD, p 77
30 Akhir Sa^{c}a, 20 November 1938, AR, pp 104-5
31 Papadopoulo, pp 231-2
32 AW, pp 47-8
33 In the foreword to Adham, p 8
34 Mandur 2, pp 89-90
35 Husayn, pp 125-31

2 The View from the Ivory Tower

> In many ways an artistic nature
> unfits a man for practical existence.
> (R. L. Stevenson, New Arabian
> Nights)

The start of the Second World War saw Hakim engaging in politically unexceptionable fiction, memoirs, essays and poetry in The Temple Dancer (Raqisat al Ma^{c}bad, 1939), Al Hakim's Donkey (Himar al Hakim, 1940), The Song of Songs (Nashid al Inshad, a 'dramatized verse rendition of the original, 1940), From the Ivory Tower (Min al Burg al Agi, 1941) and The Sultan of Darkness (Sultan az Zalam, 1941). The first is a rather worthless novel, an account[1] of an imaginary[2] affair of the heart in which he humiliates himself and makes the earliest admission of his reputation as 'the enemy of Woman'. The second, misleadingly entitled, recounts the course of his negotiations with a French film company which, in 1939 - advised by Fasquelle, the publishers of the French translation of The Soul's Return - commissioned him to write the script for a documentary on life in the Egyptian rif and how his summer in Lucerne and the Hautes Savoies and the outbreak of war extricated him from a job which he was too lazy to take seriously. The book, trite as it is, furnishes insight into his character and ideas at the time.

Sultan of Darkness is devoted to crushing criticism of Hitler - to whom its title refers - to Hakim's concern (pessimistic in the main, but hopeful at the end) at the threat posed to mankind and to spiritual and artistic values by the advance of science, industry, economic theory, nationalism, dictatorship and militarism, and (briefly) to his philosophy of 'balance', which is most fully exhibited in Action and Response and seems to have been developed from Huxley[3] and Taha Husayn.[4] It consists of essays, short stories and a play entitled The Angel's Prayer (Salat al Malaika) which, probably influenced by the journey to earth of Mephistopheles in Hakim's beloved Faust, has some worth as a reflection of his opinions on the war and as a pointer to the chief of his post-revolutionary themes, but little intrinsic value. Lop-sided in construction (it is made up of six scenes, five of which occupy five and a half pages of text or less, while Scene Two is twenty-one and a half pages in length), unreal in atmosphere and ingenuous in intent, it stops just short of mediocrity. In Scene Two the angel, who has descended to earth to try to terminate the war, is given an apple by a girl. Hitler and Mussolini, with whom he pleads, think it is a bomb, but he manages to retain possession of it until his return to heaven. The apple, which holds the book together, enables the angel's closest heavenly friend to say that he has been expelled from earth 'with an apple like Adam was expelled from heaven'.

From the Ivory Tower is an apologia for Hakim's hibernation to escape the storm of criticism he had aroused in 1938 and 1939. Its title was ironic, being chosen because he was now being accused of living apart from the real world, an accusation which Abd as Subur[5] characterizes as, in effect, ridiculous, and Naqqash[6] refutes emphatically. Shukri,[7] on the other hand, taking 'the real world' to mean party politics, supported it until 1952. Hakim himself does not admit the charge in the book but, on the contrary, constantly explains[8] that the ivory tower he would build, if he chose to build one, would be a kind of 'think tank' in which intellectuals could formulate creative proposals for the betterment of the world; it would not be for them to talk high theory among themselves in, for they would never withdraw from life but make frequent sorties in order to mingle with all types of people and guide them by their example. Unfortunately he later changed the emphasis and admitted that Shukri had been right: in the foreword to Under the Green Lamp (1942) he confessed that he did not feel that he was involved in the mainstream of existence, spending 'my days in an ivory tower, my nights beneath a green lamp'. In Action and Response (1955),[9] after the phase had been left behind, he said that the tower had been meant as a place in which thinkers could escape from party politics and the exploitation of politicians. Though <u>Literature is Life</u> (1959) takes a non-committal line,[10] the Ivory Tower was indeed a cerebral refuge from unpleasant reality and one about which Hakim did not succeed in covering up the (by no means shameful) truth by seeking excuses in highsounding theories. <u>From the Ivory Tower</u> itself must appear to the layman a difficult, long-winded, introspective and rather boring work, but to the student of Hakim it is of great interest as a concrete symbol of the policy of self-banishment which he embraced for a while and which led to the irrealism of three long plays of the '40s.

The first was <u>Pigmalyun</u>, which was written and published in 1942. It was 'borrowed from the legends of Greece', but more immediately inspired by Jean Roux's painting 'Pygmalion et Galatea', which Hakim had seen in the Louvre,[11] and then by the film of Bernard Shaw's version of the story. The painting stimulated Hakim to compose '<u>Twixt Dream and Reality</u>, and Shaw provoked him to undertake a more ambitious variation on the theme, such as he had long been anxious to compose. In his undated preface, which was his first of any length and from which the foregoing facts have been culled, he places <u>Pigmalyun</u> squarely in a dramatic category which he terms 'intellectual': 'My characters are thoughts perpetually responsive to ideas and clothed in symbols ... The gulf between me and the stage has widened, and my only bridge for transmitting these works to the people is publication.' This statement makes it obvious that he had not begun to recover from witnessing <u>The Cavemen</u> mangled about in 1935 and that he still felt incapable of writing for the Egyptian theatre as it then was. By the norms of the 1940s <u>Pigmalyun</u> was grotesquely deficient in action. In the preface Hakim tells a sad story: 'The director of the theatre said to me, "Do you know what I do before deciding about a play by you? I read it at home to my children and if they like it and don't fall asleep I take it on".' Hakim knew that, faced by this kind of mentality, <u>Pigmalyun</u> would not be staged then at any rate.

The story is simple and striking and its unities of action and place, and near unity of time, are unusual in a drama by him. Pigmalyun is a Cypriot sculptor who carves a statue of Galatia which is 'much more beautiful than a woman and much more perfect than a woman'; despite, or possibly because of, his misogynistic character, he asks Venus to give it life in order that he may love it. The goddess, in collusion with Apollo, grants his wish, Pigmalyun doubts whether he will ever make – or be able to make – another statue, and the live Galatia, having failed to extract from him an unequivocal assertion that he worships her more than his last and finest statue (now her, though she does not yet realize it), abandons him for Narsis, his great friend and protege. Narsis does not think of her as a real person - 'She will always be the toy I watched him make. I'm amazed that Pigmalyun can love this thing he made with his own hands' - and Pigmalyun is soon reunited with her by Apollo, who has told her the truth of her creation. This worries her somewhat, for she is not sure whether or not, as the product of a human's imagination ('I am only your dream'), she is merely a figment of it or a being in her own right. Pigmalyun, for his part, is, from the moment of her 'birth', dissatisfied because he finds that Galatia the woman, her innocence, sweetness and devotion notwithstanding, lacks the perfection of Galatia the statue ('I didn't make a woman with a broom in her hand'), and because she cannot be both his beloved wife and his sculptural masterpiece:

> 'Both of you tear at my heartstrings. Both of you are in conflict. She by her splendour and timeless beauty, you by your nature and transient beauty. She is Art, you are my wife ... Everything about you is limited, everything about her was limitless.'

More worryingly still, as Galatia points out to him, she will age and die and thus destroy all trace of his genius. In front of her he indicts Venus and Apollo with short-changing him by swapping his perfect and immortal work of art for a fallible, mortal woman and appeals to them to take back their property and return his to him. This having been effected, he is consumed by obsession with the question of the comparative importance of art and life and by guilt at having killed his wife. He is drained of inspiration and cannot remain in his studio to be haunted by his crime. Venus suggests that Galatia should be brought back to life, but Apollo persuades her that this would only set off the same circle of events again. They and Narsis watch the sculptor, crying 'I'll make a better one' and declaring that he has won the battles against himself and against the gods which were hindering the true efflorescence of his talent, smash the statue to pieces. In vain did Narsis try to console him with the thought that the living Galatia only existed in his mind and that the statue was the only reality; correctly did he predict that, if he destroyed the statue, he would die because he would simultaneously destroy his soul.

<u>Pigmalyun</u> is perhaps Hakim's most flawless gem - an exquisite, poetic, imaginative and economical play enrobed in a fine, exotic atmosphere. Its moral - like that of <u>When we Dead Awake</u>, where it is

52 Tawfiq al Hakim

very differently presented and in which art's triumph is total, as it is not here - is that art and life cannot co-exist; the true artist must not allow himself to become involved in life (love). The variant of the Greek version of the Phoenician story is pleasing, and the enjoyable antics of Venus and Apollo are outwardly reminiscent of Amphitryon 38. The play, whose characters are divided into two unequal teams representing life and love (Galatia, Venus, Narsis and his girl-friend Ismin) and art and thought (Pigmalyun, Apollo) - the sculptor of course ends up in neither - has been severely attacked by Mandur, who rightly sees Pigmalyun as 'a portrait of his inventor, the romantic, dreaming litterateur in his ivory tower far from the battle of life'. He contrasts Hakim with Shaw, who knew all about both the sweetness and bitterness of existence.[12] (Sayyid Qutb also comments[13] on the obvious autobiographical resemblances between Hakim and his sculptor.) He speaks of 'the weakness of (the play's) dramatic power',[14] describes it as a mixture of 'symbolism and unbridled romanticism'[15] and complains that the addition of Ismin to the dramatis personae of the legend has set the structure of Pigmalyun awry.[16] His first two points were not generally subscribed to, and the last is incorrect: Ismin and Narsis together balance Pigmalyun's erratic devotion to art in a way which is highly effective and which Narsis could not have done without a partner of like opinions. Mandur misinterprets the play's conclusion by saying, en passant, that it was grist to the mill of those who maintained that Hakim was wedded to art and would never marry,[17] for it is by no means certain that, had Pigmalyun been spared, he would have succeeded in controlling his urges in the direction of life and love. Those who believed that Hakim would stay single were soon to be proved wrong; Hakim, in his conviction about Pigmalyun's non-stageability, was also wrong, but he had to wait rather longer to be undeceived.

Ali ar Ra^{c}i, uncharacteristically, intervenes[18] to widen the area of discussion. Taking three of the major plays together he detects in each of them a contrast between 'a statue' and reality. The Decian Priska, Shahrazad and the marble Galatia are in the former category, to which is opposed a phalanx composed of the Priska of the new Tarsus, Shahrazad when she is not being perfect and the human Galatia. This suggestion serves usefully to illumine Hakim's continuing doubt about his true role.

In the same year as Pigmalyun, Under the Green Lamp (Tahta'l Misbah al Akhdar), a collection of literary and anti-female essays, appeared; several of them, not always with the same titles, are reprinted in others of his anthologies, a proceeding not uncommon with his publishers. Next came Life in Bud (Zahrat al Umr, 1943), in the introduction to which he declares that he has 'dropped out' of society and intends to give up the rest of his life to art. Thus he confirmed the widely-held interpretation of the significance both of the ivory tower and of his last play. His next, also in 1943, was Solomon the Wise (Sulayman al Hakim), which is in marked contrast to Pigmalyun. It is the last of the best of those of his dramas which had their sources in the classics. Its origins, according to one of the versions of the short preface, are the Qur'an (portions of Suras 27 and 34), the Pentateuch and The Thousand and One Nights. Mandur provides[19] a breakdown of the aspects of the play which stem from these various sources and adds to the list 'The Song of Songs', from which, exaggerating greatly, he claims that whole pages have been taken. In his preface, Hakim says that, as with The Cavemen, Shahrazad and Pigmalyun, he utilized these prompters of his inspiration 'to project a picture in my mind - no more and no less'. The resultant picture is magnificently exotic, full of atmosphere, colour and action, and macabre, and no mere synopsis can do any kind of justice to it.

The play begins in San^{C}a, which Hakim has situated on the sea. A fisherman lands a bottle which, when opened, is found to contain a jinni (genie) who had been imprisoned in it for failing to help 'the prophet Solomon' to carry building materials from Tyre for the temple in Jerusalem. He is not pleased at his release, because he has had to wait so long for it, and, as an earnest of his irritation, invites the fisherman to choose as his reward the manner of his death. His tune rapidly changes when ships of Solomon's fleet come into view, however, and he persuades his rescuer to incarcerate him again and plead with the King for his pardon.

Solomon's wazir and other notables disembark and set about searching for the royal hoopoe. They are soon joined by Solomon himself. The bird quickly reappears and informs its master, 'greater than all the kings of the earth in riches and wisdom', about the Queen of Sheba. Having given a demonstration of his mastery of the languages of the animal world the King despatches the hoopoe with an invitation to her to come to visit him. At this juncture the fisherman arrives and craves permission to enter Solomon's employ. His plea is granted, the bottle and its contents are assigned to him, and he sets the jinni free again in the knowledge that he will be held accountable for the actions of his ward.

The scene changes to Sheba, where the Queen, Bilqais, is chairing a meeting to decide what to do about Solomon's message. Like the queen in Fate of a Cockroach, she is far more positive and intelligent than her male advisers and has to provide her own counsel. Out of curiosity, she determines to answer the summons and to take with her to Jerusalem a captive prince, Munzir, who is secretly betrothed to her maid but with whom she herself has fallen into unreciprocated love, a situation which has deeply hurt her.

The third scene takes place in Jerusalem, as do the final four. With Bilqais approaching, Solomon suddenly conceives the desire to seat her on her own throne beside him. This is the sort of chance the jinni, who constantly protests that he was created for grandiose, not petty, matters, has been waiting for. As the reception party close their eyes at his instructions, he retrieves the throne from Sheba in the nick of time. When Bilqais arrives, Solomon, who is nervous, discerns that she loves another. Despite this, and his possession of thousands of wives and concubines, he becomes totally enamoured of her. The jinni foresees no problems about putting matters to rights. On the strength of this assurance and after trying to undermine Bilaqis by taking her on a tour of Jerusalem on a magic carpet engineered by the jinni, Solomon threatens her with the forcible conquest of her heart when, on their return, she - as Layla did to Sulayman in Modern Woman - makes it clear that friendship is as far as she is prepared to go. He accordingly gives the go-ahead to the jinni's plan. This hinges on Munzir, who is petrified and placed in a marble basin; only when it is full of tears can he become flesh and blood again, and when he does the first woman to meet his gaze will win his heart. Bilqais does not know this but is at once discovered weeping before the 'statue' of her lover, having abandoned her state visit in favour of an unceasing vigil. Every evening, Solomon, who charged the jinni to do nothing to harm her, comes to observe the scene and to mock her, at which she is regally angry. When the basin is within a few tears of being full, in accordance with the plan he arrives to tempt her away with talk of miracles and the jinni to enlist the vital assistance of Shahba, Bilqais's pure and self-denying maid who, though herself in love with Munzir, has throughout her mistress's watch been in loyal attendance on her. He convinces her that, for one reason or another, Bilqais may not return, information which sets the maid weeping copiously. The jinni leads her to the basin, which is soon brimming, the prince awakes and his love for her is reinforced. Solomon returns and scoffs at the sight while Bilqais faints away.

The Queen comes to accept the position calmly but changes her ideas about Solomon's suit not at all. She is, however, generous enough to be sorry for him and to maintain her friendship for him at its former level. By the time she says good-bye, however, Solomon is a different man. His hair has gone grey and he is sad and ashamed at having stooped so low. (The jinni has suffered for it and been put back into his container.) He declares her friendship to be more than he deserves and they part singing its praises. After she has gone he dozes off, having ordered the fisherman, whom he has not disciplined as he promised that he would, to ensure that he is not disturbed. After many apparently comatose months in the bedroom he had had specially built for Bilqais he is, with the fisherman's permission, visited by the wazir: his stick has disintegrated, having been eaten away by armies of termites, and he has been thrown out of his chair. He is, of course, dead, his demise through the intervention of the insects he claimed to understand so well having twice been hinted at. As the fisherman is about to go back to Sanᶜa, the jinni, now under no restraint since 'the lord of mankind and the jinn' is no more, offers him the throne, might, glory and wealth of Solomon, but he is not interested because Bilqais's 'No' was more than a match for them.

At the end we are overpowered by the gruesome but cathartic spectacle of the death of the King, which is the magnificent climax of a memorable play with serious faults, of which the chief are the too prominent part accorded the fisherman and the overdone knockabout duologues between him and the jinni. Hakim has told us[20] that we are to see in the story Solomon resisting the temptation to use the jinni's irresistible powers to gain his desires. We do not do so, and the main theme of <u>Solomon the Wise</u>, whether Hakim would agree or not, is that the summit of human might and riches is, in this instance at least, impotent to sway the promptings of a woman's heart. A notable passage[21] support this view. It could be made out that Hakim is here demonstrating again the uncooperative nature of woman, but there is in fact no misogyny in evidence: Bilqais - beautiful, brave, noble, totally upright and, like Anan in <u>Expulsion from Eden</u>, who is a special case, and Shahrazad, able to scorn the desires of the male - is indeed perhaps a portrait of the kind of partner he himself was seeking. But the theme is not a major factor, for it is the atmosphere, the brilliant cut-and-thrust of the dialogue, the humour and the breathtaking scenes - the jinni in the bottle, the prince turned to marble, the basin of tears, the King committing suicide before the very eyes of his courtiers - which make the drama the (unrecognized) <u>tour de force</u> that it is. It has, sadly, been little noticed by the critics and not acted by an Egyptian troupe, perhaps partly on account of inhibition about its Jewishness. It would be difficult to perform adequately on the stage, but would make a memorable film.

Solomon the Wise crowned the achievements of the Ivory Tower, from which its architect now emerged to resume his confrontation with contemporary life.

REFERENCES

1   Repeated with variations in Mallakh, pp 237-59
2   TAY, p 197
3   SD, pp 16-17
4   Hourani, p 328
5   Subur 1, p 112
6   p 60
7   Preface
8   Eg, p 35
9   p 100
10 pp 108-11
11 Hakim in Al Ahram, 29 November 1968
12 Mandur 2, p 57
13 Kutub wa Shakhsiyyat, pp 119-21
14 Mandur 2, p 27
15 Ibid, p 54
16 Ibid, pp 54, 56
17 Mandur 1, pp 111-2
18 Ra i, p 55
19 Mandur 2, p 64
20 AR, p 35
21 pp 138-9

3 In Step with the Masses

> What miracle can recreate this
> country when it's in this condition?
> (From the Ivory Tower)

In 1943 Hakim abandoned the civil service in order to become a full-time writer. The next phase of his career was similar to his post-Paris and pre-The Cavemen one in that it gave birth to short and long, classically-inspired, symbolic and realistic plays - plays, however, of generally lower quality - but unlike in that it was to culminate in acceptance instead of disaster. In an attempt to reach a wider readership[1] than heretofore he devoted his bread-and-butter efforts of the next eight years to the pages of the newspaper Akhbar al Yawm. His first play to appear in it did so in 1945,[2] preceded by The Sacred Bond (Ar Ribat al Muqaddas, 1944) and My Donkey Said to Me (1945). The former, made into a film after the revolution,[3] is a novel built around the character of Hakim in his Ivory Tower phase (he refers to himself throughout, in the third person, as 'the Monk of Thought') which betrays clear signs of having been provoked by memories aroused in him by the publication of Life in Bud. In it he seeks to ape the principal male part in Anatole France's Thais and endeavours, like another Pygmalion, to fit the heroine into the role of Thais herself. It starts off as if intended to display the wide range of his literary learning but, once it gets into its stride, turns into a discussion of the position of women in Egyptian society, the effects of emancipation on them and the sanctity or otherwise of marriage, the 'sacred bond' of the title. The episodes and language were unus‧ frank for the period, but - pace Nagi[4] who, on account of its treatm. of the love interest, considers the book to be 'more beautiful' than any thing by D.H. Lawrence - otherwise only the pleasingly tidy structure and the seduction of the wife, which is well and tensely done, are out of the ordinary and, indeed, above the level of the trite. Nonetheless this probably ranks third among the novels. Its conclusion is that there are holier ties than matrimony. My Donkey Said to Me (Himari Qala Li), which should have been called I Said to My Donkey, is a completely self-centred and almost entirely worthless volume mainly made up of duo-logues and scenes about its author, the Second World War (eg a playlet mocking Mussolini in captivity) and Egyptian society, potiticians and women. It contains some of Hakim's severest criticism of the last two, but this is so exhibitionist and glib that it becomes boring and counter-productive. (We learn subsequently, in Al Hakim's Stick, that the donkey defected afterwards and, suitably enough, went into politics.)

In 1946[5] Hakim entered into a marriage which, despite his forebodings ('I dreamed I was married. What a catastrophe.')[6] and expressions of non-intent (' ... I shall never marry.'),[7] has proved a happy one[8] and yielded a son and three daughters.* Mandur celebrated the event by remarking, rather patronisingly, that it did not affect his creative flair and, tardily, that it brought him out of his ivory tower, or bottle (an allusion to that inhabited by the jinni in Solomon the Wise), onto the plains of life.[9] About his wife all that can be said is that Jamal Muhammad Ahmad describes her as a lady of the peasant class from Hakim's own natal area[10] and Mallakh[11] states that she is a sister of Dr Muhammad Lutfi Bayyumi, one-time Dean of the Tanta Medical Faculty.

King Oedipus (Al Malik Udib), which seems to have been begun in 1945/6, was published in 1949. It was adorned ten years later by a 44 page preface, Hakim's longest, in which the discussion ranges widely. With regard to King Oedipus itself, 'I recalled Seneca's falling-short, Corneille's failure and Voltaire's feebleness in comparison with Sophocles, and I became giddy,' and apprehensive when he contemplated the lack of success of contemporary writers who had tackled the theme.

---

* Isma^{c}il, Zaynab (after Hakim's 'patron saint', but also known as Suzy!), Nura and Naga. (Mallakh, pp 8, 81 and 266 and Naqqash, p 77). Isma^{c}il was at one time said to be a talented musician. (Al Ayyam, Khartum, 8 August 1972).

Of the poets with whom he was familiar, Yeats and Hofmannsthal had not advanced at all on Sophocles. Among the prose writers were Cocteau and Gide. The former had adopted an inappropriately Shakespearian approach, while Gide's method, which had stripped the story of its dramatic splendour, had been that of the modern European who, following Voltaire, 'this sceptical scoffer', and Nietzsche, proclaimed man, not God, all-powerful. He steeled and encouraged himself with the thought that he could profit from their mistakes, and says that he felt it possible to cloak a Greek play in the Arab intellect, to do, in fact, the reverse of what he had attempted in <u>The Cavemen</u>. He chose for his experiment <u>Oedipus Rex</u>, 'the Greek tragedy I consider the least steeped in religious mythology, the purest and most straightforward, and the closest to real life in its unadulterated humanism,' because Oedipus was a character, like Praksa, whom he saw as suitable to be moulded for his own purposes and

> 'For a reason which may appear strange. I pondered long and perceived in it something which did not occur to the mind of Sophocles. I perceived in it a struggle not only between man and fate ... but also the same hidden struggle which took place in <u>The Cavemen</u> not only between man and time ... but also ... between the actual and the true, between the actuality of a man like Mishilinya, who left the cave, found Priska and (fell into reciprocated love with her), and the truth about him. 'Everything was ready to invite them to a life free of care and worry. If there was an obstacle between them and this beautiful actuality, was it not the truth? - the truth about this man Mishilinya who made it clear to Priska that he was her ancestor's fiance. The lovers tried to forget this truth, which sullied actuality for them, but they were ... unable to rid themselves of (it). Oedipus and Jocasta are no different from Mishilinya and Priska ... '

His version of <u>Oedipus Rex</u> represented his final flirtation with the Greek classics. Like so many of his more weighty works, it has received little attention in Egypt, where - as in the Arab world as a whole - the impression might easily be gained that he has written only three plays, <u>The Cavemen</u>, <u>Shahrazad</u> and <u>Pigmalyun</u>. It has, however, been staged in Carthage in about 1970. Mandur is the sole critic to devote much space to it, and he has nothing favourable to impart: it 'is regarded as one of the weakest of his dramas, not only in relation to Sophocles, etc., but also ... to Tawfiq al Hakim himself ... He begins his play by revealing all its secrets and surprises and then sets aside these explanations to embark upon a superficial and dull implementation whose construction is no better than Andre Gide's.'[12] He charges the author with weak characterization, which leads to diminished impact and audience appeal,[13] with inconsistency, with a 'painful moral decline' evidenced by the fact that, in his view, the version is heretical, and with causing Oedipus to lose all our sympathy.[14] Our only reaction to his final conversation with Jocasta, which resembles those of Mishilinya and Priska, is, he declares, disgust.[15] 'The play was not a dramatic success, nor was it sound from the intellectual, abstract angle. Its failure was complete and utter.'[16] Hakim, wise after the event, says that he knew that this would be the case.[17]

Much of what Mandur says is justified, though it should be remarked that Sophocles gives away his 'secrets and surprises' more quickly than Hakim does and that, in the judgement of this writer, Oedipus's fate is no less cathartic in the Arabic play than in the Greek. The former is, however, very close to the original and, for this reason, is not to be included among Hakim's best: its derivative nature is readily apparent, long passages having been translated word for word. There are minor differences in detail and major divergencies in emphasis, but 'the lord of tragedy'[18] is throughout in obvious attendance. Hakim's play is much the longer and less bare. It gives some, novel account of the domestic life of Oedipus, Jocasta and their children, and confers on Antigone an expanded and touching role which supplies appealing symmetry. But this, while perhaps bridging the gap between a hypothetical Egyptian audience and the stark intricacies of the legend, adds nothing of force or positive originality. Though the humiliation of the King is now entrusted, in place of the gods, to a more prominent Tiresias, an evil, sneering, Nietszchean character disapproved of by its creator,[19] the story remains in essentials the same. This is despite Hakim's vain attempt, explained in the preface to <u>Fate of a Cockroach</u>, to endow Oedipus with more resistance than Mishilinya by equipping him with a determined and persuasive mind - one which should have been able (but of course was not) to overcome Jocasta's qualms about the dictates of the truth and of the society to which she belonged[20] - and thus to heighten the tragic effect. Hakim could have done something much more exciting. Unlike Sophocles, he indicates that the downfall of Oedipus at the hands of Tiresias is to set a pattern, for Creon and the High Priest (Al Kahin) are plainly in an identical relationship to each other, Oedipus's successor, like his brother-in-law, being the puppet of his religious adviser, who can be expected to do him no good. This is an extension of the theme, and it is surprising that a virtuoso like Hakim, having introduced it, did not make it the mainspring of his action and thus write a more striking play than the one we have. In The Literary Art[21] he adumbrates a continuation of Romeo and Juliet which might similarly have been worth pursuing.

In 1950 he published collectively, under the title Plays of Social Life (Masrah al Mugtama^C), most of those he had penned for Akhbar al Yawm, plus others not initially featured in its pages. Though their feel is realistic as the title indicates (they have on the whole a markedly unreal air), the result is a Comedie Humaine in miniature or, closer to home, a Mahfuz trilogy with a shorter timespan. Ar Ra^{C}i has described it as 'a complete panorama of Cairene life'[22] and Jacques Berque as embodying 'en saynetes naturalistes les problemes de son pays'.[23] Mandur awarded it his seal of approval as being suitable for the stage because of its social themes, but noted that some men of letters, critics and producers considered it journalism rather than art and preferred Hakim's intellectual plays.[24] (Whatever he wrote up to this time he could not but be wrong.) Mandur, who may well have felt his view of the advantages of marriage to Hakim confirmed by the sparseness of misogynistic sentiment in Plays of Social Life, has, with Ar Ra^{C}i and Berque, taken too casual a stance. Though it concentrates on (political) corruption, the position of women and, without hatred or propaganda, the war for Palestine, the anthology is by no means solely concerned with contemporary social and political questions. Rejuvenation is not. The Producer (Al Mukhrig), about an Othello who ceases to distinguish between his stage and real identities and kills Iago, can hardly be said to be. Least of all is The Anthill (Bayt an Namal), an eery fantasy which has been translated into French, Italian and Spanish and (ironically, considering Mandur's reasons for deeming Plays of Social Life to be stageable) performed in Madrid. All in all, though containing Rejuvenation and Death Song (Ughniyyat al Mawt), a Synge-like[25] jewel which has been compared with Lorca's Yerma,[26] the collection is not especially remarkable, and two of its three long plays are among its least memorable items. The Peaceful Nest (Al Ish al Hadi), though it improves vastly as it develops and has some amusing conceits and a well-drawn supporting character in Qanbariyya, is of little moment, except to those curious to know how the institution of marriage affects writers, and is not good drama. Mandur, who says that it has been televised as a farce in the colloquial,[27] with justice describes it as light-weight, shallow, artistically naive and passe in theme.[28] The Thief (Al Luss), which is not a melodrama as Ar Ra^{c}i maintains,[29] has a number of touches which betray the craftsman's skill but do not rescue it from mediocrity; performed in 1949 and then banned after pressure from capitalists allegedly of the type portrayed in it,[30] it attacked the Faruqi aristocracy sharply and hinted for the first time at post-revolutionary attitudes by introducing the theme of the value of labour. The best of the three is <u>If Only Young People Knew</u> (<u>Law Arafa ash Shabab</u>), which was written in 1948, dramatised a topic found earlier in <u>My Donkey Said to Me</u> [31] and changed its name to <u>Rejuvenation</u> (<u>Awdat ash Shabab</u>) when it was produced. It explores the natures of time and reality and is a worthy member of the group of plays built around these matters; it also displays a growing preoccupation with science, a preoccupation which was far to outlast that with labour.

Luwis Awad has subjected <u>Plays of Social Life</u> to sneering and inaccurate ideological criticism. In an error-strewn lecture delivered at Harvard and printed in <u>Al Adab</u>[32] he opined that it and <u>The Anxiety Bank</u> were Hakim's only works with a social purpose. He added, 'When he wanted to burn incense to the revolution ... he deviated from his private path to write 21 one act plays, published them in a book and said, "This is my present to the revolution. Now allow me to continue my life in peace, writing about my legends, my interests and my personal philosophies."' A more ill-informed and prejudiced sentence has yet to be devoted to Hakim.

<u>King Oedipus</u>, <u>The Peaceful Nest</u>, <u>The Thief</u> and <u>Rejuvenation</u> were the last long plays Hakim composed before 1954. By then the Republic had come into being and, with it, marked changes in his dramatic emphases, so that Mandur[33] was able to affirm that the revolution completed the release from himself which his marriage had begun. The percipient observer would have noticed that, long before, in <u>The Angel's Prayer</u>, <u>The Thief</u> and <u>Rejuvenation</u>, he had started to turn his attention to subjects which were of increasing importance to the people at large in their run-up to the revolution and were to be of immediate and abiding concern to their leaders. He was greatly to underline his philosophical solidarity with the new rulers of his country in the years ahead (the next five particularly), but even now was, in total contrast to the misfit prewar period, a promoter and latent partisan of the ideas which they and their people were to share.

REFERENCES

1. Ra^{c}i, p 60
2. Ibid, loc cit
3. Sa^{c}ad ad Din Tawfiq, p 122
4. Adham, p 224, Mallakh, p 222
5. Mallakh, pp 266 and 287, is alone in dating this event 1944
6. MDS, p 93
7. Ibid, p 99
8. Papadopoulo, p 234, Mallakh, p 266
9. Mandur 2, p 56
10. Oral communication, 16 March 1972
11. p 224
12. Mandur 2, p 75
13. Ibid, p 38
14. Mandur 1, pp 112-4
15. Mandur 2, p 74
16. Ibid, p 76
17. Postscript, p 222
18. LL, p 35
19. Papadopoulo, pp 241-3
20. AR, p 94
21. pp 224-31
22. Ra^{c}i, p 62
23. In UNESCO, p 31
24. Mandur 1, pp 108-9
25. Anthony McDermott, 'Death Song: Tragic Lament for the Two Egypts', New Middle East, June 1972, p 22
26. By Johnson-Davies, Fate of a Cockroach and other plays (back cover)
27. Mandur 2, p 162
28. Ibid, loc cit
29. pp 66-9
30. ARD, p 81, where Hakim places these happenings a year earlier
31. pp 133-44
32. November 1972, pp 2-7
33. Mandur 2, p 56

1 Coming to Terms

> ... the reviver of literature.
> (Gamal Abd an Nasir on Tawfiq al Hakim)

Taha Husayn was Egypt's Minister of Education from 1950-2, and in 1951 Hakim became a Ministry civil servant again, this time, following the illustrious Lutfi as Sayyid at a distance, as Director-General of the National Library (Dar al Kutub), a position which allowed him plenty of scope for writing.

The early fruits of the 1950s owed nothing to his new job, however. The first was a collection of interesting, if disparate, articles and imaginative pieces from the period 1924-48; entitled The Literary Art (Fann al Adab, 1952), it is a valuable source-book for Hakim's philosophy and autobiography, even though none of the items in it is dated. The second - the staging in late 1952 of the clever and suspenseful playlet called The Chest (As Sanduq) - and the third (the production of at least one of his dramas during the 1952/3 theatre season in Algeria)[1] were the harbingers of his re-entry in force onto the Egyptian stage, which was yet a little further delayed by Memories of Law and Art (Min Zikriyyat al Qada wa'l Fann) and Show me Allah (Arni Allah), which were published in 1953. The former, later shortened and retitled Justice and Art (Adalatun wa Fann), is a miscellany of light autobiographical episodes, one of which had already appeared in My Donkey Said to Me, in which the law predominates, and the latter a varied and attractive anthology of short stories. Another sign of renewed recognition in prospect was the success abroad of Pigmalyun which, in a translation by Maria Grobmann,[2] was performed at the Salzburg Mozarteum in December 1953, and received with acclaim by the Austrian press.[3]

Hakim had been among the audience at Salzburg.[4] He returned to Cairo to find himself on the brink of disgrace, Isma^{c}il al Qabbani, the then Minister of Education, having included him among a number of his officials he wanted to see pensioned-off because they were unproductive. The list came before the Council of Ministers where, according to Luwis Awad,[5] Gamal Abd an Nasir, who was at the time Prime Minister, protected Hakim from this purge and 'emphasized (his) standing in modern Egyptian literature and ... the respect in which he was held in literary and artistic circles in Europe.' In Hakim's words,[6] he clinched matters by saying, 'Are you asking us to dismiss a writer just back with laurels from Europe? Do you want them to say we're savages?' Though it was the Minister who was dismissed, it seems likely that Hakim had, in fact, put his writing before his official duties. (One of them, ironically, was to sit on a panel to choose the best films of 1950-1 and thus help to keep the flagging cinema going.)[7] We have it from Mandur[8] that throughout his civil service career his major preoccupation was with his own work.

Three notable events rapidly followed this crisis. His long-overdue election to the Cairo Arabic Language Academy occurred on 17 May 1954, on Abd an Nasir's orders according to one source,[9] who is perhaps to be believed on the point: he filled the vacant seat of Abd al Aziz Fahmi, who was an undergraduate with his father,[10] and his welcoming address was delivered by Taha Husayn, who had undertaken the same task rather earlier for Mahmud Taymur. Next, eleven days later, Abd an Nasir inscribed for him a copy of The Philosophy of the Revolution in these words: 'To the reviver of literature, Ustaz Tawfiq al Hakim, in anticipation of a second, post-revolutionary return of the soul.'[11] (The allusion to The Soul's Return requires no amplification.) Finally, Soft Hands (Al Aidi an Na^{c}ima), an unhappy dramatic blend of social humour and disingenuous socialism which shows its author trying to get to grips with the thinking of the revolution, was published. It was heavily censored initially but nonetheless caused a volte-face in attitudes towards Hakim and his work. Mandur, for instance, praised it for its ideological soundness.[12] He maintains that it directly preceded Isis so that, ignoring Her Majesty and the likelihood that Death Game came before The Thorns of Peace, he could lump it together with The Deal and The Thorns of Peace to prove that Hakim had at last seen the light. Given his earlier hostility, it was nice of him to go to such lengths. Soft Hands would have been a much better play without the grafted-on ideology, which its author seems rather to resent: on three separate occasions he decides that he and his reader are bored with it and jettisons it with a flash of irreverent humour. He had, nevertheless, contrived to win acceptance at last, for those who wanted to, and did not detect his sceptical approach, could see in his continued flirtation with the theme of labour and his scorn for Faruq's hangers-on the correct convictions of a true son of the revolution. Most of his plays were suddenly found to be actable after all.

There were three more publications in 1954.* Al Hakim's Stick (Asa al Hakim), written before the revolution, comprises discussions, like those of My Donkey Said to Me and somewhat resembling those of Beverley Nicholls and his Irate Reader in No Place like Home, between Hakim and his celebrated walking-stick. A wide range of facets of modern life is pessimistically reviewed, home and international affairs are subjected to critical scrutiny and Hakim's mounting distrust of science is exhibited. The book, one of his most absorbing of the type, is divided into two parts, the second[13] switching the searchlight towards the life after death: the two converse, in the main to little effect, with favourite characters (not necessarily revered) of the author, such as Eve, Cleopatra, Jeanne d'Arc, Napoleon, Qasim Amin, Tagore and Hitler. The present writer has not seen Reflections on Politics (Ta'ammulatun fi's Siyasa),[14] but accounts of it suggest that it is composed of essays of the previous decade which display a post war return to political concern with Egypt and novel and surprising views on the situation at home prior to the revolution. Her Majesty (Sahibat al Galala) is a play which belatedly attacks one aspect of ex-King Faruq's conduct of his affairs, of which it gives an accurate portrayal. It has a scene, in which the hero telephones to the heroine, who is in a different part of Cairo but whom Hakim spirits onto the stage beside him, which hints at the flashbacks and 'shadow plays' of Journey into the Future, The Tree Climber, Food for Every Mouth and A Hunting Trip. Its serialization in Akhbar al Yawm began in 1954 and stretched into the following year. Most strangely, it has not been noticed by the critics.

---

* Mallakh, p 292, mentions a fourth, a novel called Ships of the Sun (Marakib ash Shams), but provides no information about it.

In 1955, Shahrazad, which was to have been put on by the Egyptian National Theatre at the 1954 Paris Drama Festival but was withdrawn when an Israeli company was learned to be participating,[15] enjoyed success abroad. It was broadcast and repeated in March, on the BBC's Third Programme, in a translation apparently of one of the French editions,[16] with Margaret Leighton, John Gielgud and Carleton Hobbs in the lead roles;[17] with Death Wish (Arafa Kayfa Yamut, one of the Plays of Social Life), it was performed at the Comedie de Paris[18] in November.

It would have been unthinkable for Hakim to fail to make use of the legend of Isis and Osiris, as he did in the same year. He had always clearly intended to do so, mentioning the goddess in Volume 1 of The Soul's Return, bringing her several times into dialogues in Shahrazad - on the title page of which a saying ascribed to her is quoted - and narrating one version of her story - not that he eventually dramatised - in The Sacred Bond.[19] The theme of Isis (Izis), a philosophical development on Soft Hands, is political, and the play makes indirect comment on the administration of Abd an Nasir. The plot is simple and affecting. At the start Isis's husband Osiris is King of Egypt, but more involved in improving the lot of his people through scientific research of his own than through taking political measures. He strives to maximise the irrigation potential of the Nile to the detriment of his royal position, which is speedily overrun by his brother Tifun[20] who, after a period of corregnum, arranges for him to be abducted and thrown into the river in a trunk. He is picked up by a passing fishing boat and taken to Byblos, where he becomes an agricultural adviser to the King, to whom he does not reveal his identity. Isis tracks him down and brings him back to Egypt, where they live in hiding with their son Huris. Osiris pursues his researches until his spreading fame enables his brother to catch up with him again and have him finally done away with. Isis determines that their son shall unseat his venal and tyrannical uncle. She organizes a lengthy programme of preparation for him and, when she thinks he is ready, enlists the aid of the Shaykh al Balad, the top official who was instrumental in bringing about Osiris's downfall but has now turned against Tifun, to set up a confrontation between uncle and nephew. At this, Huris's martial instruction is shown to have been woefully inadequate but, on the point of killing him, Tifun is persuaded by the Shaykh, in spite of their bad relations, to put his nephew on public trial. The hearing, like that conducted by King Balpirus in Praksa II (both scenes must have been written at about the same time), does not go smoothly for its organiser, and Huris's salvation and title to the throne of Egypt are clinched by the opportune arrival, planned by Isis, of the King of Byblos and his conclusive testimony to Tifun's cruel and illegal treatment of Osiris.

Isis is a good story, pleasingly rounded-off by its deus ex machina-like ending; it is a genuine addition to the literature of the legend which, though it treats it in somewhat uninspired fashion, makes the utmost, atmospherically speaking, of the legend's natural physical assets (the Nile and the Levant coast), resembling in this Solomon the Wise. The cast includes a large number of rich, colourful and witty supporting characters to whom no reference has been made in the synopsis above, but who contribute much to the effectiveness of the drama. Hakim does not write plays merely to retail engaging yarns, however. On this occasion his primary purpose has been to use the well-fleshed bones of his plot to ask a number of pertinent political and philosophical questions. Was Isis's action in making use of the tainted services of the Shaykh al Balad, the murderer of her husband, justified by the end it brought about? Further, was she right seeing that Huris, unlike Tifun, had exhibited none of the qualities of a ruler? Is ruling a task which can properly be entrusted to a hereditary succession, or should the ruler be the one most fitted to the job, irrespective of his birth and connections?

It is possible, of course, to read far more into a work of literature than its author intended. Arab critics of Hakim, however, err on the side of caution in the main and are rarely struck by, or perhaps have not found it politic to give public utterance to, interpretations above the level of the mundane. If Hakim has been handicapped by being immeasurably too intelligent for his audiences, he has also suffered from the lack of enterprise and imagination of his critics, who have largely failed to read between the lines. In the same way as, incredibly enough, none of them has mentioned the political purpose of Isis - except, in the case of Mandur,[21] to say that the play is concerned with the struggle of the normal and the ideal, or the bad and the good, in politics! - the crucial role of the Shaykh al Balad has gone unobserved. Reminiscent of several villains in Spanish literature - the mayor in Calderon's El Alcalde de Zalamea or the Corregidor in Alarcon's El Sombrero de Tres Picos, for example, - his part is that of the successful and unattractive coat-turning rogue and he is probably a political symbol.

Ali ar Ra^ci has little of assistance to say about Isis. He describes it as the final version of Praksa II, speaks of its novel-type form[22] and compares it with 'the political, masses-orientated art ... (of) Bertold Brecht'.[23] Mandur, delivering his initial verdict upon it, calls it

Hakim's only interesting and actable intellectual play;[24] on reconsideration he maintained that it was not really intellectual or abstract at all.[25] He praises its author for giving the legend a realistic character, which guaranteed for Isis not only a future on the stage but also 'a reasonable popular welcome',[26] and considers it to be 'among his best plays'.[27] His predictably favourable view of the removal from the legend of as much as was 'feasible of its mythical, extraordinary events'[28] was, he reports, not shared by Awad and other leading critics, who attacked Hakim for omitting prominent features of it, such as the rebirth of Osiris.[29] Reactions in general were varied, both when the play was published and when, only a year later, it was staged:[30] perhaps as a sop to criticism, Nabil al Alfi put back some of the missing highlights in his production,[31] which occurrence showed that Hakim had indeed returned to the theatre and presaged for him an almost uninterrupted presence, lasting sixteen years, there. It seems to this writer that in his adaptation (based to some extent on Plutarch) of the Isis legend he did not overdo the artist's privilege to be selective[32] and that his usual imaginative approach was of some benefit.[33] What may justifiably be regretted is the de-deification of the chief personae, which substitutes extraneous and anachronistic material for the remoteness and mystery of the original and, as in King Oedipus, does nothing for the drama.

Hakim's other publication in 1955 was Action and Response (At Ta^caduliyya) which, purporting to be guidance to a friend on the author's philosophies of life and art, appears to be an attempt to popularize a series of concepts of some naivete with which he has ever since been associated and which have made the inclusion of the word 'balance'[34] ineluctable in any reference to him. The book is useful in that it gives fresh insight into a number of his plays, notably The Cavemen, Shahrazad, Pigmalyun and Solomon the Wise. Farag regards it as the key to his philosophy and ideas.[35]

The following year the Higher Council of Arts, Letters and Social Sciences was constituted and Hakim left the National Library to become a permanent and full-time member of it, with the rank of Under Secretary. His pen remained active. The first of his two titles in 1956 was The Deal (As Safqa), a play which is of note not for itself but for the aims his postscript indicates that he had set himself in writing it. These were to find answers to four long-standing problems of the drama. The chief was language. As the Arab theatre developed into a phenomenon which could not be overlooked, playwrights and audiences became understandably exercised about which of the two possible languages

- the classical or the colloquial - should be its vehicle of communication. Hakim cites two examples from his own work. Death Song is based in the rif where one would not expect people to speak anything approximating to modern classical, but its central character is a student from Al Azhar who, though born in the village where the action takes place, could not be realistically presented if he used a country dialect unenhanced at the least by some Cairene elegance of pronunciation and vocabulary. In this case he decided to couch the whole play in the classical, which made it 'acceptable for reading but in need of translation, for production, into the language which people can speak'. The dilemma is severe, for the classical is the language of formal occasions, of the radio and of newspapers; not even Alwan, the Azharite, would use it unmodified. Thus books, not excluding printed plays, have until recently been inadmissible if not written in the classical. On the other hand, theatre audiences jib at unrealistic language, and for the peasants of the village of Death Song to converse in anything except the colloquial would jar. His other example is The Piper, which greatly antedates Death Song and was entirely in the colloquial. This made it difficult for readers, rendered some of the characters invraisemblable because they would have spoken a higher form of dialect, and restricted the range of the play to those areas where the form of colloquial chosen would be understood. The classical, with pronunciation modifications, is familiar to the educated Arab from the Atlantic to the Gulf, but is artificial because people do not use it under normal circumstances; the colloquial is artificial except in its own locality. A theoretical answer would be for each character in a play to talk (as in Ibsen) as he would in real life, but in real Arab life there are no colloquial-classical conversations and stage ones - like those created by Farah Antun, Mikha^{c}il Nu^{c}aima, Al Mazini and Fathi Ridwan - are therefore the least satisfactory possible solution.[36] Hakim says in his postscript (though he had never revealed this before) that The Piper and Death Song were linguistically experimental; The Deal is therefore his third attempt to tackle this difficult problem. The object was

> 'to find a valid language which would not offend against the canons of the classical and be at the same time one people could speak without being untrue to their characters or their way of living - a correct language comprehensible to every generation, district and region [of Egypt] and extensible to surrounding areas. That is the language of this play. It may well appear to its reader at

first glance that it is written in the colloquial, but if he continues
reading, following the canons of the classical, he will find that it
is as logical as it could [humanly] be.'

Hakim suggests that the reader may care to go through the play twice,
once pronouncing in the fashion of the rif and then according to
the rules of correct classical. He will discover, he says, that it may
be declaimed just as naturally by a peasant as by one who is accustomed
to speak a higher form of Arabic.[37]

'If I have succeeded in this experiment it will lead to two results
- firstly, progress in the direction of a unified theatrical language
for our literature .., and secondly - and more importantly - the
closer juxtaposition of the classes of the one people [Egypt] and the
Arabic-speaking peoples by unifying the medium of mutual understanding as far as possible without violating the requisites of art.'

He did not achieve the first result, perhaps partly because his experimental vehicle - though, in feeling, a natural follow-up to Act One of
Soft Hands and to Isis - was not particularly noteworthy while being at
same time too extreme. (The language of The Deal, dubbed fus^{c}amiyya
(classico-colloquial)[38] and generally termed Hakim's 'third language',
though referred to by one critic as his second,[39] is artificial because it
is not true Arabic at all and because it overstretches the classical
syntax.)[40] There is no evidence, either, that the second was attained.
Hakim had to return to the problem, to greater effect, in The Dilemma
ten years later.

His three other aims in The Deal were to write a drama which,
catering for the fact that there are few playhouses in Egypt outside Cairo
and Alexandria, required no stage, scenery or costumes ('... perhaps
there was in this ... a reversion to the pure, ancient stream from which
the theatre emerged to flourish more than 2,000 years ago'); would
attract people of different intellectual levels and simultaneously close
the gap between drama and folklore; and, by educating audiences to
react to natural stage situations in a natural way, would tackle a problem 'peculiar to us and to our theatre' - the dependence of a play's
success on either wild laughter or tears. Ar Ra^{c}i claims that it was an
operetta in shape, designed to be accompanied by song and dance, and
that its plot was based on an actual happening.[41] Anyway, the story which
he composed as the test-bed for his experimentation, which there is no
reason to suppose realized any of his subsidiary aims, is pedestrian in

the extreme. Recalling, again, the atmosphere and incidents, of fantasy rather than reality, associated with certain periods of Spanish literature (too much should not be made of this probably fortuitous resemblance), as well as the pastoral ambience of both Soft Hands and Isis, it recounts the course of negotiations between a village and a Belgian company. The village is seeking to avail itself of an offer from the company to purchase its land. Eventually terms are agreed, despite a temporary and irrelevant hitch in the proceedings. This is caused by the chance arrival in the village, in the main square of which all visible action takes place, of two corrupt and large-scale absentee landowners from Cairo whom the villagers assume have come in order to outbid them. A favourable conclusion to the negotiations appears at one point to depend, though in fact it does not, on the willingness of one of the girls of the village to sacrifice her purity to the more senior of the feudalists. She falls in with his plan that she should accompany him to Cairo but, with picaresque effrontery, contrives to keep him at a distance and return, untouched, to her fiance, having had her would-be seducer quarantined for two days during which the deal is made. Mandur says it is 'as if she is the Egyptian Jeanne d'Arc who rescues her village from the oppression of the feudalist',[42] a statement which suggests that he has misread the play.

The Deal is noteworthy for its idealisation of Egyptian rural life, which the author of A Rural Deputy's Diary and Death Song is well qualified to portray, if not to glorify. (There are other parallels with Death Song: both discuss the concept of honour as retained in rural districts and have as their off-stage focal point the local railway station.) It throws light on the grovelling but honourable attitudes of country people to visitants from the big city and on the unscrupulousness and immorality of the latter. As a piece of theatre, however - devoid of deep meaning or ambitious ideas - it is aimed at a lowest common denominator of Egyptian taste and almost totally lacks features which could render it attractive either to those Egyptian who had been able to keep up with Hakim in his non-purpose-built plays or to people in other countries (it was seen in 1965 in Baghdad) who had been introduced to some of his better work. It is hard to escape the conclusion that in 1956 he had time on his hands but little inspiration in his head and that his grandiose postscript was engineered to hoodwink the reader into believing that he had in front of him something of major significance - he appears to have so believed, for it aroused 'intense interest'[43] - rather than a routine, unworthy potboiler. Mandur's opinion could not be more opposed. He sees The Deal, with Soft Hands, as 'the best of Al-Hakim's social plays',[44] an effective echo of the philosophy of the revolution,[45] and 'a successful drama of lasting worth':[46] 'the author has been able to give his play an eternal human value and a dramatic, profoundly novel excellence'.[47] One may to a limited extent agree about the echo, but the rest of these judgements are unbecoming in their postulant. Ar Ra^{c}i believes[48] that this 'peasant theatre-in-the-round' was a precursor of those by Yusuf Idris and Mahmud Diyab.

Hakim's other publication in the year of Suez was A Variety of Theatre (Al Masrah al Munawwa^c), a collection of twenty plays: the eight issued in 1937 as Plays of Tawfiq al Hakim, Modern Woman, The Angel's Prayer, Soft Hands, Her Majesty and eight short ones; among the last is a masterpiece entitled The Clock Strikes (Daqqat as Sa^{c}a), which ranks second only to Death Song of the one-acters. The themes are mainly social, and the miscellany is as equally deserving of the name Plays of Social Life as that which came out under that title six years earlier.

During the period 1952-6 Hakim was awarded a state prize for literature (gaizat ad dawla fi'l adab) and another, the state's prize for merit (gaizat ad dawla at taqdiriyya), which was in the gift of his Higher Council and was worth £E 2,500. (When it was proposed that the latter carry with it a pension for life, he was the first recipient to whom it was suggested that this new arrangement should apply: it is not clear, however, whether or not anything came of the idea.) In addition he had the great honour of being admitted into class one of Egypt's highest order.[49] These immense expressions of his literary and general prestige were satisfyingly complemented by the success of Soft Hands, which Yusuf Wahbi, of all people, translated into the colloquial and produced in 1957.[50] This remarkable occurence, reinforced when it became a film, starring Wahbi (with Sabah), and was shown at a mid-1960s Berlin film festival,[51] was ungainsayable proof that he and the Egyptian theatre had come to terms, that they had in fact become one. Ar Rihani was dead, and his only traditionalist rival had concluded that he and Hakim were entirely compatible. Since Hakim had also been completely accepted by the revolution, it was only natural that President Abd an Nasir should have attended the premiere.[52]

74 Tawfiq al Hakim

REFERENCES

1 Landau, p 133, quoting La Bourse Egyptienne for 1 November 1952
2 Al Hilal 76, 2, p 70
3 See the appendices to The Sultan's Dilemma, pp 188-93, for the translated notices.
4 AW, p 35
5 In Awad 1. See also Lacouture, Egypt in Transition, Methuen, London, 1958, p 460, and Robert St John, The Boss, Barker, London, 1961, p 162
6 AW, loc cit
7 Sa^{c}ad ad Din Tawfiq, p 94
8 Mandur 2, p 12
9 St John, loc cit
10 LP, p 37
11 Awad 1
12 Mandur 1, p 113, 2, pp 31, 104, 114
13 Repeated in much abbreviated form in LL, pp 201-11
14 Hakim dates it 1947 in the appendix to Food for Every Mouth, p 181
15 Landau, p 110
16 Professor Walid Arafat, oral communication, 18 April 1973
17 See an appendix to The Sultan's Dilemma, pp 181-5, for the translated comments of the Radio Times and The Times. The latter, reviewing the Cambridge production of Pigmalyun, remembered Shahrazad as 'a work of luxuriant fantasy and rich ambiguity'
18 See Ibid, pp 186-7, for a French view of this
19 pp 83-7
20 The Greek form of the name of the legendary Seth, whom Hakim had referred to as Sit in The Sacred Bond
21 Mandur 2, pp 79, 82
22 Ra^{c}i, pp 82-3
23 Ibid, p 88
24 Mandur 1, pp 114-6
25 Mandur 2, p 81
26 Ibid, pp 82-3
27 Ibid, p 82
28 Ibid, p 78
29 Ibid, p 82
30 Shukri, p 280
31 Mandur 2, p 145
32 See, for example, R.E. Witt, Isis in the Graeco-Roman World,

Thames and Hudson, London, 1971
33 Compare some of its details with T. G. H. James, <u>Myths and Legends of Ancient Egypt</u>, Hamlyn, London, 1969, for example, p 32
34 See <u>Farag</u>, pp 162-72
35 <u>Farag</u>, p 162
36 Dr Husayn Fawzi disagrees, in <u>Dawara 2</u>, pp 67-9
37 Mandur (2, p 118) did not find this to be the case. The language of the play, he believed, was colloquial.
38 <u>Muhammad al Hasan</u>, p 98
39 Ar Ra^{c}i, in <u>Ostle</u>, p 178
40 Cachia in <u>JAOS</u> 87, p 18
41 Ar Ra^{c}i, in <u>Ostle</u>, pp 167, 168, 176
42 <u>Mandur 2</u>, p 130
43 Cachia, in <u>JAOS</u>, loc cit
44 <u>Mandur 2</u>, p 31
45 Ibid, p 32
46 Ibid, p 131
47 Ibid, p 130
48 Ar Ra^{c}i, in <u>Ostle</u>, p 168
49 <u>Hiwar 20</u>, pp 128-9
50 <u>Mandur 2</u>, p 118
51 <u>Mallakh</u>, pp 92, 303
52 Olga Kapeliuk, <u>The Theater in Egypt</u>, NO. 1, 4, p 38

2 Speaking to the World

> The prospects open to the world range from the disaster of nuclear war to an age in which science can provide liberation from poverty and squalor and the basis of a new advance in the dignity and value of human life.
>
> (Mr Reginald Maudling to his constituents, 1962)

In 1957 Hakim brought out three plays of a political timbre which, to varying degrees, reflected his concern at the danger faced by the world because of the advance of science and, not noticeably inspired by Suez, at the international situation in general and the trend of events in Egypt. In line with the output of his whole career, they are of uneven quality and none of them has been performed at home. Death Game and The Thorns of Peace are trite, Journey into the Future is exciting. It is not certain in what order they were written, but they will be taken in that suggested by the somewhat unsatisfactory internal evidence.

Death Game, or Death and Love (Lu^{c}bat al Mawt, aw Al Mawt wa'l Hubb) shares with Praksa the odd featue of having been published in full in Arabic only after having issued in French. Its themes are the powerlessness of the twentieth-century individual against nuclear-age governments and the potential of love in world affairs. Its chief character is a professor of ancient history, an authority on the age of Cleopatra, who has, by undisclosed means, become contaminated by a fatal dose of radiation and is determined to have his revenge on 'them'. With only three or four months to live and no family left, he settles upon a modern Cleopatra (Kilyubatra), a dancer in a night-club he frequents and the only other figure to appear on the stage, as 'their' representative. He draws up a will bequeathing all his earthly possessions to her in the expectation that as soon as he tells her of it she, her boy friend Antonio and her manageress, none of whom is privy to the alarming prognosis of his sickness, will combine to murder him and get their hands on his money. The last laugh will posthumously be his when, in court, they learn that Kilyubatra would have inherited in a matter of months anyway, with no need to resort to violence. This is the gist of his death game, initiated to give himself the satisfaction of manipulating lives in the same fashion as he believes the great powers - and especially their henchmen, who have felt able to deal high-handedly with his do. Its progress is monitored by his tape-recorder.

The whole thing misfires because Kilyubatra falls in love with him, informs no one about the will, and indeed asks him to make out a new one to benefit poor students of his university. Convinced of her sincerity, he breaks his secret to her. She determines to stay with him until the end, thus ensuring a happier departure from this life than that he had planned for himself and at the same time taking from him his desire to act towards her as 'they' had done towards him.

At this point the conclusion of the play's first instalment has been reached. The two acts added for the French translation of 1960 or, at least, not initially made public, develop the theme no further but underscore the moral. They show the professor filling his last days with intensive work on <u>Cleopatra and Love</u>, a new book which interprets the Queen's character and deeds along thoroughly unscholarly lines dictated by his knowledge of those of his own, real Kilyubatra. His helpmeet, who may be an idealised portrait of Sacha Schwarz, fusses around him like the proverbial 'little woman' and, at the end, he is completely subservient to her.

The main theme of <u>Death Game</u>, the individual as pawn in the nuclear age, is one worthy of Hakim's talent. Unfortunately, he has found nothing of value to say on the subject in a play which is weak in plot, flat in characterization, and unsubtle in its Antony and Cleopatra allusions. The secondary theme, that the world may yet be saved by love from self-destruction - a hope he was sceptical of 30 years earlier[1] - is a profession of faith which is ambiguously presented. The professor is not saved and Kilyubatra may indeed be read as a symbol for the nuclear powers themselves. It is in any case too naive an idea (sadly, it recurs in The Thorns of Peace) to underpin a dramatic success. Hakim seems never to have made up his mind what exactly he wanted to say, and has attempted to unveil too much of his current thinking, in a piece which contains some good things. Among them are the startling revelation at the end of Act One that it is with his own life that the professor is opening the death game and, in Act Two, the smooth development of the plot, the satisfying build-up of tension and the skilfully-constructed dialogue. It is perhaps, however, an apt commentary on this arch and rather awkward protest against the bomb, founded upon an unconvincing academic whose irradiation does not ring true and is never clarified - Kilyubatra's concern for his students is a detail which also jars - that seven years were needed before the first complete Arabic edition was issued and that it has been ignored by the Arab critics.

The Thorns of Peace (Ashwak as Salam), though without any novel accessories like the device of the tape-recorder, has received slightly more attention even though it has, if anything, even less to recommend it. It is very thin and rather silly, and its dramatis personae are totally lacking in life. Journey into the Future (Rihlatun ila'l Ghad), a political parable which is in part the Arab 1984, is, on the other hand, one of Hakim's most attractive, fresh and original pieces. Set firmly in a framework of directly contemporary appeal, it was developed from chapters in The Literary Art[2] and Literature is Life,[3] and was obviously inspired by the launching of the first artificial satellite by the USSR on 4 October 1957, which filled Hakim with both joy and fear: ' ... How can science continue triumphing without unbroken peace on earth?' Structurally it is, in comparison with The Cavemen, Pigmalyun and The Sultan's Dilemma, for example, diffuse and loosely constructed, and we can agree with much of Shukri's adverse criticism of it.[4] For interest, however, it scores well. Its themes are that a human being can never renounce his humanity, that he is inexorably linked to his past and that woman is man's worst enemy. The reason for a resurgence of misogyny here can only be surmised; the others are themes for which it is difficult to see how the author could have chosen a more effective, striking and up-to-date vehicle than a space capsule first at large in the unknown and then stranded on an unidentified planet. The worth of the play has been recognized in France, where a translation was published in 1960. Journey into the Future is not merely the first entry of the space age into the theatre, which by itself would have made it notable, but also an engaging enquiry into the basics of existence (time, place, reality, humanness) and the problems of an automated society, with, for good measure, a look into the crystal ball.[5] The speed with which Hakim - earlier than any other dramatist? - detected in the satellite age one which offered him unanticipated scope is a tribute to his remarkable virtuosity, and the ability of the Arabic language to handle his technically-oriented text speaks volumes for its underrated flexibility.

In 1958 Juan Ramon Jimenez's Platero y Yo appeared in Arabic and Hakim consequently found himself under attack in Al Gumhuriyya for alleged plagiarism in My Donkey Said to Me.[6] His 'idol-breaking'[7] young assailants were Ahmad Rushdi Salih, Kamil ash Shanawi and Galal al Hammamsi, whose accusations created a sharp, if short-lived, controversy in artistic circles. Supported principally by Yusuf as Siba'i and Al Aqqad, Hakim proved overwhelmingly capable of dealing with the campaign - his defence is convincing[8] - and of defusing Salih's threat to expose many other instances of claimed literary theft by him and others. The articles he penned to divert the enemy's fire were collected in 1959, with others of the period 1952-9, as Literature is Life (Adab al Haya). They are a great disappointment, taken as a whole. The only independent non-dramatic work of his between The Deal and The Journey of Spring and Autumn (1964) should have been full of invaluable information about the impact of the revolution on his career, methods and attitudes. Unfortunately it contains nothing of the kind, but simply a hotch-potch of, for the most part, uninspired essays and imaginative pieces on innocuous and anodyne topics. The only point of real interest is his rejection of calls by some of the literary spokesmen of the revolutionary society for such phenomena as 'Art for the People'.

His emergence untainted from Salih's vendetta was aided by Abd an Nasir, who displayed irritation and decided to show where his sympathies lay by presenting to his laureate designate the republican chain (qiladat al gumhuriyya), which was normally only awarded to heads of state[9] and in his case in recognition of his services to the nation's intellectual life,[10] on 29 November 1958.[11] He thus betrayed the 'emotional impetuosity' with which he was later charged by Hakim,[12] whom the President honoured further by, six weeks later,[13] nominating as the UAR's permanent representative at UNESCO.

During the 1958-9 Cairo theatre season The Deal was staged and further praised[14] and Rejuvenation, with the script cut by the producer[15] and its language turned into the colloquial with its author's blessing,[16] was mounted by the National Theatre. Though the attendance figures showed that only 200 people a night came to see it, compared with 466 for a play by Nu^cman Ashur which the Theatre put on during the same season,[17] it was deemed to have done well; Mandur could not be blamed, however, for observing that language was not all (Ashur's play was also in the colloquial),[18] as Hakim has sometimes seemed to think. In 1959 he went back once more, on posting, to his beloved Paris in January; The Kaleidoscope (Sanduq ad Dunya), a programme made up of three of the items in A Variety of Theatre, was performed by the National Theatre; and The Thorns of Peace was published in Arabic in Tel-Aviv. The return to France was an appropriate moment for an assessment of his dramatic career to be made and, in reviewing the production of Rejuvenation, Fu'ad Dawara attempted one.[19] His most illuminating comments are that 'the theatre is an art form which is strange to our Arab 'art' - an incredible statement in view of all that his subject alone had done since 1933 [20] - and that Hakim had not yet succeeded in being a trail-blazer:

> '(He) is today still an almost lone pioneer in the art of writing plays and in the rules of play-construction, for most of our dramatists, particularly the young ones, refuse to take advantage of (his) experience in this field and do not sufficiently recognize his preeminence in our theatre. They do not begin where he left off but mostly continue to stumble along the path (he) trod before writing The Cavemen.'

France again proved a fructifying force by inspiring him to compare The Sultan's Dilemma (As Sultan al Ha'ir), one of his most important plays and possibly his most successful, in the autumn of 1959. It came out in both Cairo and Paris in the following year. It treads familiar ground - the topic of government, which Praksa, Soft Hands and Isis had already discussed in their separate ways, and the 'peace or the bomb' theme of Death Game and The Thorns of Peace. Following four plays with modern settings, the backdrop of The Sultan's Dilemma is an undefined phase of Mamluk rule in Egypt and the treatment of the subject-matter is symbolic. It opens with the Sultan facing a threat to his position from rumours that he has never been made a free man and insinuations that, as a slave, he is unfit to reign over a free people. He adopts a statesmanlike attitude, ordering his wazir, who was anxious to demonstrate that the rumours were unfounded by executing a scapegoat for his detractors, to circulate copies of his certificate of manumission. This the prime minister cannot do because he omitted to have them prepared in time for the previous Sultan to sign before he died: he suggests that instead it should be spread abroad that his master was liberated and that the qadi has the confirmatory documents. The latter, upholding the letter of the law it is his task to administer, declines to be party to this 'conspiracy'. He insists that the law must be applied and that the Sultan must submit to its provisions like everyone else. This would involve him in being auctioned as part of the ex-Sultan's estate and presents him with his dilemma: should he abide by the rules or remove the problem by killing the recalcitrant qadi? Slightly unpersuasively, he opts for the legal course.

The second and third acts see another character in a legal quandary. This is the rich and attractive widow who makes the highest bid to the exchequer for ownership of the Sultan. It has been assumed by all except her that she will sign a certificate of release. Despite two brandishings of his sword by the wazir, she refuses initially to do so because she wants to keep her prize for herself and shows up the qadi's law, which allows her to purchase and then demands the immediate return of the goods. Eventually, however, she responds to gentle pressure from the Sultan and agrees that he shall retain his position as ruler rather than become her slave, provided that he first spends a night in her company. After the whole city has passed some hours of darkness in sleepless worry lest she go back on her word, she signs without demur as the mu'azzin makes his dawn call; on the instructions of the qadi, who reveals himself to be as prone to break the law he has been so pompous about as anyone else, it is made outrageously early to forestall possible second thoughts. The widow and the Sultan part tenderly, and he gives her a Mughal ruby worth more than three times the price of her bid for his freedom.

The Sultan's Dilemma, not very adequately titled, is a glorious little play. Its theme is not one to arouse intense enthusiasm in the contemporary reader, but this does not matter because it is treated with a gentle humour and lightness of touch which encourage us not to take it too seriously and, as a result, perhaps to think about it the more afterwards. The atmosphere, with dawn scenes resembling those of Praksa I in their effectiveness, is superb and rivals that of Scene One of Shahrazad. The simple structure cannot be faulted. It has a petite and satisfying unity, it does not attempt to cover too much ground and it proceeds unerringly from its amusing opening to the pleasing conclusion. It has a purposeful allure matched only by the finest of its predecessors. A cast of comic minor characters - a bewildered executioner, a bribeable and lying mu'azzin, a ubiquitous wine-seller - contribute much by ensuring that the interest and impetus are maintained. Except for the colourless sultan and the widow, who are the only characters to remain faithful to the law, the dramatis personae parallel in function those of many a Shakespeare comedy. The delightful array of jolly minor incidents also enhances the impression. The scapegoat who is at the start about to be executed on the orders of the wazir is saved when the mu'azzin, as a variant, delays his dawn call and becomes the auctioneer charged with fetching an appropriate price for the sultan; the wazir decrees that, if the widow does not keep her promise, a crowd shall be hired to denounce her as a Mughal spy. It is all very Gilbertian. The abounding threats of imminent torture or execution, the gallery of lightweight rogues and the unblemished hero and heroine bring The Mikado to mind. Ar Ra^{c}i rightly notes the operetta atmosphere of a miniature equivalent, for richness, of a Mahfuz novel like Zuqaq al Midaqq. Hakim's achievement is far greater than his simple statement of intent - will the world choose force or the law to solve its conflicts? - might have caused us to anticipate.

It was first performed in 1961 by the National Theatre and was well received, despite the failure of Futuh Nashati, the producer, to get the humour across.[21] It has been staged in Syria.[22] The National Theatre revived it in 1969, in which year, as in the following one, the Sudanese National Theatre performed it. In 1970 at least, it was not a success in Omdurman because audiences did not take to its classical language or understand its symbolism.[23] The second point should cause surprise, for it is readily appreciable as a piece of realism alone, as Fu'ad Dawara has observed.[24] In Cairo its deeper meaning was grasped with so little effort that Egyptian audiences seemed at last to have come of age and, according to one source, Hakim seemed to have begun to be watched by other playwrights as a trend-setter.[25] The critics were unanimous in their praise. Ghali Shukri thought the play one of his finest[26] and the one which revealed him as a truly modern playwright.[27] Muhammad Mandur, regarding him as having already established the correctness of his ideological attitudes, eschewed party considerations in maintaining that 'this great play' could stand comparison with the best that the rest of the world could offer,[28] and went so far as to say that it was 'the most splendid implementation' of what he wanted to see the Egyptian theatre doing.[29] Dawara had some reservations but overall gave it as his opinion that The Sultan's Dilemma, with its skilful suspense, 'precise, engineered', symbolic framework, 'skill and charm of dialogue' and 'force and ...

sharpness of ... logic ... (which) give the mind a shake', 'has achieved (an) outstanding position among (Hakim's) other plays ... '[30]

His UNESCO tour was, at his own request, a short one, and he returned home early in 1960 to his old seat on the Higher Council of Arts, Letters and Social Sciences. Later in the year the complete Praksa came out. Acts 4-6, which were probably held back in 1939 lest the monarchy or Sir Miles Lampson saw the overthrow of Balpirus as an incitement, make the six-acter a more finished article than Praksa I. They introduce no basically new material but, like the second part of Death Game, reinforce the message. They are closer to the Aristophanean spirit than the first half of the play. Act Four is full of comic drama and includes a delightful Greek chorus episode, which Gilbert again might have written, when the three plotters realize that Balpirus is the victim they have been waiting for. Act Six, despite its potentially gruesome subject-matter, is overflowing with wit and humour. There is an excellent example of Hakim's ability to draw a figure capable of smooth and convincing development. This is rarely one of his foremost aims, since he is far more concerned with ideas than with character portrayal, but the part of Ibqirat is allowed continual and compelling growth.

It is not to be supposed from the fact that nothing from his energetic pen was converted into durable print in 1961 that Hakim was resting on his oars. His silence was more in the nature of a garnering of his strength. He had in a decade thoroughly ingratiated himself with the revolution (which the final act of Journey into the Future nonetheless perhaps seeks to caution and whose leader is apostrophised in The Sultan's Dilemma) by buttressing the realistic section of his repertoire through Soft Hands and The Deal, and acquired the confidence to address himself in a loud voice (unlike the muted call of The Angel's Prayer) to the world of the nuclear age in the plays of 1957 and in The Sultan's Dilemma. There was no sign that the world was listening to him, and he therefore turned to the enthralling and surprising tasks of his next decade. As far as the UK went, he did in fact break his silence once again, when Pigmalyun was performed in translation at Cambridge by the University's Middle East Centre and the Pembroke Players. It was commented on most favourably by The Times of 9 June, which described it as being 'of a classic clarity and precision'. It added that 'Perhaps (it) is in places a little too clear and precise for comfort' and that 'at times it suggests a preliminary outline for a play rather than the play itself'. Had he seen it, Hakim would have winced in chagrin at the latter remark.

REFERENCES

1. LIB, p 22
2. pp 257-60
3. pp 191-7, an essay which was commissioned by the Soviet Foreign Literature to mark the despatch of the first satellite
4. Shukri, pp 324-36
5. For an even farther look, see In the Year One Million, in Show me Allah, pp 85-106
6. Dawara 1, p 323, and Mallakh, pp 304-7, wrongly have Al Hakim's Donkey
7. AW, p 41
8. See Mallakh, loc cit
9. Awad 1
10. As Siba^{c}i, in a foreword to Al Kitab al Fiddi, November 1959. A photograph of the scroll is in Mallakh, p 314
11. Mallakh, p 315
12. AW, p 56
13. Mallakh, p 307
14. Ibid, p 320
15. Dawara 1, pp 52, 119
16. Mandur 2, pp 47, 138
17. Ibid, p 48
18. Ibid, loc cit
19. Dawara 1, pp 39-40
20. In Nur Sherif (ed), About Arabic Books, Beirut Arab University, 1970, p 62, Awad speaks of the post-revolutionary playwrights as having 'no Egyptian tradition in drama worth mentioning' to build on
21. Farag, pp 48-9
22. Khaznadar, in UNESCO, p 145
23. Abd ar Rahman Abd ar Rahim ash Shibli, oral communication, 26 February 1972
24. Dawara 1, p 32
25. Abdel Moniem Ismail Mohamed, rary Egypt, p 21
26. Shukri, p 372
27. Ibid, p 378
28. Mandur 2, p 152
29. Ibid, p 150
30. Dawara 1, pp 16, 32, 33

1 Experimentation and Consolidation

> The Theatre of the Absurd is a return to old, even archaic, traditions.
>
> (Esslin, The Theatre of the Absurd)

Hakim's instinctive bent towards the Theatre of the Absurd has been mentioned in earlier pages. In 1962 he took to it whole-heartedly, calling his version of it Irrationalism (Al Lama^{c}qul), which, he explained, he conceived as applicable only to the shape of a play, and not to shape and content as was the case with the Theatre of the Absurd; he meant by Irrationalism 'the presentation of the rational world in an irrational framework' rather than, as in the true Theatre of the Absurd, the presentation of an absurd world in an absurdist framework.[1] That he should have turned his pen elegantly and effortlessly at the age of well over sixty in a radically new direction - one not taken before by Arabic literature, which had been little exposed to the Theatre of the Absurd - is a further indication of his wealth of natural talent, which now displayed itself with a breathtaking self-assurance which only the leap to The Cavemen had more thrillingly exhibited. The days of stumbling along uncertain paths were over.

Irrationalism, the dominant feature of his future work, quickly caught on in Egypt and, in the opinion of one man of the theatre,[2] helped the live stage to hold its own against the competition of television, which was introduced in 1960. Hakim's first irrationalist play was The Tree

Climber (Ya Tali^c ash Shagara). It captivated critics, readers and playgoers when it appeared in print[3] and when it was performed at the Pocket Theatre (Masrah al Gib),[4] understandably arousing greater curiosity than any of its successors, some of which are in some ways superior to it. It has a preface of twenty-six and a half pages, Hakim's second longest, which attempts rather confusedly to describe the motives which led him to expose the Arab theatre to Irrationalism.[5] The gist of it is that, firstly, after his return from UNESCO, where he had decided that Egypt was not ready for the Absurd, he began to appraise the arts of the ancient Egyptians and came to the conclusion that they had already encompassed all the manifestations of modern European art; they could, for example, show antecedents for surrealism, cubism and contemporary sculpture, and had already worked along Absurd or Irrealist lines - a statement which caused controversy.[6] This, and the fact that modern Egyptians sang the 'nursery rhyme' whose opening line gave The Tree Climber its title, without being worried by its lack of meaning, suggested that there was no reason, after all, why the modern European type of play should not be at home in modern Egypt. Secondly, Shahrazad had, in the event, not served to join folklore and 'official' literature in indissoluble union: a play based to some extent on the former but framed in the most up-to-date fashion might be able to do so. Having convinced himself that Irrationalism was after all feasible, he went ahead, couching The Tree Climber in the classical language because he wanted it to be understood that it had been partly inspired by ancient Egyptian traditions in general and not by linguistic ones (which would have required the use of the popular language) and because he was not aiming at realism. The models he chose were Brecht on the one hand and Ionesco, Beckett, Vautier and Adamov on the other. (Nadir Salim makes out a case[7] for Chekhov.) It was a product of his love of the search for new artistic values and modes of expression and one of a type which - though he recommends only a limited application for it - he felt Egypt should add to its repertoire lest its art stagnate while the rest of the world struck out in new directions. He believed, however, that realism would be needed for many years to come.

The Tree Climber, though simple in structure and outward form, is more obscure in intent than its irrationalist successors. Hakim was soon to castigate those he believed traded obscurity for its own sake. He justifies his 'obscurity' in an appendix to Food for Every Mouth,[8] as being designed to shake Egyptian society out of its languor by setting before it the spectacle of its loss of direction. The play begins with the simultaneous disappearance of Bihana, the wife of a retired railway inspector, Bahadur Efendi, and, equally importantly, of the female lizard which has lived under his orange tree throughout the nine years of their marriage. After three days, Bahadur informs the police who, in the shape of a detective, quickly assume from his demeanour and evasive answers, and from the enigmatic testimony of a dervish whom Bahadur came across on one of his trains, that he has murdered his wife. The dervish states that he told Bahadur when they met that, with his wife as fertiliser, the tree would produce four different fruits per year. The detective orders digging to begin beneath it and Bahadur - crying, 'They'll kill the tree! Murder!' - to be taken into custody.

At the start of the second and last act, while the detective is supervising the excavating, Bihana returns. Bahadur, speedily released, rejoins his wife and rejoices to discover that the lizard has reappeared. He asks Bihana where she has been during the days unaccounted for but she, like an up-dated Shahrazad, will not tell although she admits that she can see no sense in not doing so. Her husband strangles her. He rings the detective, cannot get over to him what has occurred, is advised to 'forget it ... and not to worry', and prepares to bury the body in the hole under the tree so conveniently provided by the police. The dervish, who knows that exactly what he predicted has happened, pops up again, but Bahadur decides to proceed with the fertilization. During their conversation, however, the body has vanished and the lizard is lying dead at the bottom of the pit.

From this brief synopsis it will be noticed that Hakim's distinction between Absurdism and Irrationalism does not hold water. His play does, nonetheless, bear his own stamp, which takes the form of two impressive flashbacks in Act One. (The fact that both are reminiscent of that in Act Two of Ionesco's <u>Amedee</u> (1956) is no contradiction, especially as we have seen that he first indulged in the trick in <u>Her Majesty</u>.) In one flashback the family maidservant and the detective watch, without surprise, a replay of a domestic scene between Bahadur and Bihana; in the other, the detective and Bahadur view the latter, carrying out his duties on a train, coming into contact with the dervish who, unprovided with a ticket, spirits ten from mid-air, shows that he has cognizance of Bahadur's presumed intentions towards his wife and steps straight from the 'train' into the interrogation of the tree climber by the detective to accuse Bahadur of proposing to kill Bihana if he has not already done so.

There are many instances of conventional Theatre of the Absurd. One is the instruction - as for The Deal - that no sets or props, except those with which each character enters and exits, should be used. Another is the conversation which goes on and on and gets nowhere. (The play opens with one between the detective and the maid, and that in which Bahadur quizzes Bihana about her movements during her disappearance is long and magnificent. It reaches its climax in a superb passage of four and a half pages where Bahadur puts to his wife a list of possible, impossible and ridiculous places where she might have been and Bihana answers merely 'No' or, if appropriate, 'No, no', 'No, no, no' or 'No, no, no, no' to them all. It is after the last of the denials that he strangles her.) A third is the duologue in which the interlocutors each wrongly imagine that the other is talking about the same thing. Examples are the flashback in which Bahadur speaks of his tree and Bihana rambles senilely on about the daughter she never had; an interview between the detective and Bahadur at which the former is asking about Bihana's disappearance while her husband is discussing his lizard; and an interview the detective has, immediately after her return, with Bihana, who denies that in her flashback scene with Bahadur she was talking about her daughter and he about his tree and affirms that the reality was the exact opposite of this.

The Tree Climber is, nonetheless, not a thorough-going example of the Absurdist genre: it is not consistently absurd, but one of basically 'normal' type which sports Absurdist features, and it incorporates too much humour of the traditional Hakim kind. Its interpretation is difficult. Bahadur is just as obsessed by his tree and by his service on the railways as by his lizard, but the lizard and Bihana are the phenomena which engage the interest of the spectator most deeply. Does Bahadur see them as one and the same? Does Hakim mean us to identify the one with the other? Bihana is of course a puzzle. Where was she during her first absence? Where has her body gone at the end? Why is she in her dotage in the flashback scene, energetic and forceful when questioned by the detective, and insanely unforthcoming ('a wall of silence') when finally in her husband's presence again? Above all, perhaps, has the play made Egyptian society conscious of its alleged disorientation?

Ali ar Ra^{c}i has opined[9] that in The Tree Climber, as in Pigmalyun, we are being shown the simultaneous destruction of life and art. The thought-provoking if dogmatic Tarabishi offers satisfying answers to most of the questions raised above, pursues the life-versus-art theory with much conviction and compares and contrasts Bahadur, in stimulating fashion, with Shahriyar and Pigmalyun.[10] Every reader or spectator will, however, make up his own mind about the meaning, which is probably best appreciated from a literal standpoint and does not seem to be weighty. As to the Irrationalism or Absurdism of the play, the critics, while approving of it, have not brought forth much in the way of enlightening analysis. Muhammad al Hasan, the usually penetrating Sudanese, regards it as 'a strange departure'[11] Mandur reckons only the first duologue between Bahadur and Bihana as absurdist, the rest being symbolism;[12] and Shukri and Tarabishi[13] see no connection between it and the Absurd; it is hard to agree with Taha Husayn[14] that it represents nothing new. On the credit side, Abdel Moniem Ismail Mohamed considers it a masterpiece which gave the Egyptian theatre a tremendous fillip[15] and Luwis Awad - after he had earlier criticezed it at length[16] - pronounced it 'probably his most mature creation'.[17] It displays a mastery, fluency and grace which Hakim was never again to equal. A typical Hakim product, with absurdist extras, it was almost universally praised and thus reinforced his belated recognition. Jabra Ibrahim Jabra, the Palestinian-Iraqi man of letters, thinks it ' ... as funny, as surprising, as dramatically effective, as anything by Ionescu',[18] the influence of whose Les Chaises is easily discernible. This is probably too ambitious a claim. As the first Arab essay into Absurdism, however, it demands admiration and astonishment at the least, and these it has received in some measure.

Some of the statements made in Hakim's preface have been challenged. Jamal Muhammad Ahmad inclines to the view that his chief aim was to show that anyone could write Ionesquesque nonsense;[19] in support of this belief is his contempt, in an undated appendix to Food for Every Mouth,[20] for the obscurity of Beckett and Ionesco. Others have maintained that the author himself, amused by the tortuous interpretations put upon his play, said that the critics had got it all wrong[21] and that his sole purpose was to dramatise a quarrel with his wife. Ar Ra^{c}i[22] and Tarabishi[23] certainly detect autobiographical motivation. Whatever the truth of the matter, The Tree Climber is a fine work and is all the more remarkable if the true reasons for its composition are the commonplace ones.

1963, when Chekhov, Gorki, Brecht, Beckett, Ionesco and Miller were produced in Cairo, saw a further rise on the graph of Hakim's acceptability: a theatre named after him (Masrah al Hakim) was founded in the capital after much prior excitement and debate, 'an outcry unprecedented in the history of the Egyptian theatre'. He was pleased to lend it his name,[25] but fearful when Pigmalyun was selected as its curtain-raiser.[26] According to Awad,[27] whose attitude to him is in general hostile, the critics had categorised the play as 'the natural extension of his intellectual drama' and as, therefore, unsuitable for acting. They were wrong, for Pigmalyun scored a notable success. Even so, Awad would only concede that this demonstrated that, under the right conditions and 'before a small audience, of course', all the intellectual dramas could do well. Muhammad Mandur, on a later occasion, was more generous:

> ' ... how great was my amazement when I went some days ago to see ... Pigmalyun, which ... Nabil al Alfi produced on the stage of the Muhammad Farid Theatre. I found myself becoming excited ... with a twofold excitement which overcame my contemplation of the tragedy of Pigmalyun ... I discovered that this play is not merely intellectual as I had imagined. '

He now described it as a 'great, poetic, dramatic work', 'whose truth and extent the reader cannot perceive'.[28]

Hakim consolidated his reputation further in the same year with the publication of the impressive Food for Every Mouth (At Ta^{c}amu li Kulli Famm). It lacks the sparkle of The Tree Climber but is a more original contribution to the Absurdist genre, a closer approach to Irrationalism and a far less diffuse and enigmatic piece of writing. The opening situation is the drenching by Sitt Atiyat, engaged in washing her sitting-room floor, of a wall in the flat beneath. In this live Hamdi and Samira, whose marriage is unsatisfactory. He is a civil service clerical officer who vainly tries to overrate the importance of his duties, she a grudging housewife. Atiyat, summoned to explain herself, fails to see any connection between the floor-washing and its obvious effect, and storms out. Hamdi then notices that the wet patches on the wall are turning into a picture, of three people in a drawing-room. When one of them, a girl, strikes up an audible tune on the piano, Hamdi thinks he is going mad, but Samira sits down beside him to enjoy it. The play of the wall - the play within the play - gets under weigh and when a painter arrives, sent by Atiyat to put right the damage she has caused, they refuse to let him in. Later on, the wall begins to crack above the girl's head and Samira and Hamdi try, in vain, to warn her of her danger. Atiyat comes down to protest against their treatment of her handyman, but goes away satisfied by a piece of paper absolving her of responsibility for all past and future harm to the wall and with no inkling of what is going on.

The following day Hamdi and Samira, who surprisingly have not sat up all night, find that the top coat of the wall has crumbled into a heap on the floor. They are heartbroken, but spurred into action by Hamdi's thought that their friends (the play on the wall) might be recoverable if Atiyat could be persuaded to wash her floor with the same gay abandon as previously. They call her down but she will not hear of it, realizes she did wrong, and has learned to do the job without a drop of water reaching them. They beg her to wash the floor again, and this time to employ her old, 'exemplary' method - she must be skimping the business, is it too much to ask her to do it properly? Atiyat flounces out, suspecting that she is being lured into a trap. Under these circumstances, direct action is the only answer. Hamdi breaks in, soaks her floor and succeeds only in turning the wall into a waterfall. Atiyat hurries down on her return, Hamdi writes out for her another guarantee of immunity, and Samira demands that she allow them to wash her flat daily to salve their guilty consciences. Her husband's effort failed, she believes, because he soaked the floor but did not wash it. With regular access they will be able, sooner or later - by doing it in the same way, using the same brand of soap, etc. - to reconstruct the circumstances which gave rise to the 'shadow play' which so engrossed them.

The action thus far is almost wholly Absurdist. What occurs on the wall embodies most of what Hakim wishes to say to us on this occasion. The personae are a beautiful woman of forty-five and her two children, Nadia and Tariq, whose conversation embraces two topics. One is the rights and wrongs of the mother's marriage, within six months of the death of their father, to - shades of <u>Journey into the Future</u> - the family doctor. Nadia insists that the doctor murdered their father in league with her mother, announces that she will not stay under the same roof as a murderess and shames her distrait brother into doing likewise. In a different class from the domestic affairs of the household, to the resolution of which Tariq signally fails to contribute, is his antihunger project, which is discussed elsewhere.

The play on the wall, with its abrupt ending, has considerable influence on the relations of Hamdi and Samira. They were bad at the start of the play mainly because Hamdi, the self-proclaimed 'key' of his ministry, could not convincingly refute the scorn of Samira and her relations for his low-level employment. To bolster his ego he goes in for gambling and out for amusement while Samira stays unwillingly at home doing the chores. After exposure to Tariq's ideas on hunger he has become a changed man (at one stage during the play on the wall one of his cronies inconveniently arrives and is told to take his puerilities away) who is entirely devoted to carrying on his mentor's work. Samira is right behind him as he purchases a microscope with which to examine the remains of the top coat of the wall and sets out to dream the dream which, like those of Jules Verne and H.G. Wells, will lead to the reality. The sale of her jewelry for the acquisition of research equipment is done with Samira's active encouragement. They regard their life together as now being full of new interests, productive and devoid of pre-judgements, and they finally appear to us as a happy and dedicated couple. Uplifted by the concerns and intelligent converse - unmatchable among their friends - of the 'high-class' family on the wall, Hamdi sees his government job as ridiculously beneath him and Nadia has inspired Samira to take up the piano again. It is not clear how, though obviously fairly well-to-do, they are going to keep themselves in funds.

It is debatable whether or not the play on the wall is a suitable conveyance for its theme, but most readers, struck by its novelty, would probably feel that it is. The two-tier structure, even if not perfectly dovetailed, is most effective in keeping alive a basically dull, if vital, subject and it has the advantage - great, in view of the sort of audience at which Hakim was of necessity aiming - of allowing Hamdi, Samira and Atiyat, who are intellectually run-of-the-mill, to act quite naturally as interpreters of a difficult topic to both reader and spectator. Some may derive assistance in this from the language of the play, which is the 'third language' of The Deal - 'an attempt to bring the (classical) down to the level of its closest point of contact with the colloquial without becoming colloquial, and to raise the colloquial without it becoming classical'.[29] Food for Every Mouth is by no means without blemish in its construction. Hamdi and Samira's improbable abandonment of the wall drama in favour of sleep has been mentioned. At least four times the reader is halted in his tracks while Hakim freezes the action to insert information which could have been more smoothly introduced. The most glaring instance of this occurs when the wall play conveniently stops while Samira answers the door bell. More serious are the facts that the intellectual levels of the drama (high-flown on the wall, pedestrian in Hamdi and Samira's flat) are not complementary and that the less gripping of the two themes of the play within the play - the domestic quarrel over the remarriage of the mother - is, as Mandur has noticed,[30] completely aimless. The critic regards the wall scenes as a wish-fulfilment dream by Hamdi and Samira - one which they are mentally unequipped to have - and finds the transformation of Hamdi ridiculous.[31] These are valid points, though Mandur has not considered whether the collapse of the wall does not perhaps symbolise a desire on the part of Hakim for talk of scandalous marriages to be given short shrift, because they should be either prohibited or tolerantly viewed, and his belief that the world was not concerned about starvation. He goes too far, however, when he says that Hamdi and Samira's assault on Atiyat, in a frenzied endeavour to persuade her to soak her floor again and thereby resurrect the wall family, is merely padding and 'a hallucination of the Absurd ... with no excuse or necessity'.[32] The episode is absolutely brilliant and in the best traditions of the Absurd, to which the play is a well sustained and remarkable addition. Its subject-matter may be traced back to Hakim's philosophical conviction that the thinker and writer, represented here by the converted Hamdi (whom one would take to be Hakim under another name were it not for his lack of brain-power), has a role both as John the Baptist and as prophet which eventually brings about changes for the good of the world.

Food for Every Mouth was staged by the National Theatre in the year following its publication; in Mandur's opinion the conventional methods used in the production ruined it. In the same year The Cavemen was at last revived* after twenty-nine years, the National Theatre taking advantage of the high tide in Hakim's affairs and, presumably, of his blessing. The consequences could not possibly have been so grave as in 1935 but, disappointingly, on this occasion it seems to have made little impression while, as before, spectators tended to doze.[33] Mandur remarks, 'I felt ... after reading The Cavemen and seeing it on the stage that my enjoyment was greater on reading it than on seeing it ... when it did not evoke in me any strong reactions' - except, he adds, the impression that the characters were chessmen.[34] It is tragic that the finest play of the greatest Arab playwright should apparently be doomed to adorn the shelves of libraries, and instructive that it should have run to more Arabic editions than any other of his works. The third production of 1964 was Soft Hands, by the Hebrew University in Jerusalem; Shams an Nahar (see below) the fourth.

In this same year of much activity Hakim published Life's Prison (Sign al Umr), a frank, interesting and somewhat maudlin account of his strange personality, and two more plays, A Hunting Trip (Rihlatu Sayd) and A Train Journey (Rihlatu Qitar). These, written in 1962-3, are shorter than most of those concentrated on in this book and, with the poems of 1926-7, form a volume called The Journey of Spring and

---

* Dawara 1, pp 267-9, is alone in indicating a revival in 1960, when prominent writers and critics attacked it and branded it a failure.

Autumn (Rihlat ar Rabi^c wa'l Kharif). A Hunting Trip is worth no more than a bibliographical mention at this juncture, and little more elsewhere;[35] the rather longer A Train Journey has all the meaning, action (there is one most memorable scene) and atmosphere its companion so conspicuously lacks. Neatly designed, with well-drawn characters, much humour and rich symbolism, it is the third of the Absurdist, rather than Irrationalist, type. It is most attractive, highly dramatic, worthy of being translated and suitable for production anywhere. As it is, we have only a hint that it has been staged in Egypt.[36]

In 1965 The Tree Climber appeared in a worthwhile English translation, Hakim agreed that the theatre which bore his name might put on an adaptation of The Soul's Return,[37] which it does not seem to have done, and the eponymous Shams an Nahar, which happens to mean Daytime Sun, was published. (It was played before this, as noted, the previous year, in November at the Uzbakiyya Theatre in Cairo.)[38] It contains little of dramatic note, the story-line is weak, the theme is not at all gripping, it is unendurably boring in parts and it has an embarrassingly sentimental conclusion. Setting off as though en route to becoming an Arab Ecole des Femmes, it finally achieves a specific resemblance to Expulsion from Eden, The Suicide's Secret and Pigmalyun: love and serious work are self-excluding. In a short preface Hakim calls it a 'sermon', written, he hopes, in the 'pleasingly didactic manner' of Kalila wa Dimna, the fables of La Fontaine and 'the plays of Brecht'. But he does not say what he is trying to tell us. The play is not a success, and he does not reckon it a major one;[39] but it is of interest because of its resuscitation of the rather neglected subject of labour and of its parallel with Shaw's Pigmalion - the creation of an ideal which is then given its head - and is remarkable for perhaps the most egregiously enigmatic and thrilling (and irrelevant) episode in the whole of his oeuvre. In this the Princess Shams orders one of her suitors, as they approach her father's palace, to climb a tell to seek information about the route. On top he finds a village populated by ghosts with their hands outstretched. She commands him to give them bread, they come to life and point out the way, and he descends. Completely out of character with the rest of the play, the scene is nonetheless the best feature of Shams an Nahar and its extraordinary impact is not quickly forgotten.

1966 was a year of much exertion. Shams an Nahar was produced by the National Theatre, Shahrazad at last underwent the test of the live stage at home, scoring a 'succes d'estime'[40] (it is not clear whether or not it was graced by the 'musical atmosphere' Hakim considered essential for it and at which French and British composers have tried their hand),[41] and two more long plays were published. One of them was The Dilemma (Al Warta), an unexciting thriller whose source is a passage in My Donkey Said to Me.[42] It concerns the involvement, for purposes of research, of a professor of Criminal Science and Psychology with a gang of petty thieves who kill a policeman in the course of a robbery. Despite its serious intention, which is to exhibit in a legal setting the kind of conscience-searching presumably engaged in by the scientists who split the atom,[43] its only aspect requiring study is its language, which is gone into at some length in Hakim's postscript. The Deal and Food for Every Mouth had not solved his linguistic problems:

'Despite my manufacturing an Arabic simple in the extreme, for production I need someone to change it or translate it into the colloquial. This is an incredible situation. It is distressing to have to recognize the existence of two separate languages in a single nation which is striving to do away with the distinctions between its classes. Frequently people who speak living languages have reproved us for the fact that our Arabic language is on the path to extinction because the people do not speak it in their conversation. Interested parties would eagerly mislead us about the depth of the gulf between the classical and the colloquial and the impossibility of ever [reconciling] them. The fact of the matter, which I observe today and many have observed, is the antithesis of this allegation. The colloquial is condemned to extinction, and the difference between it and the classical is lessening by the day ... The normal spoken language has risen towards the level of correct Arabic.'

He goes on to qualify and expand some of this, throwing doubt in the process on 'the fact of the matter' and in general displaying less confidence over the language issue than in the postscript to The Deal. He says that in England and France the classical extended itself in order to absorb colloquialisms and assimilate 'differences' and 'barriers'; given sincerity of purpose, Arabic can do the same - he urges it to do so - by upgrading the standard of the spoken tongue in the direction of that of the written. As to the theatre, its initial aim should be to bring its language into line with that of the press.

He refuses to admit the existence of an independent colloquial, 'as though Arabic were a foreign language', and claims that most of what is thought of as such is simply abbreviation provoked by the speed of speech. The alleged gulf between speech and writing has been exaggerated by authors who have been seeking to make readers and audiences laugh by their caricatures of dialectal differences and to divide the classes on a linguistic basis. These writers are not doing their duty: in an age when standards of speech are being improved by education, the press, radio, television and the cinema, they should not be reflecting today's linguistic position but preparing for that of tomorrow, when the colloquial and the classical will be one.[44] En passant, he mentions the paradox of Shaykh Salama Higazi, in the days when Egypt was under occupation and education was scarce, addressing full houses in the countryside in the classical, while now that independence and education have arrived the theatre has ended up under the tyranny of Egyptian colloquial, which the other Arab countries feel that they must resist with their own. If such a state of affairs were allowed to continue, inter-Arab communication would be conducted on a basis of translation and the Arabic mother tongue would be dead.

His non-recognition of the colloquial is, as the precis above makes plain, a refusal to grant it the status accorded it by others, not a denial that it exists at all. The Dilemma tries to demonstrate how near to the classical much of the colloquial is by using again the 'third language', 'the ordinary language of conversation in our everyday life'. This is close to 'correct Arabic' and does not require translation into 'so-called' colloquial for stage performances anywhere in the Arab world. He expresses the hope that writers in the other Arabic-speaking countries will follow his example in order that the united Arab nation, whose establishment is so dependent upon unity of language, may come into being.

Two things particularly strike the reader of the play and its postscript. The first is that the option open to producers of The Deal, to present it in the classical or the colloquial according to preference, has now been withdrawn: The Dilemma is classical or nothing, Hakim having decided to throw his quite considerable weight behind those who believe that 'pan-Arabic' must win the day if Arabic is to survive as a world language. The second is that, although it is true that The Dilemma as it stands is comprehensible (with regional pronunciation variations) throughout the Arabic-speaking world, this attempt to uplift the colloquial to meet the classical is one that can only be applicable to Egypt. Close to classical the language of the play may be, but it bears little relation to 'the ordinary language of conversation in our everyday life' of the Arab countries apart from Egypt. It would, for example, be a waste of effort to set out to convince an Iraqi that The Dilemma, a potboiler which has been acted neither in, nor outside, Egypt, is written in anything akin to his own colloquial.

REFERENCES

1. Appendix to Food for Every Mouth, pp 176-7
2. Farouk el-Demerdash, in UNESCO, pp 134-5
3. Mandur 2, p 156. Cf Tarabishi, p 147
4. El-Demerdash, in UNESCO, p 137
5. Part of the preface is reproduced in Abd al-Malek, Anthologie, pp 420-5
6. Mandur 2, p 156
7. In AQ 1, 4, p 157
8. pp 175-6
9. p 101
10. Tarabishi, pp 146-66
11. pp 21-2
12. Mandur 2, p 157
13. Shukri, p 296, Tarabishi, pp 147-8
14. In Nadir Salim, loc cit, p 158
15. p 97
16. Muhammad al Hasan, p 71-2
17. In The Baghdad News, 13 October 1964
18. In The Journal of Arabic Literature 2(1971), p 90
19. Oral communication, 16 March 1972
20. p 172
21. See, eg. Muhammad al Hasan, p 72
22. p 100
23. Loc cit
24. Awad 2, pp 183-4. Mallakh, pp 324-6, indicates that he is going to explain the outcry but does not do so
25. Awad, p 184
26. Ibid, loc cit, Farag, p 83
27. Awad, pp 184-6
28. Mandur 2, pp 159, 161
29. Appendix, p 174
30. Mandur 2, p 169
31. Ibid, pp 166-7, 170

32 Ibid, pp 169, 170
33 Subur 1, p 91
34 Mandur 2, p 159
35 Tarabishi, pp 80, 81, is, however, impressed with it
36 Hakim, in Farag, p 175
37 AQ, April, 1965, p 192
38 Shukri, p 340, Mallakh, p 321
39 In Farag, p 190
40 Nada Tomiche, in UNESCO, pp 118, 122, 123
41 Preface to The Tree Climber, p 31. The French composer was Maurice Thiriet (Al Hilal 76, 2, p 70)
42 pp 121-31
43 Sikinat ash Shihabi, in Adib, May 1974, p 33, thinks that its purpose is also to treat the Palestine question symbolically
44 Nagib Mahfuz echoes these comments in Dawara 2, p 287

2 Under Two Presidents - Disenchantment and Recovery

> The Egyptian Army is very large and is probably the largest Army in the world.
> (Rameses, Oriental Spotlight)
>
> Are we any different from our enemies? Yes, thank God we are.
> (Menahem Begin, 26 February 1973)

The other long play of 1966, Fate of a Cockroach (Masir Sarsar),* is unencumbered by experimentation and is Hakim's last great one. It is the brilliant and original tour de force which opened his Troilus and Cressida Period, brought about by an unexplained heartbreak,[1] and is in three acts, the first of which appeared in Al Ahram before the publication of the complete work. Though Act One and Acts Two/Three are complete in themselves, the drama as a whole, though it has never been staged in toto, is in no way unsatisfactory. On the contrary, the cockroach King serves as an ample and ingenious bond between its two contrasting aspects.

---

*   This should be Fate of a Cricket, but Hakim is undoubtedly concerned here with cockroaches though, as Adil and Samiyya found in Act Two, without lexicographical backing.

100 Tawfiq al Hakim

If <u>Fate of a Cockroach</u> is an exercise in disillusion and bitterness, its chief protagonist nevertheless stems directly from Hakim's established psychological and philosophical attitudes. In <u>From Beyond</u>, the concluding item of <u>The Devil's Pact</u>, he refers to the wars of the ants and the cockroaches. In <u>From the Ivory Tower</u> he describes[2] his 'frequent' contemplation, when a youth, of columns of ants bearing cockroach corpses; he used to scatter their ranks with cups of water, which he supposed they probably regarded as well-aimed acts of God and which prompted in him the by no means unprecedented thought that perhaps humans were 'ants', whose natural catastrophes were the deeds of 'ants' yet larger than them: 'Allah is greater than we can conceive, and our senses are more ignorant about this life than we imagine.' He returns to this train of thought in <u>Literature is Life</u>.[3] In the preface to the play he declares again his interest in the insect world - one demonstrated in <u>Solomon the Wise</u> - which, he surmises, is the ancient Egyptian in him coming out: they 'used to link insects and man in one framework'. He says that he once saw a cockroach struggling to climb out of his bath and heralds one purpose of Act One of the play by continuing, 'How glorious is the sight of a determination to struggle without hope! ... (it) is, as I understand it, the crux of tragedy ... For me, sadness, catastrophes and the death of the hero are not properties of tragedy, but obligatory is (it) ... that the hero's end comes as a result of his striving with a force over which he has no power' - as, he avers, is the case with Othello but not with Hamlet. 'Every human struggle lacks efficacy before that power against which man is powerless. Nevertheless he struggles, and that is the tragedy and greatness of man.' Having expounded his theory, he correctly dismisses the idea that <u>Fate of a Cockroach</u> is a tragedy - 'it is merely a play and no more.' Containing much political criticism which is examined elsewhere, it is difficult to label.

Act One takes place in the bathroom of an Egyptian flat and is an account of an evening in the life of the Kingdom of the Cockroaches which flourishes there. The King, chosen for the length of his antennae, is alive to the threat posed to his rule, as to those of all his ancestors, by the traditional cockroach foe, the ants; also like his forebears, he is quick to evade pressure to do anything about them. His Queen constantly nags him about the problem, the non-solution of which inhibits her from walking abroad lest, should she be so unfortunate as to fall on her back, she be overrun by an enemy patrol. The King despises the ants but sees no reason why he should be picked on to force a confrontation. The regal pair have only three 'regular' subjects: the prime minister, who was unopposed for the position; the priest, enrolled on account of his habit of addressing incomprehensible remarks to the King; and the scientist, so dignified on the strength of his 'strange knowledge of things which exist only in his own head'. The King puts up with them only because they needed someone in whom to confide their tomfoolery and because he wanted to be called 'Your Majesty'. The ants' seizure of the upturned son of the prime minister brings matters to a crisis. The Queen urges action, the King - sure that he will have nothing sensible to propose - reluctantly asks the prime minister for his views, and the latter has the temerity to suggest that the cockroaches should try ant tactics and recruit a large army - of twenty - to fight them. The King scoffs at this notion - when in their long history have the cockroaches been able to muster a force of twenty? - and declares that the ants know about the organization of armies but the cockroaches are different and do not. The scientist is called in to advise but sees the question as a political one - if the King cannot solve it, what does his authority amount to? Pressed by the Queen he does, however, condescend to impart the information that, when he was very young, he did once witness ten cockroaches together, around a slice of tomato. He unbends sufficiently to state that cockroaches are conditioned against congregating because of the proven connection between their assemblies and catastrophes occasioned by such instruments of nature as moving hills and torrential downpours. The ants are too small to be targets for these perils and can therefore do whatever they choose to. The others demand a solution from him and he recommends that, for a start, the cockroaches get to know themselves and their environment.

The priest arrives and is similarly grilled. His answer is for sacrifices to be offered to the gods more conscientiously than heretofore - a response which attracts the mockery of the scientist, whom the others think has gone too far. The passing of a phalanx of ants, holding triumphantly aloft the body of their victim and singing about their 'unity', brings the quintet abruptly back to reality. The Queen scorns the males for meekly standing by, but the scientist says they have no alternative because, unlike the ants, they are not warlike; they are superior to ants and, indeed, the most superior creatures on earth. The prime minister, prolonging this self-deceiving line, adds that they have never attacked a living soul or harmed anyone, and the King backs him up enthusiastically with 'Are the ants more powerful than us? - Never! Do they know we are thinking creatures?' Only the Queen keeps her head during this hysteria, pointing out that the enemy they so despise gives them rough treatment to which they must respond. The King, closing the formal part of their meeting, sums up by concluding, to the Queen's disgust, that their only refuge is to avoid tumbling over.

The scientist proposes a tour of their surroundings, to look at the view from the top of the bath. The King seconds this practical contribution to the debate, but the superstitious priest dislikes the suggestion and, with the Queen and the prime minister, elects to remain behind. They seek to begin the enlistment of an army by soliciting the services of a cockroach who wanders by, but he rejects their overtures with contempt. The Queen and the priest criticize the King, the former repeating earlier assertions that her character is stronger than her husband's and hinting that, by virtue of being female, she possesses unparticularised special qualities.

The scientist appears up above to announce that the King has fallen into the bath; it would be suicide for any of them to try and help him. The priest, after a long delay (reminiscent of Ibqirat's lack of concern for his companions at the end of <u>Praksa</u>) while he reconciles his conscience to participation by the atheistic scientist in their joint orations, leads them in prayers for their master's safety.

At this point Act One closes. During the other two acts, while the cockroach King's writhings are never overlooked, we come back to life-size and find ourselves in an absurd, human world. The humans are Adil and Samiyya, the young married couple who inhabit the flat whose bathroom forms the territory of the Kingdom of the Cockroaches. She wears the trousers and bullies her husband unbearably. Adil is defenceless against her and, while complaining that she has robbed him of his identity, pretends that he always submits to her out of deference to the weaker sex. On the day in question, Samiyya demands, and secures, first use of the bathroom when the alarm clock rings (this, though the human early morning, is the cockroach evening) and orders Adil to start preparing breakfast. He telephones a friend, incoherently enlisting his sympathy, and later tells his wife that it was a girl he had spoken to. When Samiyya is about to run her bath, she sees her way barred by the beleaguered cockroach King. The self-pitying hysteria in which she consequently indulges, and her departure to fetch the insecticide, enable Adil to appropriate the bathroom, not so that he can get ready for work but to protect the cockroach. Samiyya can get no sense out of him as he parrots back to her everything she says through the door. She is convinced that he has gone mad (and says so to her cook, and to friends on the telephone), complains that he has never disobeyed her like this before and begins to feel sorry for herself for being, despite all her guidance, of, and support for, him, presented with so embarrassing a situation.

The doctor of the firm which employs them both arrives. Adil assumes that his mission is to kill the cockroach but, persuaded otherwise, is finally coaxed into opening the bathroom door. He will not come out but, after a violent battle with his wife, succeeds in pulling the doctor inside to observe the cause of his alleged illness. This done, having learned from Samiyya that her husband is writing a thesis after office hours, the doctor claims that he understands the case and prescribes rest and tranquillisers. This causes such an uproar from the couple - Adil insisting that the visit has been of no assistance to the cockroach, Samiyya protesting that she is still unable to bath - that he flees their dual insanity.

At the beginning of Act Three he returns, impelled by his sense of duty. He decides, in another private talk with Samiyya, that her husband's concern to shield the cockroach stems from his identification of himself with it as a fellow-sufferer at her hands. The cure is to convince him that there is no resemblance between him and his insect protege and that he is not safeguarding his identity by defending it. They agree on a campaign to undeceive him but succeed only in making matters worse. They flatter him, Samiyya claims to believe that the cockroach's personality is more powerful than her own - a statement Adil dismisses as ludicrous - promises that everything will be different in future and finally voices the doctor's theory about his behaviour. He violently ejects her from the bathroom, into which she has stolen. The doctor puts to him the theory that his wife's character is stronger than his and elicits a denial which throws the medical man into disarray. He now retracts his diagnosis, and is shocked when Adil demonstrates its inaccuracy by saying that the cockroach is so superior to him that comparisons and identifications are irrelevant. All that matters, and concerns him, is its continuing efforts to get out of the bath. The doctor now becomes engrossed in the spectacle and gives sincere expression to a wish that he were its equal. Samiyya, certain that he is as mad as her husband, inveigles them out of the bathroom and orders her cook to run her bath.

Except for the down-to-earth final scene, the action ends here, with the arrival of the insensitive domestic in the centre of the stage. Samiyya, who vowed during her husband's cries never again to claim precedence over him in the matter of the bathroom, is now in repossession of it. What has the human episode told us? Principally, it is designed to show that everyday life is naturally absurd, that how people choose to spend their time is not the business of anyone else and that interpretations of their actions - as Pirandello said less colourfully in Cosi e (se li vera) - are as likely as not to be mistaken. Samiyya does not understand any of this and is scorned by Hakim for her treatment of Adil, who is to be seen not as unbalanced but as being merely intrigued by a sight which, admittedly unremarkable enough, affords him intellectual satisfaction. He is not interested in the cockroach's success or failure, as he reiterates several times ('I must leave him to his fate'), but simply fascinated by its unflagging persistence, which similarly enraptures the doctor. He is, in any case, precluded from giving it a helping hand because Samiyya might object, her finickiness makes it impossible for him to consider despatching it in situ, and no other answer occurs to him. He wishes the struggle to continue. The author makes it clear that he approves of Adil's attitude but regards it as undeserving of special note; he leaves us to infer that, if madness is really present in the flat, it resides in Samiyya.

The end comes quickly, and with it a perfect portrayal of the mindless callousness of one school of the Arab servant class. Umm Atiyya, the cook, unaffected by the drama of the cockroach or by knowledge of all that its heroism means to her employer, runs a bath according to her mistress's instructions, drowns the King and flings its carcass into a corner. Adil is upset, but soon recovers when the doctor reminds him of his indifference to its fate and when another spectacle is set before him: a column of ants marches up to bear the corpse away, and he and the doctor settle down to watch, absorbed. Both levels of action are, however, brought to a smart conclusion. Umm Atiyya's robot-like labours engulf both the ants and their trophy, and Adil, bereft now of any consuming diversion, receives a directive from his wife to spend the day in putting her wardrobe straight. We are back where we began. The wars of the cockroaches and the ants, and of Adil and Samiyya, are to be resumed at the point they had reached before greater issues temporarily supervened. Adil had the upper hand in his conflict as long as he retained the cockroach as a weapon against his wife. Once Umm Atiyya has done her work, the period of his sway is over and his normal lot is reimposed on him - a lot which, if Ar Ra^{c}i's talk of heartbreaks is interpretable thus, may have reflected Hakim's own marital position at this time. (When Acts Two and Three of Fate of a Cockroach were staged together, the ending was changed so that Adil emerged victorious.)[4]

Act Two of the play particularly contains some brilliant Absurdist dialogues between Adil and Samiyya. Acts Two and Three both make superb dramatic capital out of little concrete material and are extremely readable and tense. They show humans behaving in an even more purposeless and irrational fashion than the cockroaches of Act One.[5] The play as a whole, far from being a tragedy, exhibits the futility and unimportance of life's petty details. Its enormous stage potential is readily apparent.

Everything's in its Place (Kullu Shay fi Mahallihi), a brief, farcical extravanganza based on two of the items in Show Me Allah and added to the original contents of A Variety of Theatre to make up its second edition, and The Wedding Night (Laylat az Zifaf), an anthology of short stories, the title piece in which has been filmed,[6] brought 1966 to a close. 1967 saw Hakim's last sustained effort, the second of the Troilus and Cressida type to appear in print. The Anxiety Bank (Bank al Qalaq), a novel-play which unevenly mixes satire, fantasy, surrealism, the thriller, farce, the comedy of manners, the picaresque, and pastoral autobiography and in the upshot achieves nothing of any value, is a stock-taking exercise in disillusion and uncertainty which Ar Ra^{c}i compares with Shaw's The Adventures of a Black Girl in her Search for God and in which he detects the influence of Mahfuz's Thartharatun fawqa'n Nil[7] on. It was ready for the press before the June War, on the first day of which Hakim contributed a poem to Al Ahram,[8] but apparently was delayed for over six months[9] by official indecision. Only a reading of it by President Abd an Nasir, whose administration is much criticized, broke the impasse, according to one source;[10] according to Hakim,[11] who intended it as a warning to Abd an Nasir about the condition of Egypt, which he understood but did not heed, it was passed by the censors only after being published abroad, an occurrence of which no details have come to light. An account of the book which is helpful as far as it goes is in Sherif,[12] and Muhammad al Hasan sums it up well.[13] Its opening is of exciting promise but, quite rightly, he says that its 'wide dimensions' are not properly exploited and that Hakim has - in his keenness to thrust his new genre upon the world ('I wish to unite the play and the novel')[14] - contented himself with a slender description of the problem he had set out to explore; his casual conclusion blunts a message he had already blurred by failing to get down to the job of tackling the question of anxiety at all. The critic believes that the use of the narrative/dialogue form shows that he had reached a literary roadblock. He rates the innovation, for which Hakim coined the term masriwayya (play-novel)[15] as one of little efficacy, a forced fusion of two incompatibles which does justice to neither and has no future. The Anxiety Bank, the first masriwayya in Arabic, is a 'monster' which is both unactable and unreadable, he says, and Hakim could have approached the phenomenon of anxiety more effectively by means of either a novel or a play.

It is debatable whether the book is unreadable, and Muhammad al Hasan's conviction that there would be no more masriwayyat was subsequently disproved by Mahfuz Ayyub's Babil al-Khati' and Mahmud Awad Abd al Al's Sukkar Murr. It is certainly true, however, that The Anxiety Bank is a strange creature, which reveals Hakim at his most bitter in his attitudes to Egyptian society and twentieth-century life. Another odd apparition to which he gave his name in 1967 was a volume entitled Our Theatre Model (Qalibuna al Masrahi), which consists of plays by Aeschylus, Shakespeare, Moliere, Ibsen, Chekhov, Pirandello and Durrenmatt rewritten by various hands, none of them, as far as can be seen, his own. Greatly abbreviated versions, they are put over by means of a narrator, two actors who are responsible between them for all the male and female roles and, in the Aeschylus, a panegyrist standing for the chorus. Hakim was patently the guiding spirit of this experiment, which he introduces with a medium-length preface. Its essence is that when, in The Piper (sic), The Deal and The Tree Climber, he attempted to put the modern theatre and the cultural traditions of the Arabs into touch with one another, he was operating in accordance with the international conventions of the drama. A demand had grown up for an independent Egyptian prototype, to create which he believed that he must go back to the point in Egypt's history where it had been uninfluenced by the outside world and had not come into contact with the play in any shape or form. This was the age of the story-tellers and entertainers whose interaction with their audiences was total. If, to their legacy, were joined the rich folk sources of Al Isfahani, Al Jahiz Al Hariri, Badi az Zaman, etc., the required framework might have been found. It had to be one which could embrace all plays of every kind ('world' and 'local', ancient and modern), one capable of accommodating European and world concepts and subjects just as the European model had been readily utilisable by the Arabs. Hakim decided that he had discovered the starting-point he needed[16] - that of pure art (direct contact between art and audience) - and claims that his chosen framework could link folklore and the most advanced theatre. His three or four players, with 'great scripts in their heads and hearts' but no stage, decor, lighting, costumes or make-up, could bring all classes of people to appreciate 'the most glorious fruits of art and thought, as he endeavoured to demonstrate in Our Theatre Model. He believed that the Arab framework could solve the problem of 'the theatre for the people' not only for the Arabs but also for the rest of the world, and felt that it had affinities with the 'anti-theatre' and the 'happening'.

The end-product of this highly artificial theory, a questionable attempt to redraw the shape of the drama as developed through the ages, is of no interest.* What admirer of Hamlet or The Cherry Orchard would wish to see them diluted and potted; what valid idea of Moliere or Pirandello would be conveyed to someone who had not heard of them and would be able to grasp them undistorted? Hakim, as often, hedges his bets by saying, rather feebly, that this 'concentrated' or 'anatomising' theatre is not a substitute for the world model, from whose progress and new directions the Arab theatre must not become cut off.

1968 seems to have been a year notable only for a poem in praise of Martin Luther King.[17] In 1969 there was talk of filming The Soul's Return,[18] The Tree Climber was reported to have had huge success in Canada[19] and 'the Canadian Television Corporation ... asked Tawfiq al Hakim for permission to screen it on its trans-Canada channel'.[20] We do not know how he responded. In March, Cairo University celebrated fifty years of achievement by their venerable old boy, each faculty presenting one of his plays (one was Act One of Fate of a Cockroach) and a Tawfiq al Hakim Festival being organized. In the same month, in his capacity as President of the Egyptian affiliate of the International Theatre Institute, a branch of UNESCO, Hakim convened a Congress of Arab Dramatists to debate 'the possibilities of the Arab theatre participating in world theatre'. The meeting, held in Cairo from 19-25 March, in the opinion of one commentator[21] had no results, made no recommendations and was a chaotic flop. It is hard to see how, under the chairmanship of a man with little active concern for the destiny abroad of even his own work, it could have been otherwise. On 14 June he gave a depressed interview to Al Ahram and on the 27th published in that paper part of the first scene of a play entitled The Moonmen (Ahl al Qamar), begun to celebrate the imminent lunar landing of Armstrong and Aldrin but soon abandoned.** It looks as if it was going to be a Swiftian performance of the Gulliver type and, if in the mood, he would probably have done it very well. In November Kitab al Hilal brought out Ar Ra^{c}i's Tawfiq al Hakim: Fannan al Furga wa Fannan al Fikr, to which the dramatist

---

* In Ostle, p 169, f.n., Ar Ra^{c}i disagrees and cites Nagib Surur, At Tayyib as Siddiqi and Sa^{c}ad Allah Wanus as practising exponents of the theory

** It seems unlikely that it was taken up again and turned into Dialogues with a Planet, which only Awad has mentioned, in Ostle, p 185

contributed the sketch of a possible opening for a commedia dell'arte piece (not conceived along lines set out in Our Theatre Model) to be called Harun ar Rashid and Harun ar Rashid and concluded by a discussion between the actors and the audience. Ar Ra^{c}i detected in it a new departure for the Arab theatre and declared his determination to have it staged. It is not recorded that it has been, and it is surprising that the critic should have expected new doors to open as a result of these six pages of unambitious text inspired by an episode in The Thousand and One Nights.

1970 began with a performance of The Anxiety Bank in April, at the fourth Festival of Provincial Theatre Groups. The inexperienced producer turned it into a play proper and it was completely unsuccessful. It was the old story, except that The Cavemen and The Anxiety Bank are ill-assorted bedfellows: the spectators, of whom 'many ... left the theatre', did not understand 'a work unsuitable for the masses of Cairo' let alone for those of Al Mahalla al Kubra, the populous industrial town where the production took place, 'who have no conception at all of the philosophical reflections of Tawfiq al Hakim,... of the anxiety which is (the play's) theme' or of anything else about it.[22] They mocked it and made a 'devastating failure' and 'artistic tragedy' of a creation 'impossible to produce on the stage'. In April also, perhaps not entirely coincidentally, Hakim wrote a letter, dated the 26th, to Abd an Nasir, who must have been hurt by the only overt sign his protege ever gave him that he disapproved of his regime. Composed following the appointment of Muhammad Hasanayn Haykal, the internationally significant editor of Al-Ahram, as Minister of Guidance, the letter informed him that, since the debacle of the June War, the nation had not been minded to believe the government's version of events and that the existing credibility gap could only be prevented from widening by the continued exertions of 'free pens' like that Haykal had wielded, especially in his Friday article, Bi Sarahatin. This protest at the loss of a comparatively robust journalistic voice, a clear denunciation of the state's propaganda apparatus, was delivered by Hatim Sadiq, Abd an Nasir's son-in-law and a member of Al Ahram's editorial board. It was treated as matter for official enquiries - showing, Hakim says, the strength of the police grip on Egypt - the involvement in its despatch of Hakim, Haykal, Haykal's personal secretary and her husband, Sadiq and Lutfi al Khawli and his wife was investigated in May, and the last two went to gaol for more than six months. Haykal's part in the affair, for the apparent initiation of which Hakim paid no penalty, seems to have been not insubstantial.[23]

In June, Hakim was elected Honorary Chairman of the Egyptian Drama Writers' Association;[24] in October it was announced that a film was actually being made of The Soul's Return;[25] and on the 23rd of that month, twenty-five days after the death of Abd an Nasir, Luwis Awad contributed an article to Al Ahram,[26] with the name of Hakim's most famous and seminal novel as its title, about the book's influence on the dead leader and the effects on its author of, as a consequence, having the President as his protector. Thus quickly was one version of their relationship placed formally on the historical record. Hakim's publication of Tawfiq al Hakim the Artist (Tawfiq al Hakim al Fannan) during the course of the year was a relative non-event. It comprised a clutch of articles, on the theatre, the cinema, painting and the rest, two-thirds of which had already been featured in others of his anthologies.

In the summer of 1971 he undertook a journey round his past, starting with the Swiss village where he and Taha Husayn had gambolled thirty-five years before. He found it utterly changed, scrapped this part of his exercise in nostalgia and made his way to Paris. There he had hoped to retrace the footsteps recorded in A Sparrow from the East and Life in Bud, but instead spent a traumatic ten days. He and his unidentified companion never slept for more than two nights at the same hotel because of pressure on accommodation, could never unpack and were constantly worried as to where they should stay the next day. He could not find his student digs, and the Paris of his twenties was not to be discovered. He did see Strindberg's The Dream at the Comedie Francaise and a film version of Death in Venice, but the cultural component of his tour was, on the whole, not uplifting. His holiday, cut short by an attack of rheumatism in the leg, was a disaster[27] - one which the French Embassy in Cairo would no doubt have been happy to prevent had he approached them, which his character obviously would not allow him to do.* It may have been of some consolation to him, on his return home, to be re-elected President of the Egyptian branch of the ITI. Under him were ten members, including Ar Ra^{c}i and Awad,[28] and his great friend

---

* Mallakh, pp 202 and 382, mentions a trip to Paris and London (he pictures Hakim in front of the Sherlock Holmes Hotel and watching a ceremonial occasion) which would appear to have taken place in 1969 or 1970. He does not seem to be referring to the journey here described.

Dr Husayn Fawzi was later named as his deputy.[29] But his chief memory of the summer must be the knowing smiles of Parisians from whom, during his vacation, he sought directions to addresses they had never heard of. They moved away from me, he says, 'as though I had turned into one of the characters of The Cavemen'.[30]

Late in his career he had become a director of Al Ahram. Persuaded by Lutfi al Khawli, who worked for the paper and worships the ground on which Hakim treads,[31] Haykal, before the Six Day War, installed him in an office with no duties other than those he elected to impose upon himself.[32] It was Akhbar al Yawm all over again.[33] One task he shouldered was the penning of his last play, This Comic World (Ad Dunya Riwayatun Hazliyya), which has not been issued in book form and of which the present writer has managed to track down only Scenes 12-17 of the Al Ahram serialization of November 1971. Their theme is the familiar one of peace versus war, with the pivots a nuclear test series and leading characters suffering from radiation sickness. The treatment of the subject-matter is symbolic, varied and gruesome, and as fresh as to be expected in a Hakim play. An attempt by an air-force commander to communicate from the grave with the 'hero' in the role of Mark Antony is most arresting. It could be that This Comic World, though it perhaps resembles Rejuvenation and The Thorns of Peace/Shams an Nahar rather closely in its framework and conclusion respectively, will eventually rank among the majors; it fits in well with the Troilus and Cressida dramas, so far as can be judged. Written in the colloquial, it began a run at Al Masrah al Qawmi as Sikandari in early 1972.[34]

At approximately the same time as This Comic World's serialization commenced it was decided that the operations of Masrah al Hakim should be divided between two sections, one still to be named after Hakim himself and the other after Georges Abyad.[35] This was appropriate and imaginative (it could also have been malicious, but there is no hint that it was) and accurately underlined the link between the man who failed to popularize a repertoire of European classics and the one who succeeded, after years of frustration and neglect, in making of the Arabic classical theatre a phenomenon which could not be ignored.

We do not know the cause of the heartbreak which fostered the Troilus and Cressida period. (There can be no doubt of its occurrence, for Ar Ra^ci, who first discerned it, was well placed to observe Hakim closely.) It might have been another campaign of innuendo that his work was mostly not original, but borrowed, but this would have been unlikely to disturb him much. The June War came too late to usher in the phase. Whatever its explanation − and this writer assumes it to have been brought on by his discontent at the state of Egypt during the final years of Gamal Abd an Nasir and the first ones of Anwar as Sadat − it lent to the output of the years between late 1966 and early 1973 a fundamental bitterness which was not in evidence before. Four further titles did not affect the position: Tawfiq al Hakim Says ... (Tawfiq al Hakim Yatahaddath, 1971) is an Al Ahram collection of articles contributed between 1955 and 1971 to a number of newspapers and magazines, notably Al Ahram itself and the invaluable Al Masrah, whose 'spiritual father' Hakim was[36] and whose demise in 1970 was a crippling blow to students of his work; and A Journey between Two Eras (Rihlatun bayna Asrayn, 1972), A Monk among Women (Rahibun bayna Nisa, 1972) and Me and the Law ... and Art (Ana wa'l Qanun ... wa'l Fann, 1973) are regurgitations.

Hakim began to emerge from his psychological trough at the time of the student unrest in December 1972 and January 1973 which formed the climax of the dissatisfaction of the younger generation with President As Sadat's 'no war, no peace' policy towards Israel. On 9 January, concerned at the situation, he called a meeting of his fellow intellectuals in his Al Ahram office and with them drew up a paper for discussion[37] about it. Out of this grew a 'Declaration by Writers and Men of Letters',[38] with 46 signatures[39] on it, which he despatched on 21 January to the Chairman of the Parliamentary Investigations' Committee with an offer to assist in any enquiry it might provoke. The Declaration, which had the same generic theme as the 1970 letter to Abd an Nasir, concentrated on the ceaseless propaganda references to a 'battle' at some indefinite date in the future which were confusing the public, who had no faith in the government controlled media and were uncertain what was intended with regard to Israel. The 'battle' had become something which no one could any longer take seriously. (Was it, the discussion paper had asked, meant to indicate a short-term military aim, or a more distant one which sought to revivify Egyptian civilization and had no immediate relevance to the problem of Israel?) The Declaration advised the President to dispel the perplexity of the people and help them to reassert their personality and strength through the adoption of a policy of candour, the permitting of freedom of thought and opinion and of dissent, and the cessation of the exploitation of influential minds as propaganda promoters. The younger generation particularly was bewildered and in no condition to fight the enemy, if that was what the 'battle' envisaged. The government should select its policies from among those favoured by the nation, which was willing and worthy of trust.

The President was angered by this demarche, which did not come to his attention until it was featured under sensationalist headlines in Kuwaiti and Lebanese newspapers.[40] (It is not revealed how they obtained the text.) Its exposure came at a delicate time when, unknown to Hakim and his colleagues, Egypt was planning the October crossing of the Suez Canal. As Sadat received Hakim to tell him that he was disappointed that a man whose works he had taken to prison, when he was interned by the British, should not be on his side.[41] He then formed an Arab Socialist Union disciplinary committee which, beginning with the Declaration's signatories (except Hakim and Nagib Mahfuz) but soon casting its net much wider, in February expelled a large group of 'ideologically unsound' writers from the ASU, by virtue alone of their membership of which body they were able to exercise their craft. In early March a greater number were transferred from their newspapers to sinecures in the Ministry of Guidance, which effectively silenced them too. The works of Hakim and Mahfuz, too distinguished to be treated in either of these undignified ways, were not to be published or performed, or mentioned by the media.

Hakim was not prepared to be muzzled in this fashion. Presumably in order to furnish As Sadat, whose own alleged 'negativism' he briefly reproves, with an example to eschew, he set down on paper his personal thoughts on the presidency of Abd an Nasir and allowed them - unwittingly, he maintains - to be leaked by a still-trusted friend to journalists outside Egypt. They appeared incomplete in a 'respectable French magazine' and (mistranslated from the French) in a Lebanese paper. The 'unpublished' manuscript circulated widely among students in Cairo, who, having taken delivery of its message, gave it much approval.[42] 'Awareness Regained' (Awdat al Wa^{c}i), as it was entitled when, after October, the President permitted it to be issued openly, describes how, consistently with the views expressed in The Tree of Ruling, Hakim supported the Nagib coup, marvelled at the speedy ouster of Faruq and, despite the curbing of the freedom of opinion, felt no anxiety at the inception of the revolution - was, indeed, euphoric about developments. No serious distrust of Abd an Nasir arose in him in the revolution's first decade and he was enthusiastic about the nationalization of the Suez Canal Company.[43] Egypt's involvement in the Yemeni civil war ('between Arab and Arab, far from Israel')[44] and, particularly, the fiasco of the Six Day War, however, turned him so totally against the President that he could not understand how Abd an Nasir had had the audacity to survive for his last three and a quarter years. It revolted him that the army pampered while the peasantry remained sick, poor and ignorant, and proclaimed by the propaganda machine to be unbeatable, should have wasted so much of the nation's resources in the Yemen and have collapsed so lamentably in June; he was even more repelled by the eventual and inevitable claim that the 1967 debacle had in fact been a triumph and by the assertions of the President, with whom the blame entirely lay, that all but he had been at fault.

Throughout the book, Hakim, who had campaigned for a statue to be erected to Abd an Nasir on his death[45] on 28 September 1970, exhorts the reader, and the future researcher, to remain impartial in his judgements on the President. He protests that he does not hold him personally culpable for the misdeeds of his regime, but people like himself for being blinded by their emotions to the defects of the revolution and for not speaking out against them. He claims frequently that he loved Abd an Nasir as an individual, for several reasons, 'perhaps the most important of them (being) that he loved me and respected my views until the last moment of his life and that from the first ... he linked my views and his, my hopes and his;'[46] he will always cherish the memory of him as a person. Though they only met once, there was a bond of trust between the President and the man he regarded as 'a spiritual father of the revolution',[47] who in his turn regarded himself as 'the prophet and advocate of the blessed revolution'.[48]

From the time of the Six Day War Hakim saw in Abd an Nasir - whom he loved but who had misread The Soul's Return and, while taking their point, failed to act on the advice of The Sultan's Dilemma and The Anxiety Bank - a man unfitted to be a politician, let alone a ruler: when he was a youth, he notes, he had embarked on, but not finished, a work of fiction which, like two of his, had a hero called Muhsin,[49] and his dreamy, emotional character was more that of a writer than of a man of affairs. He made the country 'weak in personality, devoid of self-awareness, and ignorant of the meaning of responsibility', as it still was, and he was a disaster for both Egypt and the Arabs. 'There is no doubt that he sought the good of his people,'[50] and his revolution fulfilled some thirty per cent of the nation's hopes of it, but his administration was twentieth-century Egypt's worst and its extravagances were more scandalous than those of the Khedive Isma^{c}il, who at least bequeathed the country some public buildings and railways. The reliance of his 'Hitlerian nazism' on torture, and his penchant for making Egypt look ridiculous by giving all its products the name 'Victory' (Nasr), were only fractionally less damaging than his insincere socialism and his obsession with Arab unity which, having as its object the domination of the Arab world by Egypt, 'ruined us all'. The accession to power of another like him, accorded a reverence not bestowed on prophets by an uncritical people who dared not disagree with him, had to be prevented.

In spite of the uncompromising nature of his accusations against the President, Hakim labels them provisional and subject to revision. The files of the period, he never ceases to urge, must be opened in order that Abd an Nasir's personal involvement in an era 'full of lies' may be assessed once and for all; their general display was vital, in addition, so that a new Egypt might be built, political, intellectual and social progress made, and the lessons of the immediate past learned, never to be forgotten.

The opening of the October War was a forthright response to the Declaration's doubts about the meaning of the 'battle' and enabled President As Sadat to free Hakim from the restraints he had successfully ignored - and to drop charges still pending against students who had taken part in the 1972/3 demonstrations and reinstate the outcasts from the ASU.[51] On 9 October Hakim praised the crossing of the Canal and the stand in Sinai in an article in Al Ahram, and at the same time he asked the Minister of Culture, the notable author Yusuf as Siba^{c}i (he had similarly approached the President in 1956[52] and 1967),[53] to allow him to share in the country's effort. Preferring to seek an active role rather than merely to write, because 'our nation has moved on from words to deeds', he volunteered for manual labour, suitable to his age and state of health, in a supply factory. As Siba^{c}i replied that 'Egypt says to you that your offer alone helps the cause and she wishes you always, all your life, to see (her) mighty.'[54] Now was the publication of Awareness Regained permitted to go ahead. It naturally angered Nasirites in Egypt and outside, 'as though Nasirism were a holy religion', but it was obviously a useful document for As Sadat to have at his disposal, especially as it was no one day wonder, being said to be still the best-selling book in Egypt in mid-1975.[55] Whether or not it was a volume to be proud of is another matter. It attracted much adverse comment from people, among them Haykal,[56] who charged Hakim with cowardice in attacking a dead man whom he had not dared to confront while he was alive. The accusation sticks despite the author's exoneration of himself, and his tasteless protestations that, even if he detested his actions, he loved their perpetrator. Least palatable of all are his boast that his love was requited, which is an endeavour to elevate the writer to the level of the President, and his implication that Abd an Nasir, whose inability to emulate him in the capacity of author he treats with insincere astonishment, only went wrong because he did not pay due regard to the wisdom of the works of Tawfiq al Hakim, which is an attempt to outrank him in the eyes of history.

While Hakim was coming back into political favour in Egypt, the limelight in the UK and in English-speaking circles abroad briefly caught him, as a consequence of the publication of English translations of four of his plays, The Sultan's Dilemma, Fate of a Cockroach, Everything's in its Place and Death Song (twice), and of the broadcasting of the first of them four times, in November 1973, by the World Service of the BBC, which has done something to acknowledge his suitability for radio. At home he subsequently partnered Abd ar Rahman ash Sharqawi in writing the scenario for the film 'Muhammad, the Messenger of God'[57] which has incurred the condemnation of some Arab governments and provoked the concern of others; he prefaced a diwan;[58] and in June 1974, he became President of Nadi al Qissa, the Fiction Writers' Club.[59] In the following year, along with Yusuf Wahbi and Muhammad Abd al Wahhab, he was awarded an honorary doctorate for his services to the arts by the Egyptian Academy of Arts, which had only recently instituted such degrees,[60] and brought out The Documentary Background to 'Awareness Regained' (Watha'iq fi Tariq Awdat al Wa^{c}i). This volume, by September the most popular book in Egypt,[61] is in three parts, the first two recounting and to some extent documenting the episodes, described above, of the 1970 letter to Abd an Nasir and the Declaration of 1973. Part Three is an essay which, in the highly subjective manner of Awareness Regained, reviews the history of Egypt from the British occupation to the death of the President. Its main aims are further to censure Abd an Nasir for destroying the country and to ridicule his socialism, for which he coins the term al-ishtira'smaliyya (socio-capitalism). Other aims are to show why Egyptian socialism must be homegrown and why it would be impossible for Egypt to go communist, the rise of an Egyptian Mao Tse-tung or Ho Chi-minh being unthinkable, and to reiterate the necessity for the files of the 1952-70 period to be opened.

At the last report Hakim was cured of his depression and his morale had been reinvigorated by the spectacle of his country, under the leadership of Anwar as Sadat, at least reasserting its personality. It is, sadly, unlikely that at seventy-nine and after a gap of six years he will write any more plays; it is perhaps to be regretted that so much of his old age should have been sacrificed to hollow recrimination and lost to his metier.

REFERENCES

1. Ra^{c}i, p 116 ff
2. pp 17-20
3. pp 159-60
4. Mandur 2, p 174
5. Fate of a Cockroach is the only Hakim play Tarabishi enthuses over. His reading, in pp 169-72, of Act One as a protest at man's powerlessness against the sexual might of the female is unconvincing
6. Landau, p 125, quoting Akhbar al Yawm for 5 July 1952
7. Ra^{c}i, p 136
8. Text in Mallakh, pp 358-9
9. AW, p 65
10. Awad, in Al Adab, November 1972, p 7
11. AW, p 64
12. Op cit, pp 66-73
13. pp 96-9
14. Preface to an edition not seen by this writer, according to Muhammad al Hasan, p 98
15. MAS, April, 1970, p 13
16. Cf Husayn, p 122
17. Text in Mallakh, pp 359-60
18. Adib, January and July 1969, pp 64
19. Ibid, June, 1969, p 64, where it is said to have won six awards when performed in English by the British Columbia Bauerhaus Company at a theatre festival in which 80 troupes took part
20. Ibid, loc cit
21. Muhammad Barakat, in MAS, April, 1969, pp 2-5
22. MAS, April, 1970, p 13
23. ARD, pp 5-42. The text of the letter is at pp 16-17
24. MAG, June, 1970, p 122
25. Ibid, October, 1970, p 123

26 Awad 1
27 Hakim, in Al Ahram, 6 August 1971
28 Adib, June 1971, p 64
29 Ibid, August 1971, p 64
30 Hakim, loc cit
31 Jamal Muhammad Ahmad, oral communication, 16 March 1972, ARD, p 35
32 Jamal Muhammad Ahmad, tem cit
33 Mallakh, p 287
34 Adib, February, 1972, p 64
35 Ibid, January, 1972, p 64
36 MAS, February, 1964
37 Text in ARD, p 44
38 Text in ARD, pp 46-8
39 Desmond Stewart in Encounter, August, 1973
40 Ibid, ARD, p 43
41 Ibid
42 Ibid
43 AW, p 57
44 ARD, p 58
45 AW, p 75
46 Ibid, p 104
47 Ibid, p 94
48 Ibid, p 97
49 Ibid, p 41
50 Ibid, p 95
51 Muhammad Hasanayn Haykal, The Road to Ramadan in The Sunday Times, 11 May 1975
52 AW, p 57
53 Mallakh, p 358
54 Adib, November, 1973, p 64
55 Adib, June, 1975, p 64
56 AW, pp 99-107
57 As Sahafa, Khartum, 22 January 1974
58 Adib, March 1974, p 64
59 Adib, July 1974, p 64
60 Adib, August 1975, p 64
61 Adib, September 1975, p 64

PART TWO

The Major Themes

1   The Human Reality: Time and Place

> She was the golden thread that united him to a Past beyond his misery, and to a Present beyond his misery. (Dickens, A Tale of Two Cities)

> ... Les annees ne separent pas les coeurs. (Maeterlinck, Alladine et Palomides)

> I don't like belonging to another person's dream. (Alice, in Through the Looking Glass)

> We like to think that we own the earth, but in fact it owns us, and keeps us bound to it by those chains that we ... call our own weight ... It is only out there where there is nothing - nothing nothing - that you are really free. (Nigel Balchin, Kings of Infinite Space)

Tawfiq al Hakim has been concerned throughout his careet with the subjects of time and, to a much less obvious extent, of place. His preoccupation with them, which has stimulated his most powerful 'intellectual' writing, is partly rooted in his reading of Egypt's history and in his belief that, with death and resurrection, they are the philosophical keys to that history: to the Egyptian nationalist, such as he predominantly is, decay and death are followed, after a period, by an inevitable regeneration, just as every year (time) the Nile reinvigorates the lifeless soil of its Valley (place). He does not set much literal stress on the death phase of the cycle and uses the concept of resurrection loosely, selecting time and place as the dominating themes for his enquiries into earthly reality also in the conviction that they were two of the three pillars of ancient Egypt's view of tragedy. Hakim the dramatist has composed a number of high-quality plays on the basis of them. They may be read, as they will be treated here, as completely divorced from his interpretations of Egyptian history and tragedy, and they expose the human condition to harrowing and attractive scrutiny. In several of the other plays which are not primarily designed to do this, the same themes put in incidental appearances.

Time and place (which is in close attendance even when not overtly) are topics which may be judged to be either as of consuming interest or of little or no intrinsic worth even though they are central to the mortal state. That they should have underpinned the great The Cavemen, as well as Rejuvenation, Journey into the Future and (in Hakim's view) Shahrazad, however, gives them at least international theatrical importance. Hakim on the whole keeps them ostensibly separate, but, in Journey into the Future, deals with both together.

The Cavemen is about time. It begins with the awakening from sleep in a cave near Tarsus, which perhaps owes something to Ali Baba as well as to the Seven Sleepers, of three young Christian refugees from the religious persecutions of the pagan Roman Emperor Decius - Marnush and Mishilinya, formerly his close advisers, and Yamlikha, the shepherd who owns the cave and is the most devout Christian of the three. Under the impression that they have passed a normal night, the two noblemen despatch the shepherd into the town to buy provisions. He returns empty-handed, frightened by the facts that Tarsus has altered out of all recognition and that his foray has created a stir, and is chased back by a mob of the citizenry who, seeking the source of the coins he was proffering, carry the three off to the palace. As events unfold, the reasons for these incomprehensible happenings gradually become apparent; each of the cavemen in turn realizes that his has been no ordinary sleep, that its duration has been 309 years, that life has progressed, while time for him has stood still, beyond his capacity to adapt, and that the cave is his only trustworthy reality. Although they have been canonized during the period since they fell asleep and their reawakening has been predicted and awaited, Yamlikha is roughly handled by the populace when he straightway goes off in search of his flocks, and Marnush is demoralized as he is tailed by inquisitive crowds during a vain attempt to find his house, wife and son. Only Mishilinya, a personification of the third element in ancient Egyptian tragedy, 'the heart'[1] - in contradistinction to the intellect as represented by Yamlikha and Marnush[2] - and endowed with a more adventurous and less fatalistic temperament, succeeds in establishing any kind of rapport with surroundings which are strange yet familiar. He makes himself at home in the King's palace, has himself clothed in the correct style and essays a courtship of the King's daughter, Priska, whom he takes, despite all the evidence to the contrary, to be Decius's child and his secret fiancee of the same name of three centuries before. A significant part in what transpires is played by a dream she had, the night before the resurrection of the 'saints', that she was buried alive. She is very afraid when they are brought to the palace, and her apprehension is not diminished when her tutor, Ghalias, informs her that at her birth fortune-tellers said that she would resemble her namesake, whose inherited gold cross she wears.

Hakim's leaning towards 'Irrationalism' is clearly foreshadowed in much of the middle portion of the play, when the King regards the behaviour of the saints as so inappropriate as to merit the label of lunacy and they think him unhinged. They are totally unable to communicate and rapidly reach an impasse. Yamlikha, the quickest of the three to grasp that everything has changed, goes some way towards resolving the dilemma by fleeing the uncomfortable scene at the end of Act Two:

'This world is not our world ... It is another world, with which we have no link. There is no hope for us in life now except in the cave ... The cave is the only place we own in this life. The cave is our link with our lost world ... I'm alone in (this one) ... I can feel myself sinking beneath a 300 year old tumour.'

After a third of Act Three, Marnush, who had earlier ridiculed Yamlikha's fear at being 300 years out of date, follows the shepherd back to the cave. His balance is tilted by the discovery of the tombstone of his son, who died at the age of 60 (his own two lives have added up to only half this figure) while bringing victory over paganism to the forces of Christianity:

'My boy is dead and nothing links me now to this world ... I'm young, while my son (died) an old man; Life by itself, stripped of the past, of every link and ... cause, is less than non-existence; We are ghosts ... We are now the property of time.'

The beginning of Act Three provides another example of early 'Irrationalism when Ghalias and Mishilinya confront one another without having the remotest idea of what the other is talking about. This non-conversation is the prelude to Mishilinya's first discussion with Priska who, still afraid because of the portents, her dream and the strangeness of the saints, is harsh with him. Their encounter, which resembles those of Sadiq and Dr Tal^{c}at in Rejuvenation, deeply troubles them both. Unlike his colleagues, Mishilinya has a living past embodied in the person of Priska whom, for most of the act, he continues to believe is his fiancee - a belief strengthened by his knowledge that her cross was his gift to her ancestor. When she leaves him, however, he admits to his dilemma:

> 'Priska, darling, come to me. You are she. O Lord. You are not she. You are not she. Who are you then? You? Do I sleep? Am I alive? Is this a bad dream? O God. O God. O Christ. O God, give me my reason to see with. Give me light or give me death. Awakening. Sleep. Reason. Reason. Marnush. Where are you, Marnush? Where are we? Where are we now? Dreams in the cave? Are these dreams in the cave? Is this real? Am I in the cave?'

By the end of the act, after another meeting with Priska, he is convinced that nothing can be done about the horrible truth ('I stretch out my hand to you and see you alive and beautiful before me. But an awful, gigantic Being comes between us. History! ... Our time is up, we belong to history now. We wanted to re-enter time, but history has taken its revenge') and joins his friends in the cave. Priska, for her part, is in a state of confusion, angry and jealous because Mishilinya, insincerely, compared her unfavourably with his centuries-old betrothed, and alarmed as a result of Ghalias's statement that she is in some sense the original Priska's successor.

After a further month's sleep in the cave, Mishilinya persuades Marnush and Yamlikha that the new Tarsus was a dream; the fact that they all dreamed the same one was a simple coincidence. Yamlikha ('If we go out now we shall find our world which we can live in') and Marnush are overjoyed, and this time it is Mishilinya himself who is the least convinced because his dream Priska was superior to Decius's daughter. Before Yamlikha can be sent off again for food, however, he dies of hunger, but firm in his Christianity despite not knowing whether his life was 'a dream or real'. Marnush, brought up short by the horrible realization that the clothes he is wearing are not such as were in fashion in Decius's day, soon desolately expires as well. He warns Mishilinya against harbouring impossible hopes ('We are the dreams of time ...

time dreams us') and dies declaring that his Christian faith, which was always tinged with scepticism, has evaporated. This has been their resurrection, and their eternal life is over. Mishilinya refuses to shake the hand of a pagan, and delays his own passing on the grounds that being in love cancels out his personal time loss and will enable him to bridge the gulf between him and the exciting, up-to-date Priska:

> 'We aren't a dream ... Time is the dream. We are reality ... (Time) is our dream ... with no existence without us ... Didn't we live 300 years in one night ...? Yes, we are the ones who sought to abolish time. Yes, we have defeated it.'

Priska arrives as he is on the threshold of death. She has satisfied herself that Mishilinya's missing centuries are, after all, no barrier to their love ('There is nothing to divide me from you. The heart is stronger than time') and, indeed, is seriously wondering whether she is not his fiancee of 309 years earlier.

Priska stays with Mishilinya, who soon dies, a Christian, while her proposal to her father that the cave entrance be sealed and the site converted into a temple in honour of the saints is implemented. Having thus made her dream come true, she is confident that she and her lover will be reunited 'in another age with no obstacle between us', 'or in another world'. She rejects Ghalias's suggestion that she too is a saint, and, expelling him from the cave with only seconds to spare, merely authorizes him to say that she was 'a woman who loved'.

Although according to the Hakim belief system (death, time, resurrection) Marnush's conviction that he had had his after-life was wrong and Priska's certainty that she and Mishilinya would rise again together was well-founded, their future incarnations cannot but have the cave as their venue and bring the same problems back in intensified form. In The Cavemen Hakim has demonstrated them to perfection in his story of the horrendous plight of three individuals in the position - one which is not entirely hypothetical, as the recent cases of the Japanese Sergeant Yokoi[3] and others have shown - of being out of time and unsynchronized with the society surrounding them. The play depresses though it does not purge in the dramatic sense, for The Cavemen is not a tragedy. It has a chilling impact on the reader or spectator. Yamlikha, Marnush and Mishilinya, 309 years older than the inhabitants of Christian Tarsus, have no chance at all of adjusting to the new scheme of things. The cruellest and most shocking determinant of this is the finding of the grave of Marnush's son.

Hakim sees time as one of the forces which are greater than man but against which man must fight. It is a phenomenon which cannot be treated cavalierly, and in Journey into the Future alone among this group of dramas does one of its preys escape from its clutches to any extent unscathed. Hakim's standpoint is that if your personal clock has gone wrong, as the cavemen's has, the circumstances in which you are living cannot be real for you. Nowhere has he exhibited it more starkly than in The Cavemen; nowhere in any of its successors except Journey into the Future, and there conditionally, does he offer the palliative that, if you are chronologically out of step but do not know it or try to make light of it, time will allow you to deceive it with such chicanery. Unless you can get back to the past where you belong via a lifeline leading to your own reality - the cave here does not - you are doomed; if you are reborn out of your time, your fate is even more fearsome.

In Rejuvenation, written twenty years later, he re-examines the theme in more mundane, but even more gloomy, fashion. The emphasis, as the play's title indicates, is slightly different and here is on a sub-form of resurrection. He first thought aloud about rejuvenation in his philosophical essay The Devil's Pact, where he regretted the squandering of his youth on peripheral intellectual pursuits and compared himself with Goethe's Faust, whom he wrongly believed to have sold his soul to Mephistopheles in exchange for being made young again. In the play, which has a modern background, Sadiq Pasha Rifqi, who has led a gay life but is now 80, seeks to turn back the hands of his clock ('watch', in view of the significance of his, would be the more appropriate word) in order that he may sample again the joys of his youth. When his doctor, Tal^{c}at, comes to inject him against his angina pectoris they discuss the former's research into cell renewal in rabbits, the doctor claiming that he has performed completely successful rejuvenation operations on the mammal. The Pasha pressurizes him into trying one out on him - or, rather, he dreams that he does when the injection causes him to lose consciousness for about four minutes, which take up three-quarters of the action. During them we see the practical difficulties the rejuvenated Pasha, who calls himself simply Sadiq, has to face in his time-cheating exercise. He can produce no personal documents to prove who he is because they are all half a century wrong, he cannot cash a cheque because the Pasha's account has become that of a man who has vanished without trace, and his experience over 80 years has not been jettisoned along with his senility, so that the role of a newly-graduated law student of twenty-six is a constant trial. He meets his problems with consummate calmness, however, unlike Yamlikha, Marnush and Mishilinya, even though in winning the first round against time he has driven his doctor mad and even though, after it is announced, falsely, that his body has been recovered, he has to observe his unpleasant son-in-law to-be planning the ransack of his inheritance. But in the end, and not primarily for considerations of convenience, he opts to revert to his former state. Unlike the cavemen he has gained time, but the process which is the reverse of theirs is no less unsatisfactory. An ex-Prime Minister, he is endowed with wisdom beyond his years ('the eyes of a boy ... and the tongue of an old man'), continually conscious of the degrading part he has thrust upon himself and irked by the fact that he is a misfit. He undergoes no great torment, however, and it is a fault of the play that his decision to become an old man again does not carry conviction because it is not the desperate one of a man out of tune with reality. 'You cast me into a strange world, Tal^{c}at,' he badly states.

Luckily for him the dream ends before the doctor becomes too insane to administer the antidote for rejuvenation; Tal^{c}at has long before this been pronounced to be the stepping-stone to his past (or, depending on the angle of vision, to his partly-lived future), but Sadiq is never brought quite to the point, though on several occasions he comes very near to it, of anticipating that it is about to be removed and thus made as ineffectual as Yamlikha's cave. When he awakes he gradually shakes off the impact of the dream and prepares so smoothly to resume life as the respected, senescent Pasha that when a telephone call summons him to a meeting at which he is to be asked to be Prime Minister again he responds as if nothing has happened. Time has a master card up its sleeve, however. As he is getting ready to set out he notices that his watch has stopped, his day is done and he dies in the arms of his wife.*

The Cavemen is irresistible because it is so unyielding in exposing the audience to cold horror. As a contribution to Hakim's scrutiny of time as one of the foes of mankind, Rejuvenation, though not without its telling blows, is a less concentrated performance. On the one hand we are shown the terror of Tal^{c}at's wife when Sadiq tells her the secret of who he 'really' is, a secret he has revealed to no one else and which he has hastily to represent as a joke because of her violent reaction. On the other there is a good deal of humour of a slightly farcical kind, as when

---

* A device similar to the Pasha's watch is used in The Clock Strikes, the contemporaneous and magnificent one-actor, but to rather divergent effect.

the 26 year old allows his tongue to slip and names the year of his graduation as 1887. This sort of thing is completely absent from The Cavemen, and yet Rejuvenation, which perhaps owes something to Pirandello's Enrico IV (the same contrivance as was brought to bear on the King is used to jolt Tal^{C}at out of his lunacy), is the more sombre. Its message, that no good can result from playing games with time, comes across strongly. The shock to the audience or reader of realizing that the rejuvenation was all a dream is a coup de theatre even more striking than that which shattered all illusions in The Cavemen. Muhammad Mandur complains that the transitions from one act to another are unnatural and that the play, with the dream in his opinion dominated by illogical events and unrealistic happenings, is a fantasy of 'ill-ordered inspiration'.[4] These are unfounded judgements, which are not shared by Fu'ad Dawara, who describes the production of the drama as 'another step forward for the National Theatre'.[5]

The Cavemen and Rejuvenation are the two plays which devote themselves entirely to examining the role of time in human existence, the former in the context of resurrection and the latter in that of a recoupment of years already lived. The Cavemen has a number of offspring, none of which - unless This Comic World does - has time or resurrection as its main theme, which discuss the features of various kinds of (re)birth. In Pigmalyun, Galatia's method of creation plunges her without warning or preparation into circumstances to the comprehension of which she has no aids or clues. Her downfall as a human being is a direct consequence of her inability to cope with her unsolicited problem. A Hunting Trip, which it will be remembered is bereft of dramatic value, presents us with a famous doctor, who is introduced in a state of concussion brought about either by a fall in the jungle where he is stalking big game or by a preliminary skirmish with the lion which finally catches him. He is unable to master his dangerous environment because he can remember neither where nor who he is. He becomes the butt of his past, which flashes in front of him in a series of twenty playbacks of incidents in his career illustrative of its highlights and lowest stoopings. Each of them is short and resembles the appearances and disappearances of the Cheshire Cat; none deserves a detailed mention, but it is of note that the doctor, unlike the 'hero' of Journey into the Future, has no control over them. Finally it may be permissible to detect in Soft Hands a resurrection of the type at issue here. It occurs when the Prince and Ali are trying to organize themselves in the Prince's servant-less palace and failing abjectly to adapt themselves to a situation unprecedented in their experience. Unlike the cavemen, however, they have flexible characters and speedily get their banal problem under control.

Rejuvenation has no successors, but in The Suicide's Secret there is a sketch of the major ideas filled out by both it and The Cavemen. Dr Mahmud, having by cosmetic means shed years in honour of the memory of the girl he believes has killed herself for love of him, becomes involved in an argument with his wife as to whether or not his clock has actually been put back. He has been outwardly rejuvenated, but his attitude to his new self is more that of Yamlikha, Marnush and Mishilinya than of Sadiq. He denies, like Mishilinya, that there is a 'law of age and time' and later affirms that 'age and time have no power over the soul'. Iqbal complains that his insistence that this is so makes him see her as 'a thing from the distant past, unconnected with the present ... whose age has become unsynchronised with yours.' Although this episode is neither profound in intention nor central to the play, its juxtaposition of Mahmud's fake rejuvenation and the domestic quarrel about time in relation to marriage is immediately relevant to Hakim's study of the topic.

In two of the plays the blurring of the strict lines of the time theme brings the nature of reality momentarily into focus. Neither is, in this connection, very distinguished. In Praksa, in the course of a somewhat aimless and repetitious debate between the female leader Ibqirat and Hirunimus the dictator in the third act, the first two decide that Praksa's rule and its overthrow by Hirunimus are good and bad phases of the same dream; the military man, however, for whom reality consists solely in what he has 'between his hands', attacks the philosopher for inventing illusions which are unjustified in view of the undeniable reality of 'the world, the earth and every thing'. Food for Every Mouth adopts the same kind of unserious stance. After the wall play is over, Hamdi and Samira are not sure whether or not it was not a joint dream or figment of the imagination. They ponder the matter and come to the conclusion that it must have happened because they are not equipped intellectually to have thought up the abstruse dialogue which took place in it. They are content, nonetheless, to leave unsolved the mystery of their inability to communicate with their friends on the wall, ever examine the possibility of their own existence being thrown into doubt and agree not to trouble themselves about these things.

In The Cavemen the site of the resurrection of Yamlikha, Marnush and Mishilinya was not only the (blocked) lifeline to their past; it was also the place from which to be absent was to be lost. Galatia's only comfortable locale is her plinth, and for the spacemen of Journey into the

Future it is earth. That, in these cases, reality involves being in the right place at the right time is obvious even when Hakim has laid the stress very much on the time theme, which is the more emotive of the two. It is axiomatic that disaster directly ensues, except for the engineer in Journey into the Future, once the physical equilibrium is reestablished. The same is not true of Shahrazad, which Hakim claims as his foremost 'place' play. It is so complex that no single definition can be adequate for it but, as is maintained in the next chapter, if one must be chosen it cannot but be 'a statement about woman'. The 'place' aspect is one which most critics would have missed had Hakim not insisted on its crucial role in Shahrazad, where it really amounts to very little. King Shahriyar belongs, according to Hakim, at the side of his queen. He deserts her once, thus quitting his 'right place', and returns without finding out the answers to the questions which sent him on his travels. When he abandons her for the second time he is making his final exit[6] and revealing himself to be incapable of recognizing where his human, physical base is located. He has resumed a search Hakim regards as hopeless:

> ' ... The destiny of man is completely tied to the earth, for the other hidden force [after time], which is called place, material or spiritual, has a powerful grip on man's existence. This is the core of the play Shahrazad. In this story man sought to rid himself of the earth in order to attain the sky, but became suspended between (them).'[7]

He reiterates the same point later by explaining that Shahriyar had wanted to divest himself of the instincts and limitations of his humanity and to rise free like a balloon. The propulsive forces were not strong enough, however - as they could not be, for the human body is a prison which forbids the leap to the intellectual sky[8] - and he remained suspended in space, between earth and sky, unfit for life. At the close of the play he is en route either, like the spacemen of Journey into the Future, to being lost among the stars or, if he wished, as seems unlikely, to live again, to returning to Shahrazad's side[9] and resuming an animal existence.[10]

Although Shahriyar never actually sets foot off it, the moral that 'place' and the earth are one and the same comes through, in Hakim's many clarifications if not in the play itself: a human being ceases to be one if he endeavours to kick off the terrestrial dust. But the author does Shahrazad an injustice in affixing the place plaque so determinedly to it.

Indeed it is difficult to uphold his claim, which may have been made to deflect the critics from the play's most obvious and autobiographically revealing purpose. He would have done better to allow the poetry and atmosphere of Shahrazad to speak for themselves, and to let The Cavemen, Pigmalyun and Journey into the Future - and even Rejuvenation - bear the burden, which they do perfectly adequately. It is cogently argued,[11] for example, that Pigmalyun dangles as much as Shahriyar because, though of sky (artistic) material, he wants the earth (love). It may be flippant to say so, but the cockroach King also fits the pattern: inveigled by the scientist into taking a tour without parallel, he moves out of the sphere to which he belongs and meets his fate (of which Thomas Hardy would have approved) in one to which he is a stranger.

Journey into the Future, which comprehends both time and place, clearly defines the nature of man through its pursuit of both themes, the second being the dominant one. It asks when a man is a man and when he is free and queries his ability to remain of the genus homo when independent of the earth which bred him and to throw off the shackles of his body and of the past. It does this in four environments, a prison cell, a space capsule, a planet as different from earth as could be imagined and an earth which has entered the age of automation. In the first a well-known doctor is awaiting execution, having been betrayed to the police by his wife, who was one of his patients and whose first husband he murdered out of pity for her and at her insistent request. It was apparent to him during his trial that she had used him as a pawn to get rid of her unwanted spouse, had never loved him and was intending, as planned all along, to run off with his defence counsel after he had been disposed of. Act One is mostly somewhat tedious but gathers momentum when the doctor persuades the prison governor to allow him to see his wife alone. Now was his opportunity to get his own back on her. Unfortunately for his immediate purpose, a more important matter prevents the meeting from taking place: he is given the opportunity to be a free man again if he agrees to go up in a spacecraft and transmit to earth - as, among the country's condemned men, only he is deemed qualified to do - the scientific data to be gathered during the flight. He is not told what his destination is but, while protesting at the cancellation of his wife's visit, he chooses the one per cent chance of a safe homecoming rather than the imminent death facing him.

Act Two is an enthralling account of the flight, which is the second environment. During it the doctor discovers, to his surprise, that he has a companion, an engineer who has killed a succession of wives in order to finance his research from their estates. The two do not get on, the doctor being a man of integrity despite his crime passionnel, the engineer a cynical womaniser. The spacecraft is quite out of their control, and of that of their principals on the ground, and the suspense engendered by this is skilfully blended with philosophical discussion of their position. The engineer claims that he is no longer subject to earthy laws, the doctor that the umbilical cord of their trajectory binds them to the human race and to their past. They agree, however, that, while technically free men, they are just as much in prison as they were before. Their conversations, often heated because of their completely divergent attitudes, are abruptly halted by the capsule's hard landing on an unknown planet. When, at the start of Act Three, they recover consciousness in the third environment, they begin to explore their new home, far too far from earth for their communications' equipment to be of any service. They are in their third brand of prison: the planet affords them no present (no human society, no work, nothing to allay boredom) and no future; its properties render breathing and eating unnecessary and they can neither fall ill nor die. Under these circumstances the doctor seeks to parry madness by screening flashback memories of his past, but the engineer, who has nothing in his he wishes to relive, soon tires of the sight of his companion's wife. Out of its essential human context, their life gradually becomes insupportable and they are about to attempt a mutual murder when the thought that the spacecraft may be repaired tardily strikes them. In Act Four it has contrived to carry them back to earth, but to one which, true to Einstein's 'clock-paradox', has aged by 309 years[12] during their absence, while they are only slightly older than when they took off. This presents the reader with a delightfully unanticipated twist to the story and the heroes with mental adjustments to make, like both the cavemen and Sadiq. Outwardly things are better - war has gone out of fashion and the expectation of life has lengthened so remarkably that the doctor's wife is still alive - but in their native land the majority of the people are unhappy under the administration of the progressive party, which stands for automation in every sphere of life and the overturning of moral values; the opposition party has no prospect of ever attaining power with its platform of a reversion to an old order recognisably akin to that which the spacemen knew before. They have little apparent psychological difficulty in falling into step with the new situation. Practically, however, the engineer takes to it smoothly by joining the ruling party while the doctor enlists with the opposition to fight 'progress' tooth and nail. He pays the penalty for his crime and, again on account of a woman, finds himself back in prison.

Journey into the Future convincingly answers the questions it raises: a man is only a man and can only be free when he is involved in earthly society; if he is to continue such he must learn to live with the earth, with his physical being and with his past. In addition it underlines the lessons of The Cavemen by showing again that the prognosis is unhappy for those who have permitted themselves to drop out of their right time. The doctor accordingly suffers the statutory fate. There is, however, one significant variant. The engineer, who has always been a misfit and has no past to which he can owe allegiance, gets off scot-free - a conclusion which is not as heartening as it seems, for he does so at the cost of being fated to be out of touch with each and every circle with which he is destined to enter into contact.

To enquire into the human reality via the paths of time and place would seem to be an unobjectionable proceeding for a dramatist. Hakim's preoccupation with this most marked of his non-political themes is, in any case, not unique, for J B Priestley, who is not profound or ambitious enough to be in his class as a playwright, has gained his reputation in part for his examination of the phenomenon of time. What is unique, however, is The Cavemen; it is to be doubted whether a more effective and moving play about the nature of reality has been constructed. With Rejuvenation and Journey into the Future - Shahrazad's true glory is to be discovered elsewhere - it constitutes a trilogy which is probably without peer for profundity and novelty of approach, and one which we owe to the unhappy lives of Hakim and his country.

REFERENCES

1   AR, p 35
2   See Husayn, p 88
3   '(Sergeant Yokoi) seems to be making a desperate effort to find an exit from the "time tunnel" that separates his former world from today's civilization' ... "You are different Japanese," he told reporters ... "There must be other Japanese people." (The Times, 26 January 1972).
4   Mandur 2, pp 140-1

5   Dawara 1, p 54
6   One which frustrated Hakim's intentions to write a sequel (UGL, pp 77-8)
7   LA, p 317
8   UGL, pp 75-6
9   LL, p 195
10 UGL, p 78
11 Tarabishi, p 115
12 For a comparison of Journey into the Future and The Cavemen, based on the 309 year time-lapse they share, see the writer's article in MES 5, 1, pp 69-74.

2 Woman - enigma, idol and rival

Shahriyar ... had better luck than me, for Shahrazad was by his side ... Would that I had a Shahrazad. I am alone.
(From the Ivory Tower)

How little you can know of love, if you say it mars your art!
(Oscar Wilde, The Picture of Dorian Gray)

Her ultimate political objectives are ambitious ... she does not believe in equality. "The men have had their day," she says. "We believe that the time for female supremacy has come" ... women will dominate the Lower House of Parliament while men will be permitted to participate in the Upper House. Women will replace men in the public services ... (The Times, 6 July 1977, on the founder of the Japan Women's Party)

Of the thirty-two plays by Tawfiq al Hakim with which this book is mainly concerned, the majority express strong opinions on woman, his approach to whom is sharply split between idealism, at the supernatural level, and realism of a highly idiosyncratic kind, the latter reserved for his living, female contemporaries. Woman is, for him, an enigma, theoretically capable of achieving perfection, which it is not given to man to do, but in practice riddled with far more faults and blemishes than her male counterpart could ever stoop to displaying.

The main statement of the adulatory philosophy is Shahrazad. She has preserved her position as Shahriyar's Queen for a thousand and one nights and more, unlike her predecessors who were queens for only one night after the first of them was caught in the arms of a slave. Her fertile imagination having stayed her execution, she has gradually converted her husband from an animal, 'a body without heart and matter without spirit', into an introvert who, as the play opens, has become disillusioned with the human condition and thus guilty of flouting the laws which govern it.[1] He blames her for causing his dejection and is tormented by dread of her. She is a being, he now realizes, the like of which he never encountered before and, like Adil vis-a-vis Samiyya, he is afraid lest he lose his identity beneath the impact of her personality. He refuses to believe that she is what she maintains herself simply to be - a beautiful body enshrining a heart without guile - harbours the deepest and most exaggerated doubts about her and her intentions, and declares himself no longer physically attracted to her or interested in being in love with her. Having inadvertently taken the education of Shahriyar too far, Shahrazad, for her part, does all she can to jolt her husband out of his self-torturing frame of mind but is unable even to satisfy him about her own innocence. She contrives, like Bihana in The Tree Climber who, of course, had other reasons, to defend herself in a somewhat unfortunate way which, far from allaying his apprehensions, exacerbates his distrust of her. Eventually the point is reached at which Shahriyar can see no alternative to abandoning her in favour of his old habits or of pursuits higher, in his estimation, than the search for the truth about his wife. Initially he cannot decide which course to adopt. He consults his wizard and selects a virgin, designed to be if necessary the first of many successors to Shahrazad. At the same time he plans a journey which he hopes will put him in possession of a firm attitude to life in general and to Shahrazad in particular; should it prove fruitless he will wish only to die. In the event he both murders the virgin and sets out on his peregrination. One day from home he is caught up by Qamar, his Prime Minister, a personable young man who is devoted to him and to his Queen. The journey ceases to be a lone one, and the pair travel as far afield as India and Egypt before returning to Baghdad. Shahrazad is ready for her husband, whose wanderings have neither alleviated his problems nor confirmed in him his desire for death. In order to attempt to help him in the only direction open to her, she arranges for a black slave, like the one who precipitated the bloodbath of Shahriyar's pre-1001 nights' period, to be with her in her boudoir, hidden behind a curtain, when he arrives. Her line of thought is that, if Shahriyar does not kill them both, all will be up with him; his journey having been devoid of results, he must achieve some kind of rapport, even if a bloody one, with real life or, in Hakim's words, remain dangling between heaven and earth in a state of chronic indecision. In the event Shahriyar discovers the slave and sends him packing. He re-enters at once to tell that, on his emergence from the boudoir, he was seen by Qamar who - also anxious to know the truth about Shahrazad but, unlike Shahriyar, prepared to trust her word - has killed himself. Shahriyar, regarded by one critic [2] as a Nietzschean character and compared by another [3] to Goethe's Faust, does not bat an eyelid at this, but merely gets up and says that he is going on another journey. Shahrazad asks him to give her another chance, but he ignores her and the play ends.

Shahrazad is far and away Hakim's favourite among all the characters in his oeuvre. When she became his dramatic heroine she was, as she remains, his ideal woman. He is jealous of Shahriyar and indulges in a love affair with the King's wife through the pages of The Poet, The Enchanted Palace, The Devil's Pact,[4] The Sultan of Darkness,[5] and From the Ivory Tower;[6] he always wanted to write a sequel to the play, to be called The Return of Shahriyar, but could never decide how best to tackle it or what its theme could be.[7] Shahrazad's virtues in his eyes are that she is to the ultimate degree comely, mysterious and intelligent; blameless of all the accusations which Shahriyar and others level at her and eager to recapture for her husband his former faith in his humanity;[8] politically unambitious ('I never interfered in Shahriyar's policies,' she says);[9] and devoid of menace to her creator. She is, in short, a desirable and faithful wife, a goddess[10] who, like Isis, 'performed a glorious deed for the sake of her husband.'[11] Some of the critics see her very differently. Cachia, for example, describes her as 'the symbol of worldly interests and physical appetites, a somewhat coarse Guinevere who has intrigues with her slaves'[12] - a libel which is not borne out by the text of the play; Landau[13] similarly misreads (as, of course, does Qamar), and likens her to the heroine of Shawqi's Masra[c] Kilyubatra, who is glamorous, self-centred and sensual.

Shahrazad has, overall, been variously interpreted, but incontestably it is essentially Hakim's portrait of the perfect woman. The Queen's fascination and remoteness drive him, in Strindbergian manner, to worship, which in lesser degree he offers also to Priska,[14] Bilqais (by implication only), Isis and (not in the dramas) Cleopatra.[15] The idolization is uninhibited and almost limitless because these characters, whether legendary or not, can obviously not confront him physically. Having created them he can therefore adore without risk of rebuff, and he can do what he likes with them as he does with his walking-stick (feminine in Arabic and powerless to resist), which is the instrument of his contact with Cleopatra. He rationalizes his susceptibility with some sincerity by reference to the fact that in Egypt's history of death and resurrection the means of rebirth is female. From this angle Isis, who secured the second coming of Osiris in the legend, is both eminently worthy of idealization and the culmination of Priska and Shahrazad, who partially resurrected Shahriyar:[16] 'Each ... of them is merely Isis in a new form.' The same is true of Anan,[17] in Expulsion from Eden, who is the only 'realistic' heroine to rank with the 'goddesses'.

Hakim's writing about female characters who are not candidates for adulation falls into three clearly demarcated phases. In the plays up to and including The Peaceful Nest the misogyny is most marked. Woman is, in seeking emancipation and equality of employment, a hazard to morality (Modern Woman); jealous, selfish, vain, spiteful, dominated by 'county' attitudes, and skilled above all at hitting her husband when he is down (The Suicide's Secret); pitiless (A Life is Wrecked); frivolous (A Bullet in the Heart); immoral, pushing, covetous, more exercized about her appearance than the effective use of her power, and a threat to democracy (Praksa, whose eponymous central character is not put on a pedestal as might have been expected); and brazenly liberated (The Peaceful Nest).* In contrast, the male is epitomised by Nagib, in A Bullet in the Heart, who honourably rejects the overtures of Fifi, whom he loves, because she is engaged to his friend.

Between his marriage, which, it is assumed, post-dated the composition of The Peaceful Nest, and the publication of The Sultan's Dilemma, Hakim's general view changed to one of approval. There are only two major examples of misogyny in this period. Anisa, the mother of Her Majesty, possesses every despicable human attribute a woman can have, and the spouse of the doctor in Journey into the Future is, to the detriment of his career and liberty, a temptress and trapper. (There should, en passant, be mentioned the minor but suggestive appearance in War versus Peace (Bayn al Harb wa's Salam, 1951) of Politics personalized as a woman - a grave insult, given Hakim's hatred of the profession and its practitioners.) Otherwise the ladies of this phase are out-

---

* Even Priska and Shahrazad - for overdoing the instruction of Shahriyar - are, by inference, to be construed as inefficient.

136 Tawfiq al Hakim

standingly exemplary and co-operative. They are much less stereotyped than before and range from the village heroine of The Deal, the kind and loyal nightclub dancer in Death Game and the widow of integrity in The Sultan's Dilemma, to the nouvelles riches females of Soft Hands and Her Majesty and the pre- and post-revolutionary aristocrats of Rejuvenation and The Thorns of Peace. They do not endorse Hakim's contemporary, semi-serious judgement in Show Me Allah[18] that woman was Satan's handiwork. Their hallmarks are that they are praiseworthily anxious to share in the labours of their menfolk and deploy the unsullied weapon of love to ameliorate life on earth. That, as in the case of the more terrestrial of the Cleopatras, they may also happen inadvertently to thwart their partners' aims and cloud their literary faculties would seem to be a reflection of life as a whole rather than a demonstration of Hakim's anti-feminism. The virtual extinction of this trait is clearly shown by the bland and tolerant remarks with which he chose to preface the publication of Modern Woman.[19]

In the last period we have a mixed bag. With The Tree Climber, especially when it is read with the unprinted guesses as to the reasons for its composition borne in mind, a salutary depolarisations, away from idolisation and favourable attitudes on the one hand and misogyny on the other, is detectable. The later plays on the whole consolidate it. Bihana is, for most of the time, obsessive, stupid, and troublesome; Samira and Nadia in Food for Every Mouth are, in the main, thorns in the flesh of the males they should be supporting, and the former, like Atiyat, cannot sustain for long her enthusiasm for Hamdi's project; the ladies in A Train Journey are arrivistes; Shams an Nahar is harsh in her relations with both Qamar az Zaman and Hamdan; and Samiyya in Fate of a Cockroach is - rather like Iqbal in The Suicide's Secret - an emotionless harridan who, significantly (for girls in a 'man's university' are Eves struggling with Adam for the upper hand),[20] attended the same college as her husband. On the brighter side, Samira ends her part in harmonious, if superficial, harness with her husband; Shams an Nahar has learned to behave like a lady when her play is finished; and the Queen is, even if rather conscious of her superiority to her male entourage, by far the most level-headed character in Fate of a Cockroach. Woman is no longer mysterious (Bihana is a special case) and Hakim has ceased to feel the need to worship, as is shown by his treatment of Shams an Nahar, who certainly offered material for adulation. At the time of the publication of The Anxiety Bank his conception of the opposite sex was more balanced than at any earlier stage in his career.

Surprisingly, woman as a creature with political ambitions or, at least, with aspirations to a major role in the man-dominated world outside her drawing-room is not a feature of prominence in the plays. There are a few indications, however, of the views expatiated upon in non-dramatic works. In Modern Woman Hakim drew in Layla a sketch of a young girl who, given the chance to live and do good in the countryside idealized by her father, betrays her lack of a sense of political responsibility by declaring herself concerned for nothing besides the cinemas and theatres of Cairo. Iqbal in The Suicide's Secret and Ziza in A Life is Wrecked are similarly censurable in that the former would not dream of 'burying herself' in the countryside and the latter, who resides there but does not speak the local dialect, cannot wait to get back to Cairo and makes no effort to come to terms with provincial life. (Hakim's criticism of female reluctance to serve the provinces is less than fair when juxtaposed with his own hatred of rural Egypt.) More to the point and better considered are Praksa and Her Majesty, where the female revolutionary leader and the Queen Mother attain to positions of supreme political power and influence and, respectively, fall down on the job and abuse it. The prognosis even in the case of Isis is unfavourable, for there is much to suggest that, as Regent to Huris which she is undoubtedly to become, she will be a ruthlessly unscrupulous politician. Hakim looks with horror on the prospect of women, unless they are of the calibre of Shahrazad and Bilqais, occupying the political heights, believing that their narrow and tenaciously-held interests would turn man into a slave.[21] He has devoted an important section of In the Spotlight of Thought to his fear, which Al Hakim's Donkey and My Donkey Said to Me also treat at length. In the former he says that, after the rise of Egyptian nationalism 'the Egyptian woman studied at school and university and learned how to speak at meetings and make frequent use of the words "freedom" and "equality with man,"' as she had every right to do.[22] On the other hand, having had her material chains snapped by Qasim Amin, whose services to female emancipation he praises,[23] 'she is in a sort of spiritual harem ... because her spiritual intelligence is still limited.'[24] He has always been in favour of progress for woman, but 'I ... differ with her about the meaning of the word "progress". She understands it to mean following in the footsteps of man and catching him up.'[25] How Hakim construes it is not fully revealed, but it is plain that it is not an open-ended concept for him. He believes it to be nature's 500,000 year old law that man should be in the lead, for the cave belongs to the woman and the hunting outside it is the man's preserve. He sees women trying to defy Allah's purpose, just as Eve caused Adam's expulsion from paradise with the aim of achieving dominance. ' ... Woman does not want equality. She wants the mastery' - in order to make man her cook and slave.[26] Her failure to identify her proper place, take to herself the spirit of 'the lady' who, among Europeans, is ready unreservedly to help serve humanity, and to shed her white-slave mentality have meanwhile brought about the filth and poverty of the Egyptian village. The emancipated girl from the village sets out for the bright lights of Cairo without a thought for the suffering she has left behind her.[27] My Donkey Said to Me is more specifically political.[28] Women, it maintains, defy nature by claiming equality with men. Hakim would not, however, object to their becoming voters, politicians, or ministers, provided always that female politicians had only one vote between two. Indeed, he is keen to see them in parliament, though judging that if they constituted themselves a separate party they would make the lives of their male colleagues unbearable if they were opposed on feminine matters; if they were not a separate party he would, par contre, see no advantage to them in entering parliament at all. His frivolous attitude to the female politician is, however, based on nothing more than convictions that women's real sphere is in the rif, that they can never agree with one another and that their political responsibilities would be constantly jeopardised by the attention they would devote to their personal appearance. This last has been their downfall and has prevented the educated ones among them from learning to conduct salons fit to receive the 'personalities' of the country[29] and to enhance their contact with the things of the intellect.[30] In a number of the plays an attempt is essayed to bear out this immature and narrow opinion, through the persons of women who for the most part are arrogantly self-assured and inquisitive and whose disappearances to attend to their make-up - Praksa in power is a prime example - are carefully noted. Their weakness in this matter is extensively displayed in Under the Green Lamp.

A prominent ingredient in Hakim's anti-feminist thinking has yet to be isolated. He is convinced that women, especially if they are good-looking, get in the way of creative male work, squander male time and detract from male wealth, position and fame.[31] 'The beautiful woman is the enemy of the thinking man,'[32] and if a man associates closely with her, her charms will distract him and her moon-like nature will weaken his light and increase his radiation.[33] (Nagib Mahfuz, like Hakim in many respects, entirely disagrees.)[34] He will concede only one exception to the rule, and she, predictably, is Shahrazad who, in The Poet, is equated totally with his endeavours: she and Montmartre, the seat of their then inspiration, both have the sun-and-godlike qualities of positive influence.[35] Hakim sees no contradiction in complaining that women are not sufficiently attentive to male tasks, and particularly his: to his chagrin Saniyya is a wholehearted supporter of the ambitions of the youth she preferred over him,[36] and in The Suicide's Secret, Pigmalyun, The Peaceful Nest and even Shahrazad a deep dissatisfaction with his female backing is easily discernible. This would indicate that Hakim as suitor found his calling a weapon of low calibre in the eyes of those real women to whom he had offered his love, an inference most forcibly endorsed by Expulsion from Eden. It is obviously linked with many passages in A Sparrow from the East, such as those in which Muhsin equates himself, leaving the restaurant where Suzi revealed her faithlessness, with 'Adam expelled from paradise', accuses her of having 'pushed him out of heaven' and writes to her to say that, 'dismissed from the enchanted palace of love .., I now understand Adam's situation just after he was thrown out of paradise.' More to the point, it is the story of a man of letters whose wife regards herself - or, in order to rationalize her terror of the physical side of marriage and her intuition that her talented husband will inevitably tire of her, chooses to claim to regard herself - as an obstacle to the achievement of his full artistic potential; she avers that when love and creative activity are in contention the former must ineluctably be sacrificed and therefore takes the initiative in ejecting him from the heaven of her love. Hakim approves of Anan's self-immolation to Mukhtar's art in his short note on the title-page of the play, but at the same time he deplores its effect on the author, who is an over-exposed portrait of himself. The withholding of Anan's love turns Mukhtar into a misanthropist who, though famous and devoted to his profession, has become old, sad and poor. In The Suicide's Secret the connection between love and man's strivings is not so close, but when Dr Mahmud's marriage to Iqbal, who will take no interest at all in his ambition, falls apart he sees the future for himself as consisting in a greater immersion in his medical pursuits than before. (Hakim, disguised as the writer in The Temple Dancer, retrospectively dismisses Natalia, after he has allowed her to make a fool of him, as of no worth in relation to his art.) The supreme example of his writing on this very personal aspect of the relations between the sexes, of course, is far more profound, for Galatia is both Pigmalyun's love and his art in its finest flowering.

In practice, theory and inhibition aside, Hakim is an obsessive and susceptible admirer of female beauty,[37] which is the only factor 'enabling us to forgive woman all her triviality and stupidity'.[38] Love, however, he has strong reservations about. On the one hand he can rush to the defence of Edward VIII ('... the heart of the whole world ... cried out in perplexity, "Has not man the right to love? Has the King no heart?" My answer: the King has a heart and a head. His heart is his. His head is his people's ... His heart does not wear the crown or appear before the people'). But on the other hand he unerringly holds that as an artist it is his lot to be satisfied with a severely rationed share of love. Otherwise his work would be wrecked, and therefore he must accept his portion gratefully, like a bird in an aviary which is rewarded with sugar when it performs a successful trick.[40] This philosophy is in fact timidity, as his assertions (in The Cavemen, Expulsion from Eden, and The Suicide's Secret) that love will present none of its earthly problems in the next world make abundantly plain. Though the properties he desired in a wife, who had to be beautiful (sic), characterless and not clever, and to have had a conservative education,[41] should not have been too hard to find, matrimony was always for him a state to be eluded and, if that proved to be impossible, to be entered into with enlightened care. When he dreamed, no doubt in wish-fulfilment, however, that his admiring readers had provided him with a wife he protested, ' ... How could they marry me to someone I'd never seen? This is the twentieth century.'[42] In addition to the reasons earlier adduced for his alleged wish to evade marriage was his belief, expounded in Life's Prison, that it had brought about the extinction of his father's mental energy and artistic potential. All of this encouraged him to belittle it, at least before he finally succumbed: in The Sacred Bond he categorizes it as less venerable than the relationship of a father with his son - a relationship which a woman, with her uncontrollable desires, is incapable of comprehending - or than his own link with the world of the spirit. He also, while parading himself as a theoretically ardent supporter of married love and of marriage as both holy and the backbone of society, admits that he would not scruple to co-operate with a wife who intended to be unfaithful to her husband. A further factor was his dislike of the idea of domesticity. He had revelled in being 'free of the chains of family and responsibility';[43] long after his marriage and the birth of his children he felt able to address himself to Allah in these terms: 'Put me in one of your paradises, give me ... peace of mind and tranquillity, and keep from me family responsibilities and the troubles of dependents ... Then ask the beauty of art of me.'[44] The only alternative would be for him to be treated like Prince Albert: ' ... how much I need a woman like this

[Queen Victoria] to let me read and write and listen to music while she takes charge of the burden of responsibilities and the solution of the problems of life.'[45]

The opinion of Muhammad Mandur[46] that these attitudes to women are normal ones is endorsed neither by Hakim's approach to Shahrazad and her sister goddesses nor by his real-life creed. The point of departure of this creed is his resentment that Eve, having misguidedly been introduced into paradise and then had the effrontery to eject Adam from it, should have, as he interprets it, given woman a head-start which man has continually to strive to make up.[47] That woman is the child-bearer also rankles: 'I love beauty and hate woman,' for her selfishness, tyranny, and strange logic, and for using her appearance as a weapon.

> 'The lovely woman is oppression pure and simple ... My freedom is more precious to me than my soul. Woman is the greatest enemy threatening this freedom for (she) ... is the permanent gaoler of us men. We grope around between the walls of her womb when we are embryos; we eat what she chooses to give us. When we have emerged from between those dark walls into bright and spacious life we are confined by her restrictiveness and she feeds our minds with whatever she decides to instil in us. When through growing up we escape those confines, the shackles of her arms receive us and put a collar around our necks until death. When shall we be delivered from her? When shall we be free?'[48]

From these basic prejudices Hakim's misogyny develops much at random, and in such a manner that it is impossible (as has been attempted above) tidily to compartmentalize his opinions of woman as the complement of the male, as the professional worker and as the artist's (generally untrustworthy) companion. The non-dramatic writing fills in some of the gaps, none summing up his conception of the roles of female and male better than two of the early ones.

In My Donkey Said to Me [49] the duty of women is defined. They were made in order to be goddesses and queens for husbands like Napoleon - an engrossing idea when set beside Hakim's love affair with Shahrazad - and to feel honoured by being the servants and cooks of men. This is rather less restrictive than the job description handed down by Narsis when he said, 'Women have no role in life except love.' Nevertheless woman is a 'passive phenomenon', 'for she ... reflects the light which comes to her from the sun of man's intellect.' (Man, for his part, has, surprisingly, a precisely-stated task, which is to make his labours a sacrifice to his woman - a sacrifice the material rewards of which she has no right to use to promote relationships with other men.)[50] In conformity with these guidelines are Hakim's conviction that girl graduates are 'little devils' who are dangerous because they are clever but lack the long spiritual preparation necessary for entering society,[51] and his sustained ridicule for the notion that, with their emotional and irresponsible natures, women could be wives and, for example, lawyers at the same time;[52] so, of course, is his scorn for the Egyptian Women's Movement.[53]

In a fairly recent interview[54] he said that his basic stance with regard to women had always been that they should be themselves and not copy men, and that he had always therefore been alert to any sign of them aiming at job-equality or at replacing men in their work, which he believes they aspire to do. The first half of this sounds eminently reasonable, but nonetheless his philosophy as a whole, conditioned by a deep physical and mental fear which is highlighted by his adoration of women who are inaccessible, resembles Strindberg's. His mother, together with Saniyya and Emma Durand, inculcated in him the apparently sincere and exceedingly tenacious convictions that man has never made up the ground denied by Eve to Adam and that it is his destiny and duty to wage continual war against the female horde. In A Journalistic Incident and The Gentle Sex he has warned of the consequences of a failure to do so. The former shows the male being stampeded by a woman in most humiliating fashion, and the latter, which is his most extreme portrayal of the potential male rout, catalogues the indignities to which man lays himself open by neglecting to protect his start-line. It is a sketch of a hen-pecked husband who is afraid of flying but is coerced by his wife (an airline pilot) and two of her feminist friends (a journalist and a lawyer) into accompanying her on an inaugural flight to Iraq. To underline his opinion that a professional woman cannot be an adequate housekeeper, Hakim begins the playlet by showing the husband waiting for his wife to bring her plane in in order that he may be provided with his supper.

All the 'realistic' plays which deal with the relations between the sexes follow the pattern of The Gentle Sex to some degree - with two exceptions. The first is Expulsion from Eden, Anan's unusual role in which has been touched on. The other is The Peaceful Nest, in which the scales are evenly poised until at the end they tip unquestionably in the woman's favour. This is the more extraordinary because the male of the piece is a writer, which arouses speculation that Hakim composed it as a well-intentioned caution to his wife-to-be. Qanbariyya, whose personality grows credibly and well, is at first a brazen representative of liberated Egyptian womanhood. When, however, she makes the mistake of marrying a celebrated author, to whom she was attracted rather as Desdemona was drawn to Othello, she finds that he has a heart of stone. She reaps a fate severer than that of Sacha Schwarz, for he is concerned only for his literary ambitions and is happy to risk the life of their sick child for them. Qanbariyya struggles manfully against her husband's callousness and selfishness, and proves to be a noble embodiment of the most laudable qualities of her sex. The man, for the one and only time, outdoes his female counterpart for insensitivity and ruthlessness.

Hakim's general view of woman, despite the growing sense of proportion demonstrated in his second and third phases, is not marked by the balanced kind of outlook recommended by From the Ivory Tower. The attitude of 'the enemy of woman' - unusual enough - is nowhere near as extreme as Sayyid Qutb claims ('Women [in Al Hakim's dramas] are either saintly huris or whores. The normal woman finds no place in his work.').[55] But no account could omit a clear reference to his misogyny which has more than a modicum of hypocrisy in it, although it should not fail to observe, too, that only in Shahrazad did his analysis of the female psyche by itself inspire him to great writing. His accurate depiction of some of the undoubted traits of woman - the self-assertiveness which is a by-product of emancipation, the inability, during an emotional clash, to convince even when in the right - and his quirkishly entertaining antifeminist sentiments do not together make him a dramatist of the war of the sexes whose quality matches the quantity of his output.

REFERENCES

1   AR, p 95
2   Papadopoulo, p 241
3   Subur 1, p 99
4   pp 82-98
5   pp 91-109. (Repeated in MDS, pp 26-39)
6   p 64
7   LL, p 125. (See above, p 127 and reference 6 of that chapter)
8   AR, p 35
9   SD, p 101

10 UGL, p 196
11 Postscript to Isis
12 Cachia, p 196
13 p 107
14 In The Angry Princess (The Devil's Pact, pp 71-81) he enjoys being chastised by her for bringing about the death of Mishilinya
15 Al Hakim's Stick, pp 165-72, LA, p 19
16 Tarabishi, p 69
17 UGL, pp 196-7
18 pp 64 ff
19 A Variety of Theatre, pp 534-6
20 MDS, p 87
21 The Anxiety Bank, p 94
22 AHD, p 101
23 He reintroduces him in the later Al Hakim's Stick, pp 199-207, so that he may express his shock at how far women's liberation has gone
24 AHD, p 112
25 FTIT, p 100
26 MDS, p 91
27 AHD, p 103
28 pp 87-104
29 IST, p 136
30 FTIT, p 198
31 IST, p 226
32 Ibid, p 227
33 MDS, p 105
34 Sabah al Khayr, 7 October 1971, p 26
35 The Poet, p 128
36 The Soul's Return 2, p 235
37 Passim, e.g. The Poet, p 119, The Temple Dancer, p 66, AHD, pp 11, 54, LA, p 19
38 The Devil's Pact, p 152
39 FTIT, pp 79-80
40 Ibid, pp 199-201
41 The Sacred Bond, p 243
42 FTIT, p 197
43 Ibid, p 62
44 A Journey between Two Eras, pp 36-7
45 FTIT, p 83

46 Mandur 1, p 111
47 MDS, pp 85-105
48 The Temple Dancer, pp 66-70
49 Loc cit
50 The Sacred Bond, pp 228-9
51 MDS, p 86
52 Ibid, pp 93-9
53 Papadopoulo, p 234
54 To Dawara 2, pp 26, 28
55 Kutub wa Shakhsiyyat, p 129

3 (1) Egypt under the Pashawat

> ... if you want me to name the writer whose works did a lot to turn me into a revolutionary, it was Tawfiq al Hakim.
> (Abd an Nasir to the Lacoutures, in Egypt in Transition)

Although the aftermath of the 1919 revolution engendered in him an intense distrust of Egyptian party politics and politicians,[1] Hakim's earliest extant dramatic comment on his country's governmental methods was not made until ten years afterwards, when he loosed a lightweight, but wounding, barb or two at the ruling class. Expulsion from Eden is mostly concerned with other matters, but it so happens that the wife who has Eden in her gift is the daughter of 'the Pasha', a corrupt former minister, whose idea of office is self-aggrandisement first and service last. When it begins to seem likely that he will be recalled to the administration, he indulges in a little levity at his own expense. With false modesty he says that 'when a minister joins a cabinet he loses half his brains' and when he ceases to be a member of it 'he loses the other half'. Actually offered a portfolio, he is even more cynical: 'They proposed frequently that your father should enter the government. In the end I consented, in response to the demands of duty and the fatherland.' His second daughter observes that it is exactly these words he uses whenever the summon comes.

As his reputation and self-confidence grew, Hakim felt able to scrutinize the administration of Egypt more closely, and full-scale works critical of it began to take the place of occasional asides - for instance, 'everything in existence is in truth superior to politics'[2] and 'It is better for a writer to die of hunger than to sell his soul to the devil called Power'[3] - in the years immediately preceding the Second World War. A sizeable proportion of In the Spotlight of Thought is given over to antipolitical articles written in 1937 and 1938, and the 166 pages of The Tree of Ruling, the first book devoted entirely to the genre, are a concentrated attack on politicians in general and Egyptian politicians in particular. The volume is in two parts. The first comprises five playlets which show Egyptian leaders trying to continue in paradise the underhand behaviour they had engaged in when in power in Cairo; they are guilty of contravening the rules of heaven, where the Qur'an says there will be no idle talk and no talk of war.[4] The second is a didactic tale of loose construction which endeavours to portray the deleterious effect of the selfish actions of Egyptian politicians on the idealism of the younger generation. It challenges the remoteness of the government from the people; the harmful interference of the parties in family life, children's welfare, the moral attitudes of youth, and education; the self-seeking ambitions of the politician which bar the road to progress; and Egypt's falling-short of real democracy. It calls for a revolution in the politics, morals and religion of society, and foresees nothing but the further decline of the nation unless it can breed politicians capable of retaining their integrity and a determination to rule wisely. As we have seen, it brought a storm down on Hakim's head to which Praksa I was the provocative and brave response.[5]

Praksa I shows the women of Athens taking over the city-state from their menfolk, many of whom recognize that it is floundering like a ship without sails in deep waters, piloted by depraved rulers devoted to nothing except the advancement of themselves and their friends. The coup accomplished, Praksa proceeds to conduct from her Presidential Palace a dictatorial regime as venal as that she ousted, fails to live up to her grandiose promises to the people, calls in (mainly male) advisers in the shapes of gods, Ibqirat the apparently ineffective philosopher and Hirunimus the young commander of the army, and finally loses both her virtue and her position to the last when she proves herself incapable of dealing with warlike threats from the Lacedaemonians. The third act of the play is a masterly study of dictatorship, with all its complexes and obsessions. As it begins, Ibqirat is in prison, and by the end of the play Praksa has joined him. Hirunimus, speaking in the people's name without their consent and indulging in the tedious harangues of demagogy, is fighting the external enemy with words alone.

During this fine drama, the action moves from the fourth century BC to modern times, for it cannot be doubted that Hirunimus stands as a representative of twentieth-century totalitarian rule. Hakim's understanding of the characteristics of dictatorship is profound. Hirunimus possesses the whole panoply (much talk but no deeds, persecution mania, delusions of success, the inability to support the slightest criticism, contempt for the intellect and fear of new ideas) and runs an administration based on brain-washing, thought-control, the rewriting of history, a thoroughgoing personality cult, the proliferation of unearned titles ('Hirunimus the Conqueror') and the banning of political parties. Some modern Arab rulers might almost have used him as a model. Hakim's account of his rule, the nature of which is cleverly brought out in his oral duels with his two chief captives, is superbly presented and most economically rendered.

Praksa I appears to suggest that, in the late 1930s, Hakim believed, or was driven by his anger at the prevailing situation to pretend to believe, that for Egypt even the worst sort of military dictatorship was preferable to civilian government of whatever kind. Muhammad Mandur concurs in this interpretation [6] which, if correct, sees the author at his lowest ebb in his view of politicians. On the other hand, Taha Husayn, cognisant of the circumstances from which the play emerged, affirms [7] that it demonstrated the stifling of democracy and freedom with the object of jolting thinkers into doing what they could to prevent Egypt from going the way of Hirunimus's Athens. Hakim offers no solution to 'the difficulty of ruling' in Praksa I; the interesting answer he had up his sleeve only coming to light in its second instalment.

Praksa I purged him of his most urgent feelings about the way in which his country was being run. After it he reverted to the more positive, if less entertaining, ideas of The Tree of Ruling in From the Ivory Tower. Egypt, he declared, had known great men, but now

'I hardly see ... a trace of that noble brotherhood ... The system today is for the pursuit of sham glory and quick wealth to ride roughshod over thought, for opinion to be taboo and, out of greed for comfort and the desire for a quiet life, for cowardice to cover this up. Thus the page of our history has, in these days, emptied of mighty names and our land has been overrun by titled people, a plague of decorations and chauffeur-driven cars. We all have the right to ask this question: what miracle can recreate this country when it's in this condition? Can the wrath of Allah against us be far off, since He is not vouchsafing us a leader who can bring back respect for the value of opinion, cleanse our souls of the filth of materialism, restore high and noble exemplars to their old glory and raise the whole nation at a stroke to the heights of the great creation? If that happened we should be saved. If it does not, nothing will await us but certain disintegration and a decline to the status of the slave.'[8]

Much of his energy between 1939 and 1945 was, apart from Pigmalyun and Solomon the Wise, spent on studies on the rights and wrongs of the Second World War, and only in the latter year - except when he castigated Egyptian politicians for continuing to feud while free nations were being crushed by barbarism[9] - did he redirect his attention towards Egypt. In My Donkey Said to Me he resorted to ridicule in implying that her politicians were donkeys who, unlike their animal namesakes, worked for themselves exclusively and not for those they had undertaken to serve.[10] (He repeated this innuendo in 1954.)[11] In Reflections on Politics he went further and became more constructive. One article in it,[12] originally published in 1946, called for swingeing taxation to finance a social revolution. Another,[13] of the following year and entitled 'I am not a Communist, but ...', suggested that the government become the guardian of the interest of all and recommended that the relations of capital and labour should be regulated in accordance with the workers' slogan 'participation in profits'. It is to be presumed that Reflections on Politics as a whole gave the impression that his social and political attitudes were not going to fall short of compatibility with those of the coming revolution. Meanwhile, he wrote The Thief, still seeing no sign of the longed-for great one. The establishment of Israel in defiance of feeble Arab resistance emboldened him to attack the leadership of his country again, speaking now in total concert with the younger generation. The play, staged as a whodunit with Yusuf Wahbi in the leading role,[14] deceives us into believing that the title refers to Hamid, a young man who is anxious to set up on his own after being unjustly dismissed by his bookseller employer and who tries to break into a Pasha's house in order to acquire the necessary capital. It emerges, however, that it is the Pasha - a capitalist, exploiter of workers, swindler and womaniser who egregiously sports the outer garments of integrity - who is the thief and is Hakim's chosen representative of the governing class he wishes to expose.

The Pasha's step-daughter, Khayriyya, falls vertiginously in love with, and into betrothal to, Hamid, but their progress towards a secure marriage is not smooth because of the Pasha's lust for the girl. The play is at pains to contrast his mode of life with that sought by the young couple. Their aim is one of honourable endeavour together: Khayriyya, whose vocation is also selling books, agrees completely with Hamid when he says, 'It seems to me that there is now no hope for people like us ... except in self-supporting, respectable work.' Their ambitions in this direction are also thwarted for a time by the Pasha, who had earlier placed at the head of one of his companies a young man whose sister he coveted. He so arranged matters that the business was operated fraudulently from the day of its foundation, and when he tired of the girl he was able to jettison her by exposing her naive and innocent brother. When he aspires to Khayriyya, who rejects his advances, he plans to ensnare her by putting Hamid at the head of the same company and giving them a grand house to live in. (These machinations are similar to ones in Modern Woman, Master Kanduz's Property - Imarat al Mu^{c}allim Kanduz, one of the Plays of Social Life - and The Anxiety Bank.) Khayriyya, soon married, now encourages him to hope that she will make available the favours he demands because she sees his help as the only means to a reasonable future for Hamid and herself. The Pasha gets his deserts when, her pledges unmet and his wife called in to assist in the protection of the family honour, he is shot and killed by his first puppet company boss.

The cruel, ruthless Pasha is thoroughly discredited by the author. The younger generation comes out of the affair almost equally badly, however, for although they are given the excuse that their exploitation by their elders is responsible for all their misdemeanours, it nevertheless remains true that the play opens with Hamid engaged in burglary, that Khayriyya tells lie after lie to keep her step-father at arm's length, and that both are unashamedly intent (contrary to their high-sounding protestations) on lining their pockets whether legally or otherwise. Their attitude to the Pasha resembles that of Isis to the Shaykh al Balad and again raises questions about ends justifying means.

The Pasha was not, of course, a politician, but he was the type of man whom the pre-revolutionary rulers of Egypt emboldened to flourish by their misdeeds, and thus a credible target for Hakim. In The Thief, in contrast to what he had held to be the case earlier, he maintains 'that the ruling class and the blemished younger generation were almost equally censurable for a disgraceful state of social and political affairs. His last word before the revolution was in Hard Work has its Reward (Li Kulli Mugtahidin Nasibun, 1951, one of the sketches in A Variety of Theatre), which is a devastatingly-funny demonstration of the consequences of a dishonest regime for civil servants.

His only post-revolutionary dramatic comment on the age which was abruptly terminated on 23 July 1952 was Her Majesty. He looks back on Faruq, with a scorn which a musical production[15] might have made the more telling, building his play upon the monarch's choice of an already engaged to be one of his consorts. She is Wigdan and her husband-to-be is Hamdi, a popular musician who has his own band. Her insufferable mother, Anisa, is involved in the massive embezzling activities of her husband, Ridwan, which have enabled them to live above their station but cause them to dread a knock at the door. When it comes, it brings with it the announcement that Faruq has that morning seen Wigdan and Hamdi buying the wedding ring and as a consequence has decided to make the girl his queen. Hamdi gives in to the unopposable without a struggle, because he does not wish to stand in the way of his fiancee's elevation. He goes without saying good-bye to her or asking for the return of the ring. Anisa unpardonably misrepresents his behaviour to her daughter and, with her sheep-like husband, gloats over their luck while Wigdan weeps in their presence. Ridwan speedily finds himself promoted to the rank of Pasha, Anisa is decorated with the Order of Perfection, Wigdan remains unhappy and confused, and Hamdi is summoned to supply ud music for the royal engagement party. Just before it begins, Faruq transacts a few items of business, arranging for a million pounds of the state's money to be deposited in one of his Swiss bank accounts and vetoing ministerial development projects.

After the marriage, Hamdi bends his musical talents to the composition of songs attacking 'the savage' while Wigdan persuades Faruq not to have him killed or put in an asylum. The whole uncomfortable situation is saved by the sudden appearance of tanks in the streets, the overthrow of Faruq, Wigdan's divorce, and her marriage to Hamdi. Having made up her mind that her daughter could do worse for the moment than marry her 'singing bird', Anisa, who now refers to Faruq as 'that bullying, adulterous rake' while continuing to address Wigdan as 'Your Majesty', does her spiteful best to find a richer alternative husband for her daughter so that she and Ridwan may resume their life of luxury; she offers Hamdi a large sum if he will renounce Wigdan. Exasperated and sapped by his wife's scheming, to which he sees no end, however, Ridwan removes a suitor in prospect from the scene and, perhaps galvanized by an embryonic revolutionary conscience, confesses to the police the swindling operations of himself and his wife. A detective arrives, as the play closes, with a warrant for their arrest.

The only feature of real note in Her Majesty is its author's misogynistic attitude towards Anisa, which has been touched on elsewhere. The play is lightweight, and of small value as a denunciation of the monarchy, of which there is little account apart from descriptions of the outdated formalities of the court and of such of the King's financial and marital selfishness as is summarized above. Its purpose, no doubt to some extent realized, was to convey oblique flattery to President Abd an Nasir, whose policies and actions were soon themselves to undergo the test of Hakim's microscope and in the upshot to be vilified as those of the ex-King never were. Hakim had not felt the need to deploy against them the weapon of sustained political analysis which was already part of his armoury and was soon to be levelled at the revolution.

REFERENCES

1 LP, pp 166-7
2 IST, p 140
3 Ibid, pp 143-4
4 Suras 19, 52, 56, 78, 88
5 Sami al Kayyali, introduction to Adham, p 8
6 Mandur 2, p 92
7 Husayn, pp 129-30
8 FTIT, pp 53-5
9 SD, p 41
10 MDS, pp 78-9
11 Al Hakim's Stick, p 7
12 p 141
13 pp 154-5
14 Shukri, p 391
15 Ra^{c}i, p 84

3 (2) The Deception of the Revolution

> The people ... applaud ... every new ruler on his first day.
> (Praksa)

Except for The Tree Climber and A Hunting Trip, all the plays of the period since 1952 are political in intent and most of them are far more absorbing than those discussed, with Her Majesty, in the last chapter: they are of vastly higher quality, and concerned with matters which were, and are, of world interest - the Egyptian revolution, its leaders and policies. At first they expressed support in vague terms for the policies but, from the first equally, were more or less critical of the leaders. As the criticism of them mounted, their policies were more and more found wanting, so that by the end the revolution and its makers were alike condemned.

The earliest examination of the revolution was made in Soft Hands, which was written after the new regime had firmly established its authority and gone some way towards the development of its pragmatic ideologies. It has among its cast a character, the hero, who is at one point an Abd an Nasir symbol, and its chief purpose is to contrast the idle luxury of the ruling class of Faruq's day with the work expected of it in a revolutionary age. They are personified by Prince Farid, who has had his wealth confiscated, possesses a palace in Cairo which he cannot afford to run but is forbidden to sell, and has no productive talent or training. His only assets are his limited ability to gain credit by brandishing his officially untenderable title, his suavity and his daughters;

the girls are, however, of little actual value to him since the elder, Marfat, has eloped to marry Salim, the man who used to service her car, and the younger, Gihan, following his excommunication of her sister for mingling princely blood with that of a plebeian, has taken up residence with them. Farid has an Iagoesque foil (broadly similar to Tiresias in King Oedipus and Sha'ban in The Anxiety Bank) in Ali Hamuda, who has a PhD in linguistics which was largely based on research into the usage of a single preposition and is also unfitted for any worthwhile role in the new society. Each has to undergo various exercises in humiliation before being salvaged by the Prince's despised son-in-law. Farid falls in love with a commoner who turns out to be Salim's sister, and Ali with Gihan. As a further degradation, both the ladies insist that the decision whether or not their suitors are worthy of them must be taken by Salim, whom, since he has succeeded in life solely as a result of the efforts of his own hands, they regard as the only true child of the revolution among them and therefore the real head of the family. It is when he assumes this task, in the fourth and final act, that Salim appears garbed in the clothing of Abd an Nasir and endowed with his unequalled democratic virtues. The family into which he has married, plus Ali, are made to stand as representatives of an expectant Egyptian nation, their future is in his hands, an appeal can go no higher than him, the atmosphere turns into that of a totalitarian state, spies are everywhere and, in due course, judgement on them is handed down as in a 'people's court'. Just before it is, while the ambience of personal rule is continued for a little longer, Salim's father informs the anxious petitioners that his son had his wise point of view fixed from the start. Then the play dissolves into bathos. Salim lectures them about the dignity of labour and then announces that he approves of both projected marriages since the Prince and Ali will be able to maintain his sister and sister-in-law respectively by means of jobs in his company which are in his gift. Is this a jeer at, as seen by Hakim, the disappointing quality of Abd an Nasir's decisions, at the ineffective use he has made of his omnipotence? The suspicion that it is is reinforced by the fatuous nature of the jobs in question and the ridiculous qualifications Farid and Ali have for them. The police-state passage is of course ominous, occurring as it does so soon after Nagib and Abd an Nasir's seizure of power. There is further brave comment on them when the brothers-in-law seem at one juncture to be identified with the revolutionary leaders themselves on the morrow of their triumph, when in Act Two, alone in Farid's palace, they discover themselves confronted by problems - cooking, cleaning, putting out the dustbin, answering the doorbell - with which they are completely unfamiliar. Hakim was more reckless still if he meant us to read them throughout as symbols of Abd an Nasir and, perhaps, of Nagib in a play which expounds the bold views that current talk of work was puerile and that Abd an Nasir (whose presence on the opening night of the play's production has been noted) had not yet grasped what he was about. Hakim felt it necessary to justify his own position, pointed to by his title, with regard to the labour question. In his last long harangue, Salim says that industrial output is 'the national wealth which must guarantee the fruits of the intellect which represents civilization ... There must be rough hands so that soft hands may exist beside them.' This, which runs directly counter to the ideas set forth on this relationship in <u>The Sultan of Darkness</u>, was Hakim's excuse for not ceasing to exercise his pen while paying insincere lip-service to the laudable nature of physical and manual exertion.

<u>Soft Hands</u> is a bad play which fails to fulfil the promise of its superbly dramatic opening. It falls into the class of domestic comedies published by Hakim in the 1930s, most closely approaching the mixture of the excellent, the trite, the didactic and the autobiographically revealing which made up <u>The Suicide's Secret</u>. Its juxtaposition of ideological instruction and the comedy of manners is not felicitous, the transitions from the one to the other jarring so badly that the reader is almost always conscious of the artificiality and frequently staggering naivete of the former.

<u>Isis</u> looks at the revolution through the other end of the telescope, and through a rose-coloured one at that: Osiris does duty for King Fu'ad, Tifun for Faruq, Huris - clearly marked out to be a puppet ruler - for King Ahmad Fu'ad, and the King of Byblos, who saves Egypt from injustice and corruption, ingratiatingly for Abd an Nasir. Two pieces came next in which Hakim viewed the value of labour with more genuine favour than in <u>Soft Hands</u>. In <u>Death Game</u> he does so only en passant, by causing the 'soft hand' professor, galvanized by Kilyubatra, to say, 'When a man ceases working he enters upon death. Work is life;' but Act Four of <u>Journey into the Future</u>, which pictures a society in which employment is next to impossible to obtain and reviles the policies of the party which bring the doctor to his inevitable fate, heftily endorses the revolution's commitment to labour.

<u>Praksa</u>, issued in full in 1960, reverts to adverse attitudes. The three acts which Hakim could not print before the war indicate that he then assessed administering Egypt as too daunting a task for any individual or collective leadership to tackle: the only way (or, at least, the next one to experiment with, no other springing to mind) was to entrust it to the whole people with a philosopher (himself? - elsewhere he admits

156 Tawfiq al Hakim

to serious reservations about this) to guide them. The fact that these
opinions were penned in 1939 is unimportant, for he held them to remain
valid in 1960, thus registering a further loss of confidence in the President.
Act Four demonstrates that Hirunimus is, unlike most modern
Arab dictators, just a cowardly lion. His cossetted army has been
routed by the Macedonians* and is marching on Athens to avenge itself,
he believes, on him. Overcome by a sudden wish to hand authority back
to the civil power, he has Praksa and Ibqirat hurriedly released from
prison. The former, who dares not rule alone a second time, revives a
proposal, made in Act Three by Ibqirat, that they should govern as a
troika, but the philosopher objects that this by itself will not save Hirunimus
and that they will need a protective figurehead. Opportunely
Praksa's neglected husband, Balpirus, arrives to take her back home,
and the three create him king on the spot; Praksa informs him that his
only function will be to smile at people at parties. In Act Five, having
persuaded Hirunimus to arrange a truce with the Lacedaemonians and
constructed a system of government which brings the city to the brink of
bankruptcy, he turns determinedly uncooperative with the schemers and
has them put in gaol. The final act relates the superbly realistic 'legal'
proceedings at which the three are charged, not, as they had anticipated,
with endangering the security of the state, but with adultery in the cases
of Praksa and Hirunimus and with being an accessory after the fact in the
case of Ibqirat. Unfortunately for Balpirus, the trial is a miscalculation,
the people are swayed by the oratory of the defendants and the philosopher
takes over. Asking the populace how they can possibly consent to remain
corruptly ruled, he counsels them to try being their own masters. Acclaimed
by the crowd and deaf to the appeals of Praksa and Hirunimus, he
ends the play instructing them how best to set about the mission he has
given them and preparing to be their adviser and friend.

There was little cheer for the President in this, but he could have derived
some from The Sultan's Dilemma, in which we contemplate a ruler

---

* In Praksa I they were Lacedaemonians, as they remain in Act Five.
The juxtaposition of the Macedonians and Ibqirat perhaps suggests
that Hakim has mistaken Hippocrates, the man of medicine, for
Isocrates, the renowned pamphleteer whose 'Address to Philip' (of
Macedon) appears to have sought to divert that monarch's attention
away from the attractions of conquering Athens.

who bases his actions on the law of the land and who, in the face of much encouragement to err, refuses to employ force as an instrument of government. The chief officers of state, on the other hand, are a set of law-twisting men whose method of solving every problem is to draw the sword and above whom the Sultan towers as a being of vast integrity. In the present context he is both Abd an Nasir and a warning from Hakim to the President, who (he perhaps hoped) would not only construe the Sultan as a portrait of himself but also, if he felt the cap did not fit entirely satisfactorily, model his deeds on those of the Mamluk by eschewing violence and permitting the law to rule both him and Egypt.

The next play was much less hopeful and restrained about the leader. A Train Journey is a most interesting, and jolly, piece of theatre and one of Hakim's very finest performances. An ancient engine hurtles through the night, provoking its one-legged fireman to reprimand the driver for taking risks with the lives of his passengers. As it approaches a signal, he tells him to stop because it is at red. The driver insists that it is green but, nevertheless, grudgingly pulls up. The two peer at it and still disagree, and a great debate ensues, first between two pairs of passengers and then among the travellers as a whole, as to how the colour should be defined. The driver, constantly apprehensive because he knows there is an express behind, is for taking a risk and going on, but the division of opinion inhibits him. The only solution, he eventually agrees, is for him and the fireman to go to the signal box, a kilometre down the line, in order to consult the man in charge of the levers. While they are away the passengers throw off all restraint, like the Israelites as Moses was receiving the Ten Commandments, and engage in a frenzied communal dance. When they return they bring no news: the signal box, its windows broken in a storm the day before, has been abandoned. On yet closer inspection the signal is, after all and rather feebly, seen to be showing no colour at all, having also been wrecked. Despite the fireman's concern lest the track ahead be washed out, the driver now will brook no opposition to proceeding, only a businessman - anxious to buy the engine as scrap and prepared throughout to advocate any course which would ensure that it became such - offering dissent.

In a short preface to the book of which A Train Journey forms part, Hakim warns against a search for meaning in the play. He himself, however, has guardedly suggested in an interview[1] that the train may be a symbol for life, to which in the last resort people will always cling even though they may differ about some aspects of it. Ghali Shukri quite rightly declined to follow Hakim's advice and interpreted the play as a comment on the Egyptian revolution, for which the engine stands, the express being a personification of the nation's youth.[2] If he is correct – and his elucidation rings true – Hakim is hardly being complimentary in depicting the revolution as tearing along unsafely in the charge of a leader who is dangerously slow to make up his mind and weak in the handling of his subordinates. Shukri believes further, however, that the fact that Hakim makes the driver resume the journey is an expression of his confidence in him. This is unlikely, for here he would seem to be repeating and reinforcing his conviction that Abd an Nasir was not the great one on whom the salvation of his country depended. The consequences for the revolution of vacillation and disagreement at the top are a bewildered younger generation, a reversion to popular purposelessness and the re-emergence of exploiting capitalism and 'reaction'.

<u>Shams an Nahar</u> returns in undistinguished fashion to the themes of work and the responsibilities of the ruler. It adds considerable glorification of the peasant virtues. The eponymous heroine is a princess and woman of action who, a Modern Woman in a different setting,[3] refuses to be married off to a prince or a notable just to suit her father's wishes and bring him peace of mind. She insists that all, of whatever station, who aspire to marry her should have the opportunity of an interview, and as a result chooses the least prepossessing of those who come forward, Qamar az Zaman, an itinerant frequenter of desert solitudes. The compact sealed, he refuses to wed her until she has made something of him, which he decrees that she shall do on his home ground. Disguised as a soldier, she follows him out of her father's palace and, for the first time in her experience, is made to look after herself unaided, live rough, find fuel and food, and cook. The regime imposed upon her by Qamar, whose philosophy is moderation in all things – except in his treatment of Shams – allied to self-help and a clear conscience, has the effect of changing her while, contrary to his stated intention, leaving him much as he was before. Strengthened in character and imbued with his ideals, Shams arrives (after a long, tedious and pointless episode with a pair of treasury robbers which takes up most of the second of the play's four acts and holds up the action badly) with her fiance at the castle of the Amir Hamdan. The Amir, a candidate for her hand who has not heard that the competition is over, does not recognize her and appoints her his personal guard. She rebuffs Qamar roundly when he protests at her enlistment in this capacity.

Shams is next seen bringing Qamar's philosophy to bear on the Amir, journeying to lodge his application for her, as the three trudge through the wilderness. The abandonment of ease is proving beneficial to him, as it earlier was to her. When they near her father's palace she advises him to complete the trek alone, thus giving herself the opportunity of bringing matters to a conclusion with Qamar. She admits that he has made a better woman of her but sees this as an obstacle to marriage, for she is his creation. Qamar, who would not take her when he had the chance, makes no reference to the fact that it was she who was supposed to be guiding his development and not the reverse, and now asks that she choose between him and Hamdan. She replies that, while she attaches great hopes to the Amir as the saviour of his corrupt country - a task for which she has now fitted him - she wants to marry her mentor and live with him wherever he wishes. At this he becomes coy, maintains that he has not the right to monopolize her, and insists that she go back home to reform her father's manner of ruling. This mission comes before everything else and he abruptly imposes it on her. She reluctantly agrees with him and they part sentimentally.

In the stage version, which was the original one, Hamdan reappears after his fruitless foray to the palace just as the pair have resolved to unite. He is understandably furious, but reacts positively when Shams informs him that it is his duty to strive for his people and be a progressive revolutionary. This leaves the way clear for her to marry Qamar, which she explains that she must do because he created her, and furnishes an ending which could be expected to appeal to an Egyptian audience more than to readers and was insisted upon by Futuh Nashati, the producer, because he felt it more appropriate for a revolutionary-age princess to marry a peasant than to be allowed to pledge her troth to one of her own, outdated class.[4] It is the better conclusion since, if love and a mission are mutually exclusive, Hamdan is the obvious person to be deprived of the former. If, however, one of the intentions of Hakim's sermon was to inscribe this incompatibility among the eternal truths, he has left the introduction of it far too late - until the final scene - for it to arise naturally from what has gone before, and it does not escape the observer that, in the play as acted, Shams sees it as a truth not applicable to herself married to Qamar. As to the work theme, it is too unambitiously and feebly presented to make anything other than a ridiculous impression.

Muhammad Mandur confusedly detects symbolism in Shams an Nahar:[5] Shams is the Egyptian revolution, uncertain whether to ally itself solely with those who created it (Qamar/the people) or with those it has created (Hamdan/co-operative ex-aristocrats). There is little basis for such an interpretation and, even if it were tenable, it would not alter the fact that

Shams an Nahar, which he compares unfavourably with Shaw's Candida,[6] is a thoroughly unsatisfactory piece and unworthy of its author.

After Shams an Nahar, with all its faults and rambling confusions, Act One of Fate of a Cockroach comes as a shock. It puts before us the spectacle of a Kingdom which cannot raise an army (it could not, in any case, train one) and in which self-deluding propaganda masquerades as action; a despotic King, without self-respect or ideas, who is devoid of any sense of duty and scornful of the advice of his ruling clique; and a prime minister who cannot see plans through, a scientist who is unscientific, impractical, arrogant and uncooperative and a priest who is irreligious, hypocritical and haughty. Putting them all to shame is the Queen. Hakim's striking and vicious account of the Kingdom is so presented that the ordinary Arab spectator or reader ought to be able to assimilate the satire effortlessly. It is, nevertheless, doubtful whether the politically unaware Arab would grasp that it is not about cockroaches at all and, if coaxed into the theatre, would not be on the retreat within a short space of time. If he missed the satire he would, however, also be denied the humour and vivacity which make the act a continual joy. It is an anti-Egyptian (perhaps anti-Arab) parable: the Kingdom is Egypt, which has not studied its problems with the necessary seriousness and depth and substitutes slander and lies for the considered demarche; the King and his sensible Queen are respectively the Egyptian President and people, whom Hakim is not complimenting by dressing up as cockroaches; and the non-existent cockroach army is Egypt's.

It is remarkable that in Fate of a Cockroach, the product of a broken heart, the author should have so controlled his contempt and bitterness as to give us not only a drama, but also a political document, of value. The play is an inspired, thoughtful and vigorous denunciation of Egyptian (and Arab) politics and policies as he saw them in the years immediately prior to the June War and his last direct dramatic word on Abd an Nasir.

The Anxiety Bank is a statement of the damage wrought on Egypt by the fifteen years of the revolution. Extremely pessimistic, it is built round the quest of a young man, Adham Sulayman, for a purpose in life, and it aims to portray, like Mahfuz novels of the period, the unsatisfactory social and political backdrop to such a search. Because of its unusual form (ten 'chapters' alternating with ten 'scenes'), it makes less impact than it might otherwise have done. It has an extraordinary, and auspicious, beginning, but rapidly returns to more conventional paths and, in the end, offers little that is memorable. The first chapter observes Adham, rootless, penniless and quick-witted, gaining unauthorized entry to a nightclub, where he contemplates his fellow men. Their basic condition he judges, despite outward appearances, to be one of insecurity: he describes their escapist activities when they abandon themselves to a frenetic dance, uttering the while such contemporarily meaningful cries as 'twist', 'hully gully', and 'shake', and talking of the Beatles, and regards them as the victims of mass hysteria induced by mass insecurity. Leaving the place after the contents of a soda syphon have been expended on him, he chances upon Sha^{C}ban, a failed former fellow-student of the Law College, on a bench on the Nile Corniche. Although Adham writes the occasional newspaper article, both are in effect unemployed and destitute; Sha^{C}ban is a gambler who has already married several times and is forever in need of a cigarette. At this unpropitious time of night Adham succeeds in interesting him in a project he has long brooded upon, the foundation of an Anxiety Bank. The most widespread social disease being anxiety, the bank would offer assistance in combating it and at the same time provide the two of them with the wherewithal to continue to exist. It would make available high-price curative services at charges reducible for treatment received from clients - for Adham and Sha^{C}ban are not themselves free of the malady - at therapy sessions. Maintaining the contemporary tone established in Chapter One and ignoring the fact that neither of them is remotely qualified to administer the counselling publicised, Adham decides that their wall-advertising shall say, 'If you suffer from anxiety, let us cure you. If you don't, come and cure us.'

The Bank's first customer, Munir Atif, is, though they do not realize it until much later, an intelligence agent in the pay of masters whose identities are not disclosed and who espies potential in the enterprise. He installs the pair in sumptuous quarters which are designed to enable him to bug their conversations with clients, who start to turn up in Scene Six. Their causes for anxiety are, in the main, trivial in the extreme, and Adham and Sha^{C}ban have no need to fall back on psychological knowledge they do not possess. When Adham, whose attitude to the venture is throughout idealistic, and Sha^{C}ban, who has joined in it for the libertinage it allows him to indulge in, discover what game Munir is playing, they are afraid that if they report him to the police they will themselves be viewed as aiders and abetters of his activities. The book closes inconclusively and abruptly as they try to make up their minds what their best course of action would be.

The Anxiety Bank is an incredible work couched in a form of uncertain utility and making little overall sense. It has, however, the virtue of contriving to demonstrate that all the (petty) anxieties it relates stem from deficiencies in Egyptian society. Such was Hakim's aim in this piece of political writing. The atmosphere of fantasy and immaturity, the flippancy and cynicism, the robot-like characters - all intensify the picture of gloom he undoubtedly tried to paint. The insensate euphoria of the first chapter and a skeleton in the cupboard, in the shape of the mad, confined sister of the woman who responds so admirably to Sha^{c}ban's physical demands, make isolated contributions. The result is a strangely effective account of Egypt at a time of social disillusionment, which the Beatle-type extravagances imported from the West and set up as a shield against hardship and reality, do nothing to allay but, on the contrary, help to aggravate. The language used by Hakim, which is markedly uninhibited compared even with that of <u>The Sacred Bond</u>, and his frequent resort to neologisms are consistent with the description of a decadent society.

While sparing the President personally, the book is uniformly condemnatory and needles the revolution throughout: the Agricultural Reform laws are a source of continual apprehension, the redistribution of the land has miscarried as it was obvious that it would, government offices are havens of rest and idleness for the venal and bibulous of the nation, Islam is being undermined. Perhaps worst of all, no one knows what a socialist is or is supposed to be and everyone has to keep looking over his shoulder to make sure that his words or actions are not being recorded as ideologically improper. On the other hand, the people are forever detecting what they imagine is unsocialist behaviour in their rulers but are unable to do anything about it. The great one has not saved the nation.

In this series of plays the ringing leitmotif, not overpowered by the early flattery of the President and the erratic approval of aspects of his socialism, is Gamal Abd an Nasir's failure to bring anything but harm to the country he claimed to wish to rescue from inequity and corruption. (His tolerance of the strictures of his favourite author is astonishing: if he and his staff were deceived by the subtleties of <u>Soft Hands</u>, <u>Praksa 2</u>, <u>A Train Journey</u> and <u>The Anxiety Bank</u>, they could hardly have avoided drawing the appropriate inferences from <u>Fate of a Cockroach</u> and been expected to overlook them because their tone was more regretful than angry.) There is, however, no suggestion that Hakim would wish to see the restoration of Muhammad Ali's dynasty or had identified an alternative great one. He did not, in short, cease to be a revolutionary, even if one who believed that the new order had gone badly wrong, and his commentary on the Abd an Nasir era is therefore doubly and uniquely valuable.

REFERENCES

1. To <u>Farag</u>, p 175
2. <u>Shukri</u>, p 356
3. <u>Subur 2</u>, p 30
4. <u>Mallakh</u>, p 321
5. <u>Mandur 2</u>, p 175
6. Ibid, p 176

4 Egypt, the World and the Bomb

> The nature of peoples is one throughout the world. (The Documentary Background to Awareness Regained)
>
> We are sons of God possessed by a devil. Which of these two contending spirits in us is going to prevail? (Arnold Toynbee, Between Oxus and Jumna)
>
> I suppose the whole idea of Israel began as somebody's dream! I read once in a book that the Chinese have a saying: What is so real as a dream in the heart of man? A million Palestinians dreaming of one day going home could be a beginning. They could make it happen if they dreamed hard enough! (Ethel Mannin, The Road to Beersheba)

In the preface to Plays of Social Life, Hakim says that The Burdensome Guest

'centred upon a lawyer on whom ... a guest descended to stay for a day. He remained a month. No stratagem or other means was of any use in getting rid of him. The lawyer was deprived of everything except a desk for his work. If he relaxed his vigilance for a moment or went out for an hour the guest would pounce upon new clients, claim to be the owner of the house and take from them what he could of advance fees. It was an occupation and an exploitation. The one always leads to the other.'

This approach to the British presence in Egypt sounds engagingly Pinteresque; Mandur[1] speculates that it not only symbolised the takeover but ridiculed it as well. The spirit of The Cavemen, written eight or nine years later, is a contrasting one of dignity. In this moving picture of Egypt under our hegemony, which is neither ridiculed nor begrudged, the cave stands for her past and the foray and retreat of Yamlikha, Marnush and Mishilinya for her awakening, after the long Ottoman night she has fled, to find the strange and anachronistic British holding sway over her and her decision that accommodation with them is impossible. Hakim gently chides his countrymen for reaching this conclusion too hastily and, failing to attempt with sufficient determination to get the measure of it, merely running for cover from the new situation despite their possession, in Priska, of a key to it. He hints, through Mishilinya's acceptance, too late, of her finally profferred love, that under the right circumstances and probably far in the future, relations between the two nations could become close and fruitful.

His general attitude to the UK is not, however, quite the simple, typically Arab one these two plays suggest. In accord with it, he admires the 'kind and honourable' British people[2] and, in greater measure, suspects and dislikes British policies, past and present: he derides the presumption of those who incarcerated Napoleon on St Helena;[3] declares the colonisers of Egypt to be men 'who did not in reality represent any human race';[4] characterizes the British politician as unable 'to subordinate the interests of his nation and the ambitions of his country to international, humanitarian principles';[5] charges the UK with playing 'politics in a time of peace and prosperity' between the wars 'as a change from golf', to which game he regards Lloyd George, Baldwin and Chamberlain as having been addicted;[6] lambastes 'the country of democracy and freedom' for being the first to recognize the conquest of Abyssinia by Italy, 'the symbol of dictatorship and authoritarian power';[7] indicts her for seeking to partition Egypt on confessional lines as she later succeeded in doing with India;[8] and, in 1946, goes so far as to call for an armed struggle against (British) imperialism.[9] But in contrast to this catalogue of denunciation of postures and actions of British governments are significant instances of warm approval - his championing of Edward VIII, which has been referred to earlier,[10] his astonishment that the master of the world should be content to be called plain Mr Churchill,[11] and his praise for Queen Victoria, in whose reign Egypt was seized. He comes near to granting her the worship rendered to his chosen goddesses. He extols the strength of will which allowed her to keep distinct her duties as Queen and her devotion to the Prince Consort, 'a clever man of broad intelligence' whom she left 'to kill his time by reading and playing music'. He respects her for being a reader herself ('I admire kings and rulers who read. That is how they learn the needs of their people') and for using the novels of Dickens as guides to the areas of poverty and suffering where her influence was most required.[12]

His ability to see more than one side, albeit somewhat quirkishly, of the British performance is not surprising in one who, in A Sparrow from the East,[13] declared that 'a mother has no right to raise her child in enmity and hatred' of a foreign people, as he had been brought up to execrate the British. He has succeeded to an unusual degree in remaining open-minded, demonstrating his achievement not least by the paucity of his commentating; of which there has been almost none since the beginning of the Second World War. He only reverted to dramatic criticism of the UK more than twenty years after The Cavemen, in Isis, which, bearing in mind the probability that it was composed during the period of Anglo-Egyptian relations dominated by the Canal Zone crisis, it seems natural to interpret as, in this context, an outline statement of the impact from the 1930s to the 1950s of the UK on the leadership of Egypt, the turncoat Shaykh al Balad standing for HMG. His only subsequent political comment on the UK (Suez provoked no outburst) occurs in The Anxiety Bank when, in talking of Speaker's Corner, Adham declares that it could only exist among the British and that 'Allah has bestowed two blessings on the English. The first is their cold character, the second their saying what they do not do.'

His views on Egypt in her broader international setting are attractively presented through the political symbolism of A Train Journey. The enigmatic signal and the unmanned signal-box may be assumed to stand for Soviet guidance in an even less reliable phase than usual and - though opinions on this differ and notwithstanding the divergent explanation of it in the last chapter - the express believed to be following fast behind the marooned train to personify the USA or the West in general, poised to gobble the country up at the first opportunity. Fate of a Cockroach is much more wide-ranging. Act One, which again hints that Soviet experts

The Bomb 167

are unsuitable for Egypt, expresses the contempt of the Egyptian people (represented by the cockroach Queen) for the lack of initiative of their leaders (the King and his male advisers) vis-a-vis Israel (the ants):

Prime Minister: I think, Sire, that we can deal with the ants by using the weapons they employ.

King: What are their weapons?

Prime Minister: Armies. They attack us with their huge armies. If <u>we</u> could combine and mass in large numbers it would be easy for us to attack them, divide them and crush them with our great feet.

King: A ridiculous idea.

Queen: You ridicule it without discussing it?

King: It's obviously unacceptable and absurd.

Queen: Let him finish and then judge it.

King: Continue, I'll discuss it. Go on. Tell me the size of this army of cockroaches you wish to mobilize.

Prime Minister: Say twenty strong. Twenty cockroaches together can trample underfoot and smash a long column of ants, or a whole village. A town.

King: Undoubtedly, but ... Has a column of twenty cockroaches ever been formed in the whole of our long history?

Prime Minister: No, but we can try.

King: How can we try? We're different from ants. Ants know about drawing up columns. But we cockroaches, we don't understand organizing.

Prime Minister: Perhaps by teaching and instruction ...

King: Who's going to do the teaching and instructing?

Prime Minister: We must look for someone to do it.

King: Marvellous! We end up looking for a teacher and an instructor. Tell me this, then. If we found the teacher and instructor, how many generations of

King (contd):	cockroaches would it take before the cockroach nation had been taught and instructed to march in step?
Prime Minister:	That, Sire, is outside my competence. I've only been giving my opinion on a plan of action. Others must come in on the details.
King:	Who else is there? ...
Prime Minister:	Our learned scientist, for example ...
Queen:	Now, scientist. Have you ever seen ten cockroaches in one spot?
Scientist:	Yes, once. A very long time ago. When I was an adolescent. A number of cockroaches gathered in a kitchen one night around a bit of tomato ...
King:	That's a useful thought. If we could produce a bit of tomato cockroaches would assemble round it ... In other words, the only means of getting the cockroaches together is food.
Scientist:	Quite right, in theory ... I have pondered on this at length ... The fact is that a definite connection between the gathering of a number of cockroaches in one place and the occurrence of certain kinds of calamity has always been observed.
King:	You mean the moving mountains?
Scientist:	Exactly. And the rains which choke and exterminate ...
King:	You're saying, then, that our fear of these calamities has made our race, from time immemorial, afraid of coming together in large numbers?
Scientist:	Precisely. And from this has arisen our habit of each going alone in different directions, a simple instinct of self-preservation.
Prime Minister:	But the ants are completely different.
Scientist:	The ants, because of their small size, can do whatever they want.

In Acts Two and Three, the symbolism extends further and its interpretation is much more hazardous. Perhaps, however, the struggle around the King is one between the USA (Samira) and the Soviet Union (Adil), with the latter in the ascendant as long as the King is powerless - and in any case content to leave him to whatever fate may have in store for him - and the former on top when first the cook and then the ants overrun him. The cook is the UK and France, who threw Egypt to the Israelis ten years before Fate of a Cockroach was published, and the doctor is a Soviet satellite country opposed at the beginning to the Soviet line but eventually persuaded to conform.

Fate of a Cockroach contains neither Hakim's first, nor his last, observations on the USA. In A Sparrow from the East he had, unusually, compared the American people unfavourably with their politicians, led by President Wilson - also lauded in My Donkey Said to Me[14] - with his 'fourteen points ... made up of love and peace. For the oppressed of the world he had the air of a Christ, of a new Saviour ...'[15] Hakim was contemptuous of Americans he encountered when a student in Paris for having 'no soul, no taste and no past'[16] and for what he saw as their obsessive desire to show off their wealth.[17] On the other hand, in one of the playlets in The Tree of Ruling[18] he allowed one of his characters to liken Roosevelt's lend-lease to the 'law of loaning and leasing' practised by Egyptian politicians to avoid effort and responsibility, and thus adopted the standard form which leads Arabs to distinguish between foreign governments (bad) and peoples (good). He swung back again, in Literature is Life,[19] to accuse Americans in France of destroying the life and culture of that country. Finally, in an article in Al Ahram,[20] he said that he had not visited the USA and had no wish to and spoke of 'the Vietnam war and its ugliness'.

In a series of five plays, which grew directly out of pre-war and wartime works like The Tree of Ruling (the first of his books to reveal his fear that an unreformed world would speedily succumb to the bomb) and The Sultan of Darkness, he mounted a campaign for peace on earth; he showed in The Angel's Prayer, which was the precursor of the later plays, that he felt able, and called upon, to be a spokesman for all mankind. Dedicated 'To the Friends of Humanity', it recounts the frustration of an angel's attempt to persuade earth's two tyrants (Hitler and Mussolini) to give an ear to the people's pleas for peace and desist from mass destruction. In Scene Two he meets three members of the human race - an orphan girl who has soldier brothers, and a refugee chemist and a monk who are disillusioned with science and with religion respectively; the chemist sees his vocation as one related to the improvement of the lot of mankind and not to the perfection of weaponry: 'May God curse science, which is happy to snatch the food from the mouths of human beings in order to put it into the mouths of guns.' The conversation the four have is largely abstract and, in atmosphere, far from the realities of the war. From participation in it the angel spirits himself into a hall where the tyrants are poring over a map and dividing the world up between them. He invites them to open their hearts to the merciful influence of heaven, but this appeal gets him no further than a military court, to which he says, 'My family is everyone because all men are brothers.' He is convicted of being a security risk and is shot by a firing-squad after exhorting its members to strive for the good of mankind and delivering a Christ-like message of forgiveness. Back in heaven he greets the prayers for his safe return with the comment that it is for 'the miserable people of the earth' that his angelic colleagues should be praying.

The play could obviously have no effect on the course of the war, and neither could the episode in My Donkey Said to Me in which [21] Hakim, imagining himself Egypt's delegate to the post-war peace conference and speaking for a world family, advocates a united globe with four freedoms - freedom of speech and opinion, freedom of worship, freedom from need and poverty, and freedom from oppression and slavery. When the war ended he turned his attention obsessively towards the atomic and nuclear bombs, initially in the reinterpretative comment, appended to the second edition of Solomon the Wise, in which he detected in the jinni a symbol for the atom bomb, 'that dreadful force', and the supremacy, in the post-war world, of unfettered might over reason; he deplored the fact that armaments had run ahead of man's ability to control them with his stunted intelligence and concluded with a plea that, while the jinni could never be eliminated, man should do his utmost to keep him in check. (This theme is developed in The Literary Art [22] and Literature is Life [23] and repeated in Action and Response.) [24]

A 'note' annexed to Isis is the link between The Angel's Prayer and Death Game, The Thorns of Peace, Journey into the Future, The Sultan's Dilemma and Food for Every Mouth. In it Hakim makes vague prophecies about the conflicts which the conflicts which the advance of science will inevitably give rise to and the likelihood that science will emerge untamed from them all. With this warning in mind we turn to Death Game. The professor apostrophises his fellow intellectuals 'who do not allow an individual to play the death game but ... do permit all the nations to ... You said nothing while they were playing with my life. Keep silent then while I play with the life of someone else.' His vengeance will reflect in a small way the moeurs of 'this detestable age'. He expatiates to Kilyubatra on the intolerable nature of the modern world: 'I and you and every human being and every child and every animal may be overtaken by a dreadful death without being in a battle zone.' In soliloquies he assails the countries which own the bomb and those who manage it for them: '... Those who allow radiation to escape are greedy, ambitious and terrified, and attached to a detonator. When it fires it will cause absolute destruction, and no one will get anything;' 'In our modern era the whole world is committing suicide.' In the first four acts of the play these platitudinous sentiments slowly lose ground before his reciprocated love for Kilyubatra, but the professor still bursts out periodically in feeble, naive and sometimes self-contradictory rages:

> 'The whole of the human race wants that quiet, peaceful brook, and fears those stones which fall from the sky ... But those stones do not fall ... by themselves ... There are people on earth who release them into the sky so that they fall down onto their brothers on the ground, with their flames, their smoke, their dust and their fatal rays ... It is a spiritually deformed world, stricken with a self-inflicted disease - bad relations between the nations. How could beauty survive in such a suffocating atmosphere? ... Every human being, like every nation, wants to destroy everyone else and then wash his hands while talking of love, goodness, co-operation and hope - pretty words beautifully drawn on a stage curtain and followed by the death game.'

Despite all this, in the two acts published after the original edition of the play, the professor lives out his days in tranquillity, Kilyubatra's love for him and her scepticism about the correctness of his vision of the way the world is going ('Believe me, the world is full of hearts which trust to love and are capable of preserving all beautiful things') having overcome his bitterness. And yet there remains the suspicion that Kilyubatra represents the powers: she does not destroy him but by her wiles, as seen from this uncharitable angle, she contrives to divert him from the course he had charted in order to unleash his individual assault on those who possessed and misused the atom.

Like <u>Death Game</u>, <u>The Thorns of Peace</u> has a cheerful conclusion. It has more to it than its predecessor and, as a consequence, is less single-minded in its treatment of peace than at least the first four acts of <u>Death Game</u>, whose assertion that love can solve international problems seems a rather silly spectacle. The matter in hand is introduced as two young friends in the Egyptian Diplomatic Service bewail the lack of that concord which everyone longs for, and discuss a submission they are to make at a UN conference in Geneva. They are doubtful about the value of conferences but determined that this one, presumably on the subject of disarmament or a test-ban treaty, will achieve something. In the second scene of Act Two the diplomat cast in the role of hero excites the euphoria of delegates, and attendant journalists, by having his proposal, endorsed by every nation present, considered to be a victory for goodwill on earth and a turning-point in history - somewhat ingenuously and improbably, it eventuates: all have overlooked the absence on the day of the two Great Powers. Pressed by the journalists, the diplomat says that the peoples of the world wanted the conference to succeed, for 'all peoples desire progress along the road to peace;' he mentions a theme which was henceforth greatly to preoccupy Hakim ('Is it not extraordinary that man should travel in space towards the moon while not travelling towards harmony on earth?') and in his state of rapture declares that now the second target will be reached before the first. Speedily his hopes are dashed for, in the event, the two Powers decline to support the motion. The diplomat tells the journalists that ' ... thorns have been scattered on the path to peace ... The peoples love each other and act peacefully towards each other while their leaders scheme and prepare.'

Marching with the diplomatic activity have been the hero's difficult fiancailles, which mirror the international problems the play is about. They come right in the end, just as, in this optimistic work, Hakim intends us to be convinced that the world will sort itself out to the advantage of all: love is the key to peace, and the last scene shows the couple, about to be married, making ready to set off for Geneva to labour hand in hand for international harmony. This sentimental and idealistic conclusion, taken in conjunction with other aspects of the play, confirms what has been clear throughout - that if The Thorns of Peace was a serious attempt to tackle a subject of urgent gravity, it failed badly because of its inappropriate lightness of tone and touch. It does, however, have the merit of being unadulterated by flippancy, unlike an unaccountable episode in My Donkey Said to Me [25] which treats the post-Second World War settlement as a matter for repelling levity.

In Journey into the Future Hakim demonstrates the consequences of putting the exploration of space before the establishing of a contented earth. The journey - not, admittedly, to the moon - is a futile exercize which separates gloomy views of the contemporary world and of the world of the future. It is true that during the long absence of the spacemen earth has outlawed war, but it has not learned to be happy.

That, in these three plays of 1957, Hakim was genuinely anxious about the future of the globe is proved by the very fact that he published them consecutively; by the earlier impetus lent them in Show me Allah[26] and The Literary Art,[27] in which he respectively attacked the honour accorded the inventors of the bomb and expressed his fervent wish that writers and thinkers would try to bring peace to the earth by joining together to influence the UN; and by the appearance in 1958 of an article which is reported to have been summarizable thus:

> 'TAUFIK EL-HAKIM CALLS UPON WRITERS TO PREVENT THE DESTRUCTION OF THE WORLD. The well-known Egyptian author and dramatist, Taufik el-Hakim, published an article in the Egyptian paper Al-Akhbar in which he calls upon the writers of the world to prevent the destruction of the planet we live on. The statement says: "After the dispatch of the artificial satellite a new era in the life of our world began. This world is only one of many in the universe to which man aspires. Our fate and the fate of our culture are in the hands of politicians of varying beliefs, who are likely to bury us and the heritage of generations with a snap of their fingers. Only the writers of the world can correctly assess the importance of preventing this catastrophe."'[28]

This appeal was the Ivory Tower in action.

In The Sultan's Dilemma, Hakim persevered with his campaign, now employing a didactic tone hitherto absent. He asks in his preface, 'Is the solution of the world's problems to be had by recourse to the sword or to the law ... to force or to principle?' and adds, 'Those who hold power - and theirs is the deciding of the fate of the human race - have in their right hands the atom or hydrogen bomb and in their left the law and principles, on one side rocket bases and on the other the United Nations ...' In causing the Sultan to submit good-humouredly to the law's demands rather than get his way by violence, he challenged earth's contemporary and future kings and presidents to emulate that example.

During his UNESCO tour he drew up a document,[29] notable for the extreme vagueness of its details and in the event not tabled, which proposed that that body set up a Peace Plan Office. The ideas it contained had already been hinted at in The Thorns of Peace, and they are expanded upon in Food for Every Mouth, a work of much less restricted scope than The Sultan's Dilemma and one painted on a larger canvas. Its hunger theme

- not its most memorable feature - is developed through the wall-play, one of the three participants in which - Tariq, a collaborator at Zurich University on a project to eliminate hunger from the earth and the immediate descendant of the chemist in The Angel's Prayer - is completely dominated by a determination to provide every human mouth with food. The project has been demonstrated to be theoretically feasible and capable of guaranteeing mankind enough to eat, adequate clothing, housing, and protection from exploitation. Its practical application is, however, quite another matter, for its implementation requires that all the nations stand shoulder to shoulder, adamant that it shall succeed. Of this there is no sign, for 'those who are concerned to have power over people and peoples do not regard the eradication of hunger as convenient to themselves. Hunger is their weapon of economic domination and they choose to devote their efforts and wealth to the improvement of weapons of destruction which spread hunger wider.' Tariq and his professor can only wait, in the hope that the world's conscience will awaken and allow their plan to be put into operation. Though Tariq naturally realizes its urgency, they seemingly have no thoughts at all of possible positive steps they might take to win international acceptance for it.

With the collapse of the wall's topcoat, the project becomes a symbolic pile of rubbish, whose only legacy is the consuming preoccupation with science it has provoked in Hamdi; his new and untutored interest is encouraged by considerable, willing sacrifices on the part of Samira. He is now working on Tariq's plan, of which no details were given, and dreaming the dream which may lead to its fulfilment:

Hamdi: In the past the idea of travelling to the moon didn't enter people's heads. But they used to gaze at the moon and dream about it and long for it, and imagine and picture it in their minds ...

Samira: Until the dream became reality ...

Hamdi: That's right. Every day there's something in the papers about the moon and spacecraft.

Samira: The dream has turned into reality, hasn't it? Dream and reality are linked, indeed there may be nothing at all dividing them. The transition between them is very ordinary, perhaps one single thing ... There will be no hunger. The word 'hunger' will disappear, and when children in the future hear it they will ask their mothers, 'What does this word mean?'

Atiyat: This is all very strange ...

Samira: No stranger than moon travel.

Atiyat: But there's nothing about this in the papers. No one's told me about a kilo of meat for half a mallim or for nothing ... Not today, and not in a hundred years.

Hamdi: There's the difficulty.

Atiyat: What difficulty?

Hamdi: People haven't dreamed this dream yet with the intensity with which they used to dream in the past about reaching the moon.

Samira: Why, Hamdi? Is the human race like a child which thinks first and foremost about playing and only then about eating?

Hamdi: Why don't you say that those who do the thinking for the human race and bear its burdens have never been hungry or realized that others were?

Samira: In any case, what you said just now is true, Hamdi. The miracle of travelling to the moon or to Mars stirs the imagination of people more than the miracle of getting rid of hunger.

Hamdi: Even though getting rid of hunger means the abolition of slavery from the earth. The slavery of individuals, the slavery of nations. Food is freedom.

Hamdi has no pretensions to scientific ability, but sees himself and the book he is now writing as paving the way for 'good' scientists, as distinct from those devoted to the sophistication of nuclear weaponry, who 'must find the whole world prepared to co-operate with (them). The whole world must have its imagination aflame and have lived this dream with its full strength.' Hakim is under no illusions with regard to the concomitant necessity for radical changes in the relations of the Great Powers, but views it as his duty to speak for the ordinary man, who is bewildered by their actions as they comport themselves childishly and evilly while the rest of the world impotently protests, and, by his dreams, to blaze the trail for the specialist qualified, unlike himself, to solve the problem he has stated; he identifies for himself, however, no role vis-a-vis political decision-makers. There can be no doubt that he is sincere, if out of his depth: the project is not even adumbrated and Tariq - an impractical and insufferably patronising young man - is an unconvincing participant in a scheme which is nothing if not idealistic. Hakim is also realistic, expecting his plea that the outlawing of hunger be given priority over the race to the moon, along with his many others against the non-peaceful use of the atom, to go unheard, as it has. Atiyat, bored in her final appearance by Hamdi's obsession with something she cannot grasp (like Asakir in Death Song), takes herself off to make herself a meal - 'I only had a ful sandwich for lunch' - and Samira, less pointedly, soon loses her enthusiasm for her husband's venture and is at the end almost totally engrossed by the prospect of the happy married life ahead of her.

In his most recent thinking Hakim has not deviated from his serious approach. In an imaginary interview with an American journalist[30] he said that 'a mission of peace in the hand of a powerful state is the best constructive solution for every problem', and caused his interlocutor to invite him to visit the USA in order to persuade its rulers at the highest level of the truth of this - one the journalist had already been convinced of; in This Comic World he urged mankind to unite against the testing and stock-piling of nuclear arms.

He has been accused, particularly by Muhammad Mandur, of trusting to such an extent in the potential of science as to render his philosophical view of man unpardonably negative: man is entirely dependent on its progress, therefore he can be nothing without it. This judgement is clearly most unfair, and especially so when Rejuvenation, for example, is quoted as proof of it. Although Hakim has at times, as in Food for Every Mouth, leapt at scientists as the saviours of the world, for the most part he has been careful to differentiate between the good and the bad ones, and to express extreme apprehension about what science could have in store for man. In his afterthought on Solomon the Wise he was insistent that the jinni had to be chained if it was to serve, rather than annihilate, mankind: nowhere does he suggest that the future of the human race should be handed over to science.

The total absence of hatred in his dramatic and non-dramatic writing on international affairs is remarkable: there is not a hint anywhere of detestation of Israel or its friends; his commitment to peace, leaving no room for petty rancour, is absolute. If he is without hate, he certainly sets much store by love as an ingredient contributory to the resolution of the questions he raises, which it is patent that he has done with breathtaking naivete. In the process he has composed only one play dominated by this object which will survive, and that, of course, is The Sultan's Dilemma.

REFERENCES

1 Mandur 2, p 10
2 Winder, p 11
3 SD, p 119
4 Winder, pp 23-6
5 The Tree of Ruling, pp 21-2
6 Ibid, pp 80-2
7 FTIT, pp 203-4
8 ARD, pp 66-7
9 An article of 11 September, reprinted in Reflections on Politics, pp 129 ff
10 Another instance is to be found in Al Hakim's Stick, pp 167-8
11 AW, p 23
12 FTIT, pp 82-4
13 Winder, p 23
14 p 21
15 Winder, p 14. (This is not in the Arabic editions.)
16 Ibid, p 12
17 Ibid, p 21
18 p 94
19 pp 85-9
20 25 September 1970
21 pp 52-8
22 pp 261-3
23 pp 187-90
24 p 20
25 pp 52-8
26 pp 165-70
27 pp 261-3. See also LL, pp 47-9
28 NO 1, 7 (February 1958), p 59
29 See an appendix to Food for Every Mouth, pp 186-91
30 In Al Ahram, 25 September 1970

PART THREE

Background and Assessment

with
Donkey
and
Stick

Background and Assessment

> Apart from a few dramatists in Scandinavia and France, there was less attempt to imitate (Ibsen) than is sometimes supposed. Like Shakespeare, he affected his contemporaries by the stimulus and inspiration of his example, not by the conventions which found schools.
> (Una Ellis-Fermor)

> English poetry made its first appearance already fully-formed in Chaucer; but the miracle of Chaucer is less than the miracle of Herodotus, for the English poet was heir to the long tradition of European poetry, but Herodotus the prose-writer had no predecessors ... He was the first Greek, the first European, to use prose as the medium of a work of art. His mastery of the new medium is one measure of his genius.
> (Aubrey de Selincourt)

It is to be hoped that some day Tawfiq al Hakim's achievements as novelist, short story writer (he is a very fine one), composer of one act plays, essayist and philosopher - he is no poet[1] - will receive detailed attention in English. The sheer size of his output, which allegedly is only forty per cent of what he has actually transmitted to paper,[2] censorship still accounting for some of the shortfall,[3] makes it necessary for an introductory book about him to concentrate, while glancing at his activities in other fields where this is relevant, on just one of the genres in which he has attained distinction. That selected here, the extended drama, includes twelve plays - The Cavemen, Shahrazad, Praksa, Pigmalyun, Solomon the Wise, Rejuvenation, Journey into the Future, The Sultan's Dilemma, The Tree Climber, Food for Every Mouth, A Train Journey and Fate of a Cockroach - which are worthy of international regard, whether in print or on the stage. (This should not seem an exaggerated claim when Appendix 3, which charts the success Hakim has already achieved abroad, is examined.) That many of the twelve have not been performed in Egypt is no contradiction, for it cannot be too often reiterated that his erudition, themes, methods and personality have decreed that he would rarely be able, or wish to try, to break box-office records at home. He has seldom earned acclaim in the theatres of Cairo without lowering his sights and standards or pretending to toe an ideological line, which is why plays not on the list above, such as Soft Hands, The Deal and Shams an Nahar, have added to his national reputation, while Praksa and Solomon the Wise have been withheld from the audience's gaze.

The Cavemen was so traumatic an affront to the young traditions of the Egyptian stage that it would probably have been impossible for Hakim to find even partial acceptance without the irruption of a new regime which sought to rethink all the attitudes of the one it dispossessed. (It could not stomach all his post-revolutionary repertoire, the magnificent A Train Journey being allowed to lie neglected.) Apart from The Cavemen, however, there were other factors in his disfavour before 1952. Among them were his 'ivory tower' reaction to his work's rejection, his character, his passive stance among his cultural brothers-in-arms, his misunderstood protest that some of his best plays were designed only for reading and his apparent lack of interest in their fate. Some of these applied equally after the revolution, but their effect was diminished by the changed circumstances it brought in its wake.

With his unsociability, self-centredness, self-pity, boastfulness, consuming anxiety and callousness, as well as his reputed miserliness,[4] Hakim does not impress as an attractive man. (Zaki has compared[5] him with Kafka, whose upbringing caused him to be by nature retiring, whose ill luck with women he attempted to disguise by professing hatred for them, who threw up the law to devote himself to art, who was regarded in exile, as Hakim felt himself in exile in Egypt in 1928, as an oddity and whose writings went largely uncomprehended.) His shyness is well-attested. In its most damaging form it is illustrated[*] by his failure to

---

[*] His refusal to accept an invitation to tea from Abd an Nasir does not

appear at a reception organized for him by Nadi al Qissa,[6] on 1 December 1958,[7] to celebrate the President's award to him of the republican chain, and his omission to attend any part of the Cairo University programme which honoured him in 1969 for half a century of dramatic endeavour. His excuse on the first occasion was a fear of involvement in formal events,[8] on the second - extracted by student criticism[9] - physical infirmity and the fact that he no longer went out at night.[10] Though he was contrite and cross with himself for letting the students down,[11] it is the norm with him to erect all kinds of obstacles before those who wish to fete him or enter his presence.[12] Those who have admired him seem to have done so in the face of apparent reluctance or indifference on the part of one who will not participate in social and official functions ('I am not a man for gatherings'),[13] speak in public, venture into the foreground ('a bat dazzled by lights')[14] or receive visitors readily. He holds court in his favourite coffee-house but is not among the audience at his own premieres.[15]

In a letter to this author he displayed commendable modesty in putting the record straight about the production of Shahrazad in France, which had been incorrectly reported by Landau to have been by the Comedie Francaise. Such self-deprecation is typical (there are other examples in The Devil's Pact), but so is its reverse. His self-centredness was clearly shown by a letter in Life in Bud in which he devoted only three lines to the serious illness of Andre's wife before turning lengthily to his own concerns - an action which appears to have brought the correspondence to a sudden conclusion - and by the depression provoked in him, of all people, by a talk with Jules Romains about the latest volume of Les Hommes de Bonne Volonte because he 'does not like writers to speak about themselves and what they are writing'.[16] His self-pity is frequently paraded: A Rural Deputy's Diary rues 'my poor physique and frail constitution, and my sensitive psyche', and From the Ivory Tower states that he was created only for thought, not for love or life,[17] and that destiny has in general deprived him of the happiness which falls into the laps of others.[18] This is because it is the author's lot to enjoy only scraps of earthly pleasure. When a pretty waitress deigns to smile

---

footnote contd ...

quite fit here, for he had already lost faith in him when it came and was not, he said (in AW, pp 36-7), prepared to put himself in a position where he would be expected to utter favourable opinions of his host. Inhibition no doubt contributed, however, to his response.

at him he observes that 'We tribe of pitiable litterateurs are easily satisfied',[19] and later[20] maintains that this is as it should be for 'The contentment needful to us artists, for us to undertake great works, must be limited.' But few appreciate the misery of it all:

> 'Ah, if people knew how writers and intellectuals lived ... The difference between us and the rest ... is that we thinkers realize ... what [fate] has robbed us of and what we have lost. The rest do not ...[21] We produce, knowing that our products interest neither the rulers nor the ruled and that the fruits of our minds ... will be harvested by only a handful ... Authorship is simply martydom in this country ... I have often asked myself for whom I publish my books. The answer was: I do it only for the nine or ten writers who understand me because they endure the same pain ... But we go on ... like exiles in unexplored Siberia ... We are merely exiles in the uncharted regions of our thinking, which the populace does not appreciate.'[22]

Hakim has much to be proud of, but he has several times displayed quite remarkable arrogance, for example in the prefaces to Ash^Cab, Pigmalyun and King Oedipus, in Under the Green Lamp, where he brags about his claimed prophetic gifts,[23] and when, after dismissing Pasternak as an unworthy winner, he announced his candidature for the Nobel literature prize in the early 1960s.[24] (He withdrew it, after Sartre had rejected his in 1964, and said that he would only accept such an award from the UN.)[25] Vanity is also implicit in the titles Al Hakim's Donkey, Al Hakim's Stick and, in Arabic, Solomon the Wise who, like his creator, sports a walking-stick.*

In spite of his own undoubted spiritual suffering, he gives the impression that he can be cruel in his relationships, for example by his treatment of Sacha and his attitudes to Andre's worry over his wife, filial disturbances of his concentration (The Peaceful Nest), the baby donkey

---

* He declared in a communication of September 1933 to Taha Husayn, 'We are not issuing decrees in these hastily-written letters but raising questions and offering hypotheses which dedicated researchers will collect and gather together when the nation awakes' (IST, p 70) and in the introduction to A Variety of Theatre, 'I am trying ... to do in 30 years what has taken the theatre in the other languages about 2,000 ... ' These are statements of fact, not boastfulness.

of Al Hakim' Donkey and the unfortunate cockroach King. Nonetheless, he is a popular figure with the general public, who relish stories of his eccentricities of dress and behaviour. The national enthusiasm for his beret and stick, his cats and his frequenting of coffee houses has not, however, served to promote his plays; nor, it would appear, has the 'special circle' where Nagi observed[26] him living 'like a king'. One cannot be sure to whom, apart from Husayn, he was referring particularly, for Hakim has had plenty of friends. On the list are Mustafa Mumtaz, with whom he broke when, after his return from Paris, they disagreed about the right approach to the death throes of the theatre; Kamil al Khal^{c}i, Dawud Husni,[27] and Sayyid Darwish, the composers;[28] Ahmad as Sawi Muhammad;[29] Hilmi Bahgat Badawi, a fellow student before Paris and a flatmate in Giza who became Minister of Trade and Industry under the revolution and afterwards first head of the nationalized Suez Canal Company;[30] Dr Sa^{c}id, a devout but loose-living bacteriologist initially encountered in Paris;[31] Salama Musa;[32] Abd al Qadir al Mazini;[33] Rihani; Dr As Sanhuri;[34] Mahfuz, who is in many ways similar in character, sharing his predilections for privacy[35] on the one hand and for coffee-shops on the other,[36] his proneness to substitute memories for confidants,[37] and his reputation (which overlooks his 1953 offer to forgo a fee if it would help the theatre)[38] for avarice;[39] Fathi Ridwan;[40] Salah Tahir, the painter;[41] and, most prominent of all, Dr Husayn Fawzi, 'the Egyptian Sinbad' - ophthalmologist, (marine) biologist, connoisseur of music and, though a relatively lightweight literary figure, a verse dramatist and pioneer of the modern Arabic short story - who was his constant companion in Paris,[42] whose assistance over the details of his biography Adham acknowledged in his preface and to whom, over twenty if not nearly thirty years later, Shukri dedicated his Thawrat al-Mu^{c}tazil.

Not on the list is President Abd an Nasir, whose personality and his were, outwardly, intriguingly alike. The first two decades of their careers corresponded extraordinarily closely and both left home early, nurtured precocious and deep suspicions of politicians and parties,[43] trusted passionately in the ability of Egypt to amaze the world again and composed fiction. Unlikely to have been one of the unnamed intellectuals castigated by The Philosophy of the Revolution for their lack of practical political ideas,[44] Hakim of course recommended himself to the revolution with The Soul's Return, which so impressed Abd an Nasir, and with Plays of Social Life and The Thief; the speed of his acceptance by it was vertiginous and its allure effortless. (Mahfuz, by contrast, needed a very long time to adjust and never found himself positively in the favour of the President, as distinct from his subjects.) Though not friends, Hakim and Abd an Nasir were never overtly enemies: there is no evidence that the author's disappointment with the incredibly tolerant President led to his being thought the less of or displaced as Abd an Nasir's most highly regarded man of letters.

One absentee from the list stands out: with Mahmud Taymur, the Arab writer to have been most translated,[45] Hakim is not recorded as having had any direct contact at all. Hakim's relationship with Husayn, like that with Mahfuz, was erratic, and warmer on Husayn's side than on Hakim's.[46] The inability of Husayn, Taymur and Hakim, the trio who resurrected, and rediscovered the export potential of, Arabic literature, and Mahfuz of a later generation, to cement a firm alliance must have weakened the advance of modern Arabic writing, which Hakim himself did nothing to hasten by his fitful allegiance to the deliberations of the Cairo Arabic Language Academy.[47] How he and Husayn got off on the wrong foot is told in a chapter of the latter's Fusulun fi'l Adab wa'n Nuqd.[48]

Husayn had never heard of him when, in the early spring of 1933, two of the unknown playwright's friends brought him a complimentary copy of the limited edition of The Cavemen. He read it and composed the review which has been summarized earlier, making at least one insufferably paternalistic suggestion to Hakim, who let it pass, sent him his thanks and gratification and then emerged from the rif to express his appreciation in person. At the same time he 'threw all his literary things into my lap and asked me to be his guide and patron. I agreed gladly and happily to ... this.' An open correspondence between the two thereupon commenced in Ar Risala, in which they discussed questions such as the origins of Arab literature. Then Hakim grew more demanding and, anxious to leave the rif for good, requested Husayn to use his influence to secure him a vacant post in the Ministry of Education which he thought might suit him. Husayn, to whom the Ministry was at that period anathema, advised against his candidature for the position and proposed another job more appropriate for the needs of a creative artist. Shortly afterwards he volunteered to 'present (The Cavemen) to the people' and Hakim and his friends signified delight. But the public edition came out unadorned by the introduction he had spent some two weeks on and the critic was hurt. Hakim came to apologize and followed up with a letter in French which, abjectly repentant, said that he was determined to abandon all cultural activity if Husayn remained angry with him. Husayn telephoned him, calmed him down and thought that he had re-established their relations on a basis of trust. He was soon undeceived, however, for Hakim attacked him at a writers' meeting for announcing that he was considering broadening his critical field to include contemporary writing. Nonetheless Hakim and two companions turned up again one evening with drafts for him to vet, and he was forced (more callousness here) to plough through them until late in the night although much preoccupied by the illness of a house guest. Then he contributed an article on the drama in Egypt to Al Musawwar and had to endure the indignity of Hakim, furious because he felt that he had been misrepresented in it and particularly by a hint that his plays might not be suitable for the Egyptian stage, replying in the same journal with, according to Husayn, much twisting of facts. The climax came when the critic reviewed Shahrazad and Hakim jibbed at some of the advice publicly extended to him (not in the tactless manner of the review of The Cavemen) and some of the many flattering comments about him. He despatched Husayn a private riposte which the latter rated an unique masterpiece of impoliteness and stupidity. He said in it that, as he had told Husayn before, it was Al Jahiz and not he who invented the 'new' dramatic genre: ' ... I am therefore not an originator, but a traveller on a road the East has trodden before.' No contemporary critic had, he continued, the right to assert that a literary work would live; he was not so simple as to believe one who did, for only time could decide. He therefore rejected Husayn's prediction of immortality for The Cavemen and Shahrazad. Finally,

> ' ... I have not given permission to anyone to address me in patronising tones, for I do not require it and have known for a long time what I am about. I have spent the years revising what I have written before publishing or distributing it. Likewise I do not need a critic to dictate a reading-list for me, for I have known for a long time what to read. I do not imagine you to be unaware ... that I have not read less ancient and modern philosophy ... than you ... '

In conclusion, in an obvious allusion to Husayn's offer to revise The Cavemen, he asked him to answer his various points publicly rather than compel him to take on the task himself.

Husayn's narrative of the earliest contacts between them, compiled in reaction to the playwright's extraordinary rejoinder, is clever in parts and bitter and sarcastic throughout. He calls himself, in contrast to 'the learned man of letters', 'the humble critic' and, heightening the absurdity of this, at one stage declares, 'The likes of you [the reader] and I, and the betters of you and I may not make suggestions to the Ustaz or advise him, for the Ustaz is too great for a suggester to make suggestions to or for an adviser to advise, however sincere and loyal he may be.' At least twice he states that Hakim had never dared venture into print without seeking the counsel of his friends: 'He does not publish an article in Ar Risala until I have read and passed it'. He claims to believe that Hakim wrote his letter at the instigation of his superiors in the Ministry of Education, which he had joined, as Head of the Investigation Bureau, despite his urging, and accuses him of deliberately harming him and destroying their relationship. Before concluding by objecting to Hakim's prime ministerial tone and saying that he will not reply to any future criticism of him by the dramatist, he observes, unanswerably, that the dialogues of Al Jahiz and a play are two different phenomena and that 'The strangest thing in all this is that Tawfiq should reject the praise I have given him,' which he reiterates.

This open letter, it would appear, cleared the air between them. A second indicated that a change had occurred. It[49] started off in as mocking a fashion as its predecessor but ended after the manner heralded by his use of 'Tawfiq' in it and showed that both of them had been shaken by the episode. He begins by scorning his correspondent for never resting from art and accusing him of having crowned himself the Louis XIV of literature, but then exhorts him to persevere with the drama and inspire disciples, as he is capable of doing. (He incidentally backs his demand for the Institute of Dramatic Art, set up and closed down by the Ministry of Education, to be reopened.) He concludes by noting that he has been attacked for applauding him while ignorant of the modern theatre, declaring his intention to cease to be so in order that such charges may not be made again and refusing to retract his view of The Cavemen and Shahrazad. Sadly, however, if this letter healed the breach, it did not lead to a partnership. The Alpine holiday of 1936, which produced The Enchanted Palace, is the only recorded instance of real intimacy between the two, who came together on many subsequent occasions, chiefly for duty's sake and, largely because of Hakim's aloofness, without forging a bond of mutual trust and advantage.

Though Husayn's reservations about The Cavemen and Shahrazad have been vindicated, Hakim has every right to be resentful about the theatre's rejection of the former. But he loses himself sympathy by everlastingly protesting, in ambiguous language and without qualification, that it was not designed for the stage. He must have understood by now that Arab and non-Arab critics whose opinions count have recognized its excellence, and he should have realized long ago that to keep on about distinctions between plays for reading and those for acting, to think up all kinds of reasons why Arabic literature could not have taken <u>The Cavemen</u> unto itself in the mid-1930s, and to drag in the Greeks is a pointless exercize. Some of what he says is undeniable; but the unconvincing arguments, about the need to bring Arabic letters to accept the drama in book form without making the test of the stage obligatory, must invite the unjustified thought that the whole elaborate rationale is merely a defensive reflex against the largely depressing reception by producers and, if performed, by audiences of the <u>The Cavemen</u>, <u>Shahrazad</u>, <u>Pigmalyun</u>, <u>Solomon the Wise</u>, and <u>King Oedipus</u> quintet.

From this negativism other counter-productive actions have flowed. He has been content, since <u>The Cavemen</u>, to compose and then sit back, showing no concern for a particular work to succeed and consolidate or enhance his reputation at home or abroad. This surface nonchalance and his concomitant omission to promote himself through others have militated against a forceful and sustained entree into world literature. His attitude of 'take it or leave it', illustrated by his non-involvement in the preparation of his plays for the stage (in April 1971, he admitted[50] that he had not been to the theatre for many years, not even to attend performances of his own work), has prevented him from unbending, even though, without his help, his books are more widely read in the Arab world than those of any other Arab author who will pass the test of time, and though their penetration abroad, albeit ridiculously limited, must have pleased him:

> ' ... I have not tried to establish links ... with men of letters and artists whom I should have been in touch with, especially those who have written about me or produced (my plays) abroad. I was in Paris recently in close proximity to some of them and I did not converse with one of them ... I invariably shrink from any new contact and I do not easily open the door of my self at the first knock ... This malady has lost me many opportunities and pleasures in life and art. I work, but abstain from effort to make the work successful ... If success has come to me in life, much of it has descended upon me from ... unknown and unexpected [quarters] ... I have been invited to travel everywhere, and opportunities have been provided for me to see what I should have seen and to meet people I should have met. But my ability to miss opportunities is

greater than my ability to seize them ... Though one of the characters in my The Cavemen said, "Any life is a gift [worth having], the most valuable gift bestowed upon a created being is life," I myself have, sadly, been unable to take advantage of this gift as I should have done ... I shall die asking myself, "Why was I not better than I was?" and "What is this prison which has inhibited my being?".'[51]

Bound up in his own sense of grievance, he has almost never, unlike Taymur and Husayn,[52] offered encouragement in print, except in the most general terms, to his fellow-workers or said anything about writers contemporary with him or of a younger generation;* he has only once acknowledged a debt to precursors, Egyptian or foreign, who may have influenced and assisted him. Not only had he no Arab predecessors (Mandur[53] suggests Farah Antun and Ibrahim Ramzi, and Al Hakim's Stick[54] displays deep admiration for Ar Rihani, but these can in no real sense be accounted precursors) but, despite his greatness, he has set up no Arab school.[55] It is the well-documented, surprising and melancholy case that his plays have had nothing like the effect on the outlook and methods of Egyptian dramatists of a younger generation that his fiction has had on later novelists. Only Alfrid Farag,[56] Nu^{c}man Ashur,[57] Mahfuz,[58] who only began to try his hand as a playwright comparatively recently, and Fathi Ridwan (to these names Shukri[59] adds that of Adil Kamil) have confessed that his example has guided them. The fact is that most of the post-Hakim dramatists - among whom, in addition to those mentioned, Yusuf Idris, Lutfi al Khawli, Mikha^{c}il Ruman and Mahmud as Sa^{c}adani stand out - are perhaps more natural heirs to Ar Rihani and Yusuf Wahbi than to him,[60] and thus have emulated him to only a limited extent. A pointer to attitudes is afforded by Mustafa Mumtaz, who in 1941 made it plain that he gave his recognition to none of Hakim's non-musical work.[61] While most Egyptian playwrights who are his juniors in years have initially been fired by him, and revere him,[62] only Farag[63] and, less certainly, Ridwan (who, like him, has been inspired by Pirandello and exhibits a similar concern for the freedom of the individual)[64]

---

* See LL, pp 143-7, for his views on Mahfuz and, especially, Ihsan Abd al Quddus, and TAY, p 64, for his confidence in the former, 'the Columbus of the Arab novel', as the standard-bearer of the novel and short story and in Sa^{c}ad ad Din Wahba, Farag, Yusuf Idris, Lutfi al Khawli, Rashad Rushdi, Nu^{c}man Ashur and the late Mikha^{c}il Ruman as the new generation of dramatists.

are to any degree his disciples: when Fu'ad Dawara said to Ridwan in an interview, 'I believe that your plays are almost the only extension in our literature of the intellectual theatre in which Al Hakim has excelled,' the gist of his reply was that the resemblances between them were only of the most superficial kind.[56]

Hakim's plays, not known to have influenced any non-Arab writer, are more European than Arab, which goes far to explain his reverses at home; that they are in Arabic has hampered their progress in Europe. On the whole one can only guess who the European dramatists were on whom he modelled himself. (In particular cases, of course, his indebtedness is clear, as to Ionesco in The Tree Climber.) The only clues, and they are not necessarily reliable, are the frequency with which he refers to foreign playwrights and the guesses of his commentators. His non-dramatic work continually mentions Sophocles and the three, in his view,[66] incomparable weavers of dialogue (Shakespeare, for whom his regard is high on many counts,[67] Moliere and Goethe, 'the complete, comprehensive genius'[68] and, like Shakespeare, a true playwright because he does not require a stage to make his impact),[69] Ibsen and Shaw far less, Pirandello and Maeterlinck occasionally, and Aeschylus, Euripides, Lope de Vega, Marlowe, Corneille, Scarron, Racine, Voltaire, Wilde and Brecht once or twice. In connection with the early plays he stresses the importance of the ancient Greeks to his conception of the modern Arab theatre; and Beethoven, 'the Aristotle of music',[70] Stravinsky and Mozart seem to have been significant sources of inspiration, as has been noted. All that can be stated with certainty, however, is that the influence of the pioneers of the Arab theatre on him after his juvenilia was complete was minimal and that Al Jahiz (of whose ninth century movement of renewal he sees modern Arabic literature as a continuation),[71] the Greeks and the plays he read or watched in Paris in the 1920s form the background to his work. Adham speculates[72] that Ibsen, Pirandello and Maeterlinck were the chief contributors to his characterization; Astre[73] believes that the symbolism of the last underlies the quintet; and Monteil[74] wonders about Camus and Lenormand. Hakim has only twice confirmed or rebutted the theories. In the preface to The Tree Climber he claims that it was his acquaintance with Pirandello, Ibsen and Shaw which led indirectly and selectively to The Cavemen, Shahrazad and Solomon the Wise, and traces his first Irrationalist play back to such sources as one would expect. About Shahrazad, and with the air of a man who is repeating for the umpteenth time something long settled, he lets slip the following:

'I wrote Shahrazad some thirty years ago and returned from Paris steeped in foreign cultures and sincerely believing that I had been influenced in it by the Englishman [sic] Oscar Wilde, the Norwegian Ibsen and the Belgian Maeterlinck. The years passed and the play was translated into several [sic] European languages and performed by great actors in London and Paris. I read the reviews in The Times, Le Monde and Le Figaro, and was amazed and astonished: not a single critic in London or Paris pointed to any connection between the play and the sources from which I believed that I had drawn inspiration.'[75]

There are obvious similarities between The Cavemen and Alladine et Palomides and, in atmosphere, between Shahrazad and La Princesse Maleine, but if Maeterlinck (who, like himself and Shaw, was profoundly influenced by music and at the outset of his career contemplated the stage with exactly the misgiving Hakim was to have forty years later) was his major inspirer Hakim has kept very quiet about it. It is both suspicious and indicative that in his lament for Lugne-Poë he should not have alluded to the producer's discovery of the Belgian.

If Hakim has left us in almost total doubt about the effects on his development of the example of others, he has not been backward in identifying the heritage within him which, he contends, has directed all other influences upon him. Though his Arab affiliations have asserted themselves from time to time, most forcibly during a short period which began on the eve of the revolution and lasted until he became antipathetic towards Abd an Nasir and concomitantly towards his pan-Arabism, Ancient Egypt and his conception of himself as an Egyptian first and only secondarily an Arab (he is not recorded as having visited any Arab country apart from his own, though incidental references to some of the others are occasionally to be found in his pages) have been central to his outlook. He advances from this personal starting-point to strive on paper, as he never did in real life, to gain recognition for his plays, within one familiar framework or another, by endeavouring to persuade his readers of the compatibility first of the civilizations of Egypt and the Arabs and of Egypt and Greece, and then of the East and the West and of the Arabs and Greece (and Rome). One must have every sympathy with him in this quest. Life cannot be easy for a writer in a minority language who is rightly confident that he has something to contribute to world literature, and especially not when the qualities of his race, on the 'wrong' side in a political confrontation which arouses highly-charged emotions, are stifled beneath a conspiracy of silence or falsified by propaganda.

His most comprehensive statement of where he stood and why, and of what the consequences were for his work, is, though confused, the most important of the many attempts made to demarcate an Egyptian cultural character completely distinct from those of the other Arabic-speaking countries.[76] It occurs in a letter[77] to Husayn (who disagreed with most of it)[78] of May 1933, the month of the publication of The Cavemen. He declares that the Egyptian and Arab civilizations are totally different, the former having evolved from that of India and, like it, being founded on the spirit, the soul, the heart and 'tranquillity', and the latter, while not actually having descended from the Greek, closely resembling the material nature, concentration on this life, intellect, 'humanness' and 'action' of that civilization. (The interest of these opinions is blunted because, as Husayn pointed out, he did not explain in any depth what he meant by Indian civilization or what he believed its legacy to Egypt to have consisted in.) Egyptian civilization, unaffected by Judaism, Christianity or Islam,[79] had, even if weakened by the Mughals,[80] survived intact, but the time had come to define it, disentangle it from Arab civilization and then contrive the reunion of the two as equals:

> 'What is the spirit of Egypt? What is Egypt? Our involvement with the Arab spirit has made us almost forget that we have a spirit of our own which is beating weakly beneath the weight of that other, rich spirit. Our first duty is to distinguish the one element from the other so that ... we may take the best from each of them ... It is absurd of us to see in the entire Arab civilization any inclination towards the things of the soul and of thought in the sense in which Egypt and India understood the two words ... There is no doubt in my mind that Egypt and the Arabs are diametrically different ... two sides of a dirham and two [separate] components of existence. What a great culture could come from [their] fusion ... I wish this development for modern Egyptian culture - a marriage of the spirit and the material, of tranquillity and action, of stability and anxiety, and of architecture and decoration. These are sources of an all-inclusive [code of] thought and of a harmonious civilization the like of which mankind has never known.'

Hakim discusses the civilization of Greece, a prototype of the union of Dionysius and Apollo he wished to see bind Egypt and the Arabs, but finds it on this occasion unsatisfactory because transitory, for Aristotle had split the amalgam asunder. He therefore suggests to Egypt that she and the Arabs reconsummate the spiritual-material marriage the Greeks were unable to sustain.

He revealed elsewhere[81] the long-term object of any betrothal plans ('I want the strengthening of Eastern culture as a whole and work done to lift it up so that it can stand, strong and rich, beside Western civilization') and a little later[82] exhorted his potential Arab partners to espouse it: Eastern culture had lost contact with European civilization, which he regards as the finest the world has experienced, and it was vital for it to regain it without, however, diluting its Eastern character:

> ' ... I should like to say to Arab men of letters, "Have no fear of European garments clothing your thoughts, provided that the stamp and spirit of those thoughts are pure Eastern and that the European reader feels from your works that he has before him a soul different from his and a personality different from his own even if its attire is not strange to him. The attire is no one's property: it is the property of civilization, and civilization is the child of the civilizations which preceded it."'

The reasons for his conviction that it was essential for the East not to fall further behind are given in A Sparrow from the East:[83]

> 'In spite of everything, Muhsin saw the West not as something to reject but something to incorporate. "Stripped of its arrogance," he thought to himself, "and of its sense of superior self-sufficiency, Western civilization could be the base out of which will emerge Universal Civilization. This Civilization of Man, whose location on the surface of the globe will be immaterial, will contain all that is beautiful, useful and usable in the West and in the East. After all, East and West are really only two sides of a single coin that in itself is whole. If these two civilizations could once be united into such a total civilization, man would see the dawn of true peace. But to reach that goal ... it must do ... all in a spirit of modesty, of charity and of love." It was with this hope that the young Egyptian looked to the West and to its future, which simultaneously represented for him the future of the whole of humanity.'

Having expressed his hankering to construct, with his Arab brethren, an Eastern culture which could advance arm in arm with that of the Occident, Hakim paused to consider his position. In the preface to Ash^{c}ab he asked himself why Arabic literature, so akin to the Greek according to him, had failed to take root in Europe:

> 'Ancient Arabic literature is among the most deep-rooted of literatures, and among the most skilful of them at characterization and personality-portrayal. This is not to be wondered at, for this literature sprang from a clever, creative civilization. The extraordinary thing is that most of its heritage and treasures should have remained far out of reach of the Western world which drank from the spring of the Greeks and the Romans.'

He did not attempt to answer the question but proceeded instead, in In the Spotlight of Thought,[84] to ponder the possible advantages of a rapprochement, excluding the Arabs whose thrust had been found wanting, between Egypt and Greece. In its favour was the fact that in at least one sphere they had already met:[85] the attainments of the latter in the field of tragedy fostered by the former. It should be possible, therefore, for them to co-operate again. Three years later, having flirted with the Greeks in Praksa I, he dedicated a rhapsody to them.[86] Rating 'today's modern civilization' as 'the second day after the first, Greek day' - it is unfortunate that this judgement is delivered shortly after a passage in which he affirmed that the second and last great age was that of the early years of Islam, the Greeks retaining first place - he continued:

> 'In the history of mankind there is one small, brilliant era which is truly one of the glories of man. That is the Greek age ... The miracle of the Greeks ... is that they strove to free themselves, for the first time in the history of mankind, from the pull of the past. To speak of the Greeks is to speak of the age of the appearance of free thinking and pure contemplation, i.e. thought uninhibited by traditions, authorities, religions, or even old languages ... They (were) freedom's chosen people ... Human intelligence reached the perfection of its radiance in the Greek epoch because it was exposed to the air of doubt. Doubt is the air of the intellect which enables it to breathe. For the first time man was really able to allow this air to play about the toes of the corpse of his sacred traditions ... and to remove his thinking a little from the scope of the influence of the past, to contemplate and create.'

It is after Pigmalyun, in the preface to King Oedipus, that Hakim shifts his Egyptian cargo in order, for political, not literary, reasons, to speak as an Arab. He opines that Arabic literature's omission to maintain touch with the Greek had militated against the erection of a solidly-based drama and its inclusion among genres admissible to membership of Arabic art, thought and culture. He accordingly called for a reconciliation between the Arabic and Greek literatures.* The time for translation had passed, for it would not serve to fill the current need. What was required was for Greek tragedy to be looked at through Arab eyes as, to some extent successfully, it had been viewed through those of Corneille and Racine, and for Greek subject-matter, characters and events to be reworked by Arab minds. Only thus would the marriage, vital for the future of Arabic literature in Europe, of the spirits and the tragedy of the Arabs and of Greece be brought about, and he could do much to arrange it. He claimed that his being an 'Arab Easterner' and his retention of a strong faith had qualified him to grasp - as, by implication, no one else since the Greek age had been equipped to do - the essence of Greek tragedy, which he now analysed as a religious one: man was 'not alone in existence', his destiny was determined by forces greater than, and above, himself. He had sought to capture this essence in The Cavemen, a tangible contribution to the desired cultural reunion; he believed that he had prepared the way even more by overshadowing Sophocles in King Oedipus. (One may, with justice, query this thesis - it emboldened him to mock the efforts of, for example, Voltaire while allowing Corneille and Racine just to pass muster - and, yet more, the sincerity of it as expounded in the preface to King Oedipus and less protractedly elsewhere. The thesis, oft-reiterated, is invariably accompanied by excuses for the meagreness of the popular appeal of his tragedies.)

In The Literary Art [87] he implicitly admits that King Oedipus had not done what he had claimed for it. In reaction, he rounded on the Arabs. He berates them for cutting themselves off from the heritage of Greece and Rome and isolating themselves intellectually from modern Europe as a result. Their forebears had contented themselves with being only selective transmitters of Greek thought:

---

* In his view it was not the paganism of the Greek drama but their non-comprehension of it which led the Abbasid and Fatimid translators to neglect to pass it on. They considered the Arabs the supreme poets and therefore did not look closely at Greek poetic tragedy and, presuming that it was not meant to be read, had no incentive to translate and adapt it for the theatres they did not possess. This is in part an accurate assessment, in part special pleading, for they should have known that drama did not require a stage!

> 'If they had translated and made contact with all [aspects of] the cultures of the Greeks and the Romans and mastered all their arts without skimping a single facet or ignoring any branch, an amazing thing would have happened today: Arab civilization would now be the immediate basis of all the present cultures of the Westerners and would have taken the place among them of Latin culture ... If this had happened - and would that it had - European civilization today would be more splendid and more profound than it is.'

These wild and unsubstantiable statements come near to resembling the tenor of those of Ivanovitch in A Sparrow from the East which, in the guise of Muhsin, he had felt impelled radically to modify.

By 1966, again on account of political promptings, the Arabs had been forgotten and Ancient Egypt had resumed her position of paramountcy. Hakim had fewer reservations than in 1933:

> 'My conception of the [tragic] struggle is more akin to ... the Greek [than to Shakespeare] for it is not connected with moeurs or personality. It is a metaphysical or philosophical struggle. I regard the struggle in my tragedies as a continuation of ancient Egyptian philosophy. I imagine that if the ancient Egyptians had had the theatre they would have constructed tragedy on the same idea as me. The Greeks wrestled with fate, the Egyptians with time or the loss of the self.'

Although they recognized that they would die and conceived of death as a natural happening, his forebears fought it with all their might. The doctor and the engineer in Journey into the Future, condemned to eternity on a planet where death did not exist, had thus become things, like the everlasting hills and oceans; no longer human because their term had ceased to be fixed, they had to return to earth in order to regain their character as men by resuming the feud against mortality.[88]

Hakim's vision of his place, and the place of his drama, within the cultures of the Egyptians, the Arabs and the wider world displays his mercurial nature as a theorist, tells us very little about the context of his achievements and does nothing to enhance them as he had hoped it would: Arabic and its script have proved to be too formidable a barrier to be deflected by his unconvincing glosses, remarkable for the extreme intellectualism and impracticality of their themes. They leave no room for doubt, however, about his faith in the indestructibility of the spirit of separate, different and immortal Egypt, a faith which occasionally leads him to maintain that nothing is done in art which was not accomplished aeons before by his ancestors.[89] It is not dulled by his brief Arab phase. In The Soul's Return [90] he likened Sa^{c}ad Zaghlul to Osiris, with all that that implied. In In the Spotlight of Thought [91] he said:

'I have always believed that Egypt cannot die, for Egypt has constantly worked and toiled for one aim for thousands of years - to fight death. Egypt has had her reward, for whenever death thought it had won, a Huris rose up from among her sons to cry, "Arise, O nation, arise. You have your heart, your ever true heart, your time-honoured heart." Then death retreats before a voice ringing out from the depths of the people: "I am alive. I am alive."'

In a 1948 article [92] he averred that 'the true soul of Egypt has not disappeared and will never be snuffed out. This is my faith which will not die. History will always eventually reappear and say, " ... the soul has returned."' In 1971 he referred to himself [93] as 'an Egyptian more than 5,000 years old' and thereby sealed his claim to be counted among the modern thinkers - At Tahtawi, Lutfi as Sayyid, Zaghlul and Husayn - who considered themselves direct descendants of the ancient Egyptians. As such, on a recent tour of the Aswan Dam, he could afford the expansive and brotherly gesture of announcing that Egypt's resources and achievements were the birthright of the Arabs as a whole [94] and, equally, could give expression to a call to Huris to prepare for another possible rescue journey at the time of the anti-poverty riots in five cities during the third week of January 1977. A cataclysm in Egypt, he wrote in Al Ahram,[95] would 'cause those who sit on wells of gold to sit on wells of fire'.

Tawfiq al Hakim, whose theatre was 'born in a vacuum' [96] and who is not 'a genuine representative of our stage',[97] was 'the true founder of Egyptian drama in every serious sense' [98] and 'swung our theatre into a new direction in kind and in quality, not merely in degree and level ... This was not a revolution against a heritage but the actual beginning of that heritage.' [99] More, he was the first pioneer of the dramatic art in Arabic [100] and 'No other dramatic writer in (Arabic) approaches him.' [101] 'The summit of dialogue writing in Arabic',[102] he was 'at least twenty years in advance of our artistic development' [103] and 'leaped above his time', unable to make contact with his audiences: 'Audiences could not leap with him.' [104] He brought to the theatre the respectability which it had seriously lacked before him [105] and was a mighty bridge between the two revolutions of 1919 and 1952,[106] reflecting in his work 'every intellectual and artistic current which has appeared in our life during the period from 1919 to today'.[107] Most astonishingly, this pioneer was in the world class:

> '... There rose in the sky of Arab literature a brilliant star ... Tawfiq al Hakim, who startled his time by a technique in the play and the novel which revealed a complete knowledge of (their) principles and sound construction ... originality of thought, depth of culture ... sophistication of treatment and analysis, a charming imagination and skill in the organization of dialogue. If we read his The Cavemen [and] Shahrazad ... with their artistic marvels of intellectual, social and literary worth, [we find that] they are not limited by narrow local bounds but can keep up with a standard worthy of remark in the market-place of world literature.'[108]

He is the only Egyptian to have 'created for us literary works which equal the greatest of what writers of the West have written'.[109]

These Arab assessments, which, out of deference to the blindness of Husayn and of still inadequate comprehension of the dramatic genre, misguidedly but representatively deny Hakim the title of the foremost modern Arab man of letters, are endorsed by most orientalists and others familiar with him, who have ventured opinions. Olga Kapeliuk refers to him[110] as 'the great Egyptian writer and playwright' and Von Grunebaum[111] as 'the outstanding dramatist of the Arab world'; Schoonover believes[112] that 'In a very large degree Tawfiq al-Hakim can be credited with the establishment of drama in Arabic literature,' Rubinacci[113] that he constructed 'per la prima volta nella storia della letteratura araba un teatro in prosa realmente originale' and Johnson-Davies[114] that he 'pioneered the dramatic form in Arabic writing'. In Miquel's phrase,[115] 'Tewfik, c'est le theatre majeur, sur de lui, et, comme tel, apte a tous les renouvellements': The Cavemen, Shahrazad, Pigmalyun and King Oedipus are 'Pieces intenses ... et d'une incontestable profondeur psychologique ... pieces revolutionaires dans le contexte des lettres arabes'. Landau[116] is impressed by the many-sidedness of his talent and admires his sparkling dialogue, the rapid pace of most of his plays and his enormous contribution to the improvement of Arab dramatic style. Cachia's view[117] is that ' ... Taufiq al Hakim has written a number of well-constructed plays, often with extremely ambitious themes.' Other critics there are who, rightly, go further. Papadopoulo comments[118] that the creator of the prose play in Arabic 'Perhaps ... is among the artistically greatest writers, not only in Egypt, not merely in Arabic literature, but in the literature of the entire world,' Kritzeck[119] that he has 'proved himself many, many times over as a master playwright', Vernet[120] that he is the one Arab dramatist of universal stature and Cowan[121] that his 'work deserves world acclaim'.

The judgements quoted in the foregoing paragraph are those of specialists and will not serve to place Hakim on the roll of the great playwrights, where he belongs. The orientalists cited cannot, however, all be wrong. It is high time that British Arabists introduced a play or two by Hakim into their university syllabuses, which usually suggest that he is only a novelist, and encouraged generalist critics to tell their readers (on the basis of the translations listed in Appendix 3) about him. They will not make the discovery of a flawless dramatist. He is very uneven, reality and the rule of law are the only themes in which he has excelled, his political pieces are on the whole poor theatre, in general the characterization has no depth (he has done little if anything with the 'outer shells' of Praksa, Pigmalyun and Oedipus), the rare organizational lapse jars,[122] his endings are often weak and the victories he ascribes to Egyptian technology or diplomacy are, despite the October War, occasionally irritating,[123] like some typical Egyptian comedy which does not appeal to Western taste. Withal, however, he remains the creator of a body of original and extraordinarily varied dramatic literature which must not be ignored. It has a larger sweep and less insularity than that of a Western author - of a minority tongue and culture, Hakim has had to keep abreast of events and developments in other tongues and cultures in a way no British playwright would see a need to - and deals with his major themes in an atmosphere and with dialogue which it would be hard to match, as a glance at the 1950 French translation of Shahrazad will show. It offers strong and engaging story-lines enwrapped in humour and wit of high quality. No Hakim play, however mediocre, is devoid of some feature of charm, and none is too exotic or esoteric for the British reader to appreciate. The man who has given all this to the world is of massive interest. He has something to say about everything, from his country's past to the Beatles, he is, as befits a constant and ambitious, if frequently unrealistic, virtuoso and experimenter, always open to fresh ideas, and the width of his learning is impressive. His midway position between Islam and Christianity - reminiscent of Synge's stance on Protestantism vis-a-vis Roman Catholicism and amply demonstrated in The Cavemen, in the Christ figures of The Angel's Prayer, Death Song and The Anxiety Bank, in much of his prose writing and by the absence of any greater emphasis on Islam - is that of a man who thinks in universal terms and therefore never stoops, as many might expect an

Arab to do, to propaganda.

Tawfiq al Hakim has not been produced at Baalbek, Egypt's information publications have never disseminated an accurate picture of him,[124] and the Arab critics, who so justly praise him, constantly complain that their literature is underdeveloped compared with that of the West. Arab knowledge of what he has done is as imperfect as that of the English-speaking world.

REFERENCES

1 Subur 2, p 25, Landau, p 146
2 TAY, p 134
3 AW, p 65
4 TAY, pp 65, 154, 184, Dawara 2, p 24. See Yusuf as Siba^{c}i's good-natured playlet on this trait in Mallakh, pp 85-8
5 Adib, May 1970, p 7
6 Dawara 2, p 39
7 Mallakh, p 315
8 Ibid, loc cit
9 Ibid, p 366
10 Ibid, p 369
11 Ibid, loc cit
12 See Faruq al Buqayli's experience, described in TAY, pp 48-67
13 AHD, p 143
14 Dawara 2, loc cit, quoting Hakim, Mallakh, p 316
15 Mallakh, p 315
16 Husayn, p 191
17 p 45
18 pp 66-70
19 The Devil's Pact, p 43, UGL, p 20
20 Ibid, p 47, ibid, p 25
21 FTIT, p 15
22 Ibid, pp 157-9
23 pp 201-17
24 Mallakh, p 329
25 Ibid, pp 355-6
26 Adham, p 216
27 TAY, pp 83-92. For Al Khal^{c}i see also LA, pp 55-7

Background and Assessment 199

28 LA, p 52. For Darwish see also TF, pp 18-27
29 IST, pp 133-41, Adham, p 188
30 Dawara 2, p 249, LP, pp 246-57, AW, p 56
31 Al Ahram, 13 August 1971; Journey Between Two Eras, pp 13-32, 54-6, 70-5, Mallakh, p 185-7
32 Mallakh, p 321
33 Ibid, p 288
34 AW, p 24
35 George N Sfeir, 'Najib Mahfuz: Writer with a Universal View', Baghdad News, 12 November 1965
36 Sabah al Khayr, 7 October 1971, p 25
37 Mallakh, pp 283-4
38 Landau, p 123, quoting an interview in Akhir Sa^{c}a of 21 October 1953
39 Mallakh, pp 13, 349
40 Dawara 2, pp 248-50
41 TAY, p 145
42 Al Ahram, 13 August 1971
43 Safran, p 135
44 p 33
45 Dawara 2, pp 49-50
46 Mallakh, pp 281-2
47 Ibid, p 281
48 pp 109-18
49 Ibid, pp 119-24
50 TAY, p 181
51 LP, pp 285-9
52 Dawara 2, p 50
53 Mandur 1, p 103
54 pp 65-6
55 Cf Adham, p 228, Awad, in Al Adab, November 1972, p 7, Farag, p 78
56 Farag, loc cit, Nada Tomiche, in UNESCO, p 120
57 MAG, March 1971, p 87
58 Sabah al Khayr, 7 October 1971, p 28, Dawara 2, p 282, Shukri, p 89
59 p 89
60 Subur 1, p 103, Awad, loc cit
61 FTIT, pp 146-7
62 See, e.g. Subur 1, pp 83-4, Farag, pp 78, 162, Aziz Abaza in

	Dawara 2, p 153
63	Awad, loc cit
64	Dawara 2, pp 255-9
65	Ibid, pp 249-50
66	TF, pp 113-4
67	Ibid, pp 130-5
68	LA, p 200
69	AHD, pp 156-7
70	LA, p 238
71	Preface to King Oedipus
72	p 131
73	Appendix to The Sultan's Dilemma, p 199
74	Anthologie Bilingue de la Litterature Arabe Contemporaine, Imprimerie Catholique, Beirut, 1961, p xvi
75	LL, p 182
76	Safran, pp 144-7
77	Much of it is reproduced in IST, pp 54-69
78	See Husayn, pp 91-101, and Mustaqbal ath Thaqafa fi Misr, chapters 2-6
79	IST, pp 108-9
80	LIB, p 168
81	IST, p 114
82	pp 115-6, 125
83	Winder, p 168
84	p 113, f.n.
85	See LIB, pp 88-9, for a failure to meet, in art
86	SD, pp 23-4
87	p 124
88	Farag, pp 166-8
89	See, e.g. LA, pp 35-8, 41, IST, pp 115-6
90	Volume 2, p 243
91	pp 208-9
92	Reproduced in Reflections on Politics, p 133
93	Al Ahram, 13 August 1971. See also the preface to Fate of a Cockroach
94	Mallakh, p 374
95	Reported by David Hirst in The Guardian Weekly, 17 July 1977
96	Subur 1, p 96
97	Ibid, p 101
98	Awad, in Vatikiotis, p 159

Background and Assessment

99   Shukri, p 19
100 Ibid, p 24, Ra^{c}i, in UNESCO, p 88
101 Nadir Salim, in AQ 1, 4, p 154
102 Mallakh, p 380
103 Subur 1, p 102
104 Ibid, p 96
105 Ra^{c}i, in UNESCO, p 89
106 Shukri, p 373, Galal al Ashari, in MAG, May 1971, p 45
107 Naqqash, p 60
108 Taymur, p 41
109 Dawara 1, p 322
110 In NO 1, 4, p 38
111 'Nationalism and Cultural Trends in the Arab Near East', in Studia Islamica 14, p 137
112 MW 45, 1, p 31
113 Introduction to his version of The Cavemen
114 Introduction to his version of The Tree Climber
115 La Litterature Arabe, p 115
116 pp 127-8
117 p 234
118 Appendix to The Sultan's Dilemma, pp 221, 234
119 Anthology of Islamic Literature, Pelican, London, 1964, p 97
120 Literatura Arabe, p 190
121 In Vatikiotis, p 163
122 As in Soft Hands, The Thorns of Peace, Journey into the Future and Food for Every Mouth.
123 There are examples in Rejuvenation, Death Song and Death Game
124 See, e.g. Prism Supplement II, Ministry of Culture, Cairo, 1970, p 6, which, at some length, makes The Soul's Return out to be a play

APPENDIX 1

The Egyptian Prose Theatre before Tawfiq al Hakim*

> The theatre of Tawfiq al Hakim was
> born in a void.
> (Salah Abd as Subur)

> Egyptian drama was born in its near-
> perfect form with The Cavemen and
> the subsequent works of Al Hakim.
> (Ghali Shukri)

The first modern Arabic prose play which was undeniably in accord with the traditions of the stage generally recognized by the world at large was Tawfiq al Hakim's The Cavemen. It dwarfed its few Arab predecessors, raised the standards of the Arab theatre to undreamed-of heights, and overnight introduced into the field a competitor to all playwrights everywhere.

Among the chroniclers of Arab literature there is little identity of view about the history of the theatre prior to this new dawn; of the prose drama as such they make little mention, perhaps reflecting the inconstant nature of its development. The Arabs appear to have conducted their

---

* The chief sources for this outline account of a large and complex subject are Landau and UNESCO (the contributions to Part 1 by Berque, Khaznadar and Ra^{c}i) for the period to 1847; Najm for 1847-1914; and Adham, Cachia, Subur 1 and Taymur.

earliest theatrical experiments with the shadow play, which reached them, in the twelfth and thirteenth centuries, from Java or, possibly via Mughal invaders, from China, but declined in vigour when the heart of the Arab world came under the Ottomans. The theatre did not get purposefully under weigh again until the beginning of the nineteenth century. The Napoleonic invasion of Egypt in 1798 provided the impetus, and Muhammad Ali, who assumed power in Cairo in 1807, increased the momentum of the Arab literary renaissance, the Nahda. During his long reign, which lasted until 1849, men like Shaykh Rifa^{c}a Badawi Rafi at Tahtawi were enriching the cultural soil of Egypt as the drama started to move forward on three fronts. The shadow play underwent a regeneration; the 'knockabout', which had its roots in it, sprang up in rural areas and spread to the large towns; and Italian, and to a lesser extent French, companies set about exhibiting samples of their contemporary drama in Cairo and Alexandria. The sturdiest developmental seeds, however, were planted in Greater Syria, where French and American missionary societies had actively assisted in the fostering of an intellectual rebirth in the Levant. In Beirut in late 1847, Marun an Naqqash (1817-55), a Maronite Christian who had chanced upon the theatre during a visit to Italy, wrote an Arabic verse adaptation of L'Avare (Al Bakhil) as the first play in the Western mould to be composed by an Arab; with the aid of his family, he performed it, as a musical, in his house. The venture was a success and fired him, in 1849-50, to put on the first original Arab drama, Abu'l Hasan al Mughaffal, aw Harun ar Rashid. It drew on Moliere and The Thousand and One Nights and depended less on music and verse than its predecessor had. The enthusiasm it evoked encouraged An Naqqash to obtain a firman to place his activities on a legal footing and open a 'theatre', in which in 1853 he presented his As Salit al Husud, a comic opera with linking dialogues which, dealing with contemporary social topics, was constructed of a mixture of verse and rhyming prose and again influenced by Moliere. On An Naqqash's premature death, the drama maintained its tenuous bridgehead through the efforts of the pioneer's nephew, Salim Khalil an Naqqash (died 1884), who established the earliest Arab repertory company, made up of both male and female players, and brought it to Egypt just as a theatrical infrastructure was being laid down there. In 1868 and 1869 respectively, the Khedive Isma^{c}il (1863-79) built the Marsah al Kumidi (Comedy Theatre) and the Khedivial Opera House in Cairo in preparation for the festivities to celebrate the inauguration of the operations of the Suez Canal. The first impresario to avail himself of these facilities was the interesting Egyptian Jew, the 'Molière egyptien', Ya^{c}ub b Rafa^{c}il Sanu^c (James Sanua, 1839-1912), who is at the head of a long line of actor-managers, most of whom fled from Lebanon as a result of the strife of 1860, whose careers tell the story of the drama in Egypt up to the First World War. The second was Salim an Naqqash who, a refugee, left behind him in Lebanon a theatre which continued to thrive at a repetitive and unambitious level. The others were Yusuf al Khayyat (died 1900), also an exile; Sulayman al Qardahi (died 1909), a Syrian who made actresses respectable, toured widely in Arab lands, particularly in the Maghrib, and participated in the 1891 international Paris drama festival; Ahmad Abu Khalil al Qabbani (?1840-1902), the erstwhile Marun an Naqqash of Syria; Iskandar Farah, another immigrant from Syria; the Egyptian singer Shaykh Salama Higazi (1852-1917) who, though he knew nothing of art and executed nothing of great merit,[1] is of enormous significance because he was the earliest Muslim man of the theatre and, by carrying his classical verse musicals to Lebanon, Syria and the Maghrib, blazed a trail for the drama in the Arab countries as no Christian could have done; and Aziz Id, a versatile Syrian. These figures are to be remembered as signposts on the path of progress rather than as writers, adapters, translators and producers of large numbers of plays, of which few are now worthy of notice, still fewer were either original or in prose and most were dependent for their popularity on the music which accompanied them.

The years between the British occupation of Egypt and the First World War saw a higher standard of living and improved education enlarge the circle of people who both wished and could afford to indulge in theatre-going. By 1914 the shadow play had become an upper-class vogue but had been driven off the stage proper into cafes and open places and was soon to be submerged by the cinema; the debt owed to it by Arab drama had been considerable.[2] The acted play, in verse and mostly in the shape of translated and adapted Italian and French historical tragedies and satirical comedies[3] accompanied by music, song and dance, had replaced it in the theatres; it was flourishing, and firmly embedding itself in the Arab scene. Original dramatists remained scarce. Only Nagib al Haddad (1867-99) and Ibrahim Ramzi (1884-1949), 'in the style of Corneille, Hugo, A. Dumas and Shakespeare'[4] and with music in the case of the former, had contrived, without markedly improving on him, to keep the flag raised by Marun an Naqqash flying. The irruption of the Great War brought to a close a preliminary phase, predominantly imitative in character, which had thrown up little that was both indigenous and worthwhile.

After the War* the Arab theatre began slowly to make the ascent towards the peak it was to scale in 1933. It was not a gradual climb, however, for Al Hakim's Everest was immeasurably higher than anything that had been attained before. His post-war predecessors, of whom he with his juvenilia was one, were instrumental in convincing the Arabs of their ability to write plays which would be as acceptable to audiences as the imported product, and in attracting spectators of all classes. The musical, the translated and adapted play in verse, and to a lesser degree in prose, and - making a real mark for the first time - the farce and the home-grown drama displayed tremendous vitality despite the ever-increasing competition of the cinema. Composers of original pieces rapidly asserted their authority over the adapters, and the stage achieved full acceptance, drawing to itself people, like the Taymurs, of good families. Three men dominated the period. Georges Abyad (1880-1959) was a Lebanese who had emigrated to Egypt in 1898 and been sent by the Khedive Abbas Hilmi to study in France, for a time under Sylvain, during the years 1904-10. He attempted initially to perform an exclusively European classical repertoire but later became the first man of the theatre to offer audiences a limited range of less directly derivative prose plays. His relevance to the study of Hakim is immediate. He eschewed the musical and the farce, but for both personal and financial reasons failed to seize the opportunity accessible to him to guide Egyptian taste towards the appreciation of a higher type of drama than it had been familiar with. To his great credit, however, was the encouragement of playwrights like Farah Antun (1874-1922), a Lebanese emigre whose best remembered piece is <u>Misr al Gadida wa Misr al Qadima</u>, and Ibrahim Ramzi, who penned historical works flavoured with much contemporary political allusion. Najm views this as the opening move towards the establishment of sound Arab drama, as without question it was. Abyad toured abroad much with his company and was active almost up to his death.

The champion of the musical melodrama and the play of social criticism in verse was his great rival Yusuf Wahbi, who is still alive. He studied in Italy under Chiantoni and in 1923 founded, with Aziz Id, the famous Ramsis troupe. For a time he teamed up in unlikely harness with Abyad but concentrated almost exclusively on dramas of his favoured kind, many of which he wrote, produced and starred in. Despite voci-

---

* Hakim's <u>Justice and Art</u>, pp 112-27, affords interesting sidelights on the early post-war period.

ferous audience approval of them, he could never make ends meet in the face of the radio and cinema competition which felled every prominent company except Ar Rihani's.[5] Retaining the live affection of his admirers, he moved up to more exalted regions in 1935 and there had a deleterious effect on the progress of the theatre, especially in the person of Hakim.

Nagib ar Rihani (1891-1949) was the most successful and best loved of the farceurs. The energetic Aziz Id was perhaps the first of them. Another in the same line of business was Ali al Kassar. Ar Rihani outshone all his challengers. A born comedian, he had his apprenticeship with Farah, Higazi, Abyad, Id and, in lowly roles during the First World War, with French exponents of the drama of the calibre of Sarah Bernhardt, who undertook frequent tours to Egypt. He modelled himself on the French vaudeville, creating in Kishkish Bey a satirical pundit who won most hearts. That the critics, like Husayn, considered him too lowbrow to be either respectable or an artist was of no importance, for the songs which were a feature of the often obscene and uproarious Ar Rihani show were ever on the lips of the people.

Of these three most powerful forces in the theatre between the War and 1933, the only one who may be said really to have failed is Abyad, the prose innovator. It is not without significance that, if he was remotely an heir to any of them, the post-Paris Hakim descended for him. He also inherited a legacy from Muhammad Taymur, Mahmud's actor, critic and writer brother whose life was cut sadly short in 1921 at the age of twenty-nine and whose prose pieces stand out as the only prominent landmark on the road separating Marun an Naqqash and Hakim. Gibb[6] regards him as the founder of the drama in Arabic, and Adham is of the opinion that, with him, the theatre for the first time reached European standards. His three attractive comedies, staged between 1918 and 1921, confronted the problems of everyday life with engaging realism. That they were in colloquial prose, which incidentally demonstrated that good plays had not necessarily to be in the classical, helped usefully to loosen the grip of the versifiers. Even Ahmad Shawqi (1868-1932), the 'prince of poets', followed Taymur's lead. He came late to the theatre and, when he did, wrote in verse until, in Amirat al Andalus, he felt prose to be more appropriate and thus assisted it in its recovery from the disproportionate neglect it had suffered.

When Hakim came home from France in 1928, Wahbi and Ar Rihani were in complete control of the Egyptian stage.[7] Seven years later, when The Cavemen was produced, the situation had only altered in that

Wahbi had taken charge of the National Company which performed it. (The government commendably having intervened to save the struggling theatre, it invited him to mastermind the rescue operation. The summons showed how highly his brand of drama was rated and did not inhibit him from carrying on much as before: by eroding the official guidelines he was able with impunity to offer the usual fare at home, in many other Arab countries and to the weighty Arab diaspora in South America.) With him in command, and Khalil Mutran (1872-1949), the famous poet of Lebanese extraction, as his deputy, The Cavemen could not have stood much chance. It turned an unimagined and exciting page nonetheless. With it, the Arab theatre - pioneered by Sanu^C, Abyad and Mikha^{C}il Nu^{C}aima (born 1889) according to Ar Ra^{C}i,[8] Najm, and Adham respectively, and founded by Higazi, Muhammad Taymur, and Hakim in the differing judgements of Najm, Gibb, and the author of this study - made the discovery of its first playwright of international stature, whose tragedy it is that he was born prematurely into the least developed component of that theatre, the original prose classic. It will be some time before the future path of Arab drama can be clearly descried. Wahbism and Rihanism remain strong, but if, as seems inevitable, they follow the shadow play into decline and the course of the theatre enters more universal channels, the work of Hakim, remarkable for its quality, will, with that of those to whom he has pointed the way, constitute a reservoir of lasting relevance and inspiration. It is to be hoped that ample demonstration has here been made that Tawfiq al Hakim himself had virtually nothing that was indigenous onto which to graft his own historic achievement.

REFERENCES

1   Muhammad Taymur, in Najm, pp 147-9
2   UNESCO, pp 48-9. Cf Berque, in ibid, pp 23-4
3   Ra^{C}i, in ibid, p 87
4   H A R Gibb, in 'Arabiyya' in the new edition of the Encyclopaedia of Islam
5   Sa^{C}ad ad Din Tawfiq, p 51
6   In loc cit
7   Subur 1, p 95
8   In UNESCO, pp 84-5

APPENDIX 2

The Plays of Tawfiq al Hakim

		Written	Published	Performed in Egypt
1	The Burdensome Guest	1918-9		
2	Modern Woman	1923	1952	1926
3	The Bridegroom	1924		1924
4	Solomon's Ring	1924		1924
5	The Suitor	1924		1924
6	Ali Baba	1925	1969 (part)	1926
7	Devant Son Guichet	1926	1937	
8	The Cavemen	1928	1933	1935, 1960 (?), 1964
9	Expulsion from Eden	1929	1937	
10	The Suicide's Secret	1929	1937	1937
11	A Life is Wrecked	1930	1937	
12	The Piper	1930	1934	
13	Shahrazad	1930	1934	1966
14	A Bullet in the Heart	1931	1937	
15	Muhammad	1934-5	1936	
	Plays of Tawfiq al Hakim: 7, 9, 10, 11, 12, 14 and			
16	The Gentle Sex	1935		1935
17	The River of Madness	1935		
18	A Journalistic Incident	1938	1952	1938
19-23	Playlets in 'The Tree of Ruling'		1938	
	Playlets in 'The Devil's Pact':		1938	
	24 Satan's Foe (Aduw Iblis)			
	25 'Twixt Dream and Reality			
26	Praksa I		1939	
27	The Angel's Prayer	1941	1941	
28	Pigmalyun	1942	1942	1963. Again?[1]
29	Solomon the Wise		1943	
30-4	Playlets in 'My Donkey Said to Me'	1945	1945	
35	Leave the Truth Alone (La Tabhathi an al Haqiqa)	1947	1956	

			Written	Published	Performed in Egypt
36		King Oedipus	1945-9	1949	
		Plays of Social Life:	1945-50	1950	
	37	The Anthill	1948		
	38	A Day's Work (Bayna Yawm wa Layla)	1946		
	39	Death Song	1950		1955
	40	Death Wish			
	41	Free Enterprise (A^{c}malun Hurra)			
	42	A Hero's Anniversary (Miladu Batal)			
	43	The Honourable Lady Member (An Naiba al Muhtarama)			
	44	The Hungry Ones (Al Giya^c)			?, Masrah al Hakim with Acts 2 and 3 of 79[2]
	45	I Want this Man (Uridu Hadha'r Ragul)			
	46	I Want to Kill (Uridu an Aqtul)			
	47	The Key to Success (Miftah an Nagah)			
	48	The Man who Withstood (Ar Rajul alladhi Samad)			
	49	Master Kanduz's Property			
	50	The Marrying Kind (Ashab al Ada'z Zawgiyya)			
	51	The Peaceful Nest			
	52	Platonic Love (Al Hubb al Uzri)			
	53	The Producer			
	54	Rejuvenation	1948		1958-9
	55	The Thief	1948[3]		1949[4]
	56	The Treasure (Al Kunz)			
	57	Witch (Sahiratun)			
58		The Clock Strikes	1950	1956	?, National Theatre
59		Hard Work has its Reward	1951	1956	
60		War Versus Peace	1951	1956	

		Written	Published	Performed in Egypt
61	Towards a Better Life (Nahwa Hayatin Afdhal)	1955	1956	
62	Soft Hands	1954	1954	1957
63	Her Majesty		1956	
64	Isis		1955	1956
	A Variety of Theatre: 2, 7, 9-12, 14, 16-18, 27, 35, 58-63 and		1956	
65	The Chest	1949		1952
66	The Devil in Danger (Ash Shaytan fi Khatr)	1951		
67	The Deal		1956	1958, The Egyptian Modern Troupe[5] at the Opera[6]
68	Death Game	1957	1957-64	
69	The Thorns of Peace		1957	
70	Journey into the Future		1957	
	The Kaleidoscope: 46, 49, 52			1959
71	Praksa 2		1960	
72	The Sultan's Dilemma	1959	1960	1961, 1969
73	The Tree Climber		1962	?, The Pocket Theatre
74	Food for Every Mouth		1963	1964
75	A Hunting Trip	1962-3	1964	
76	A Train Journey	1962-3	1964	?[7]
77	Shams an Nahar		1965	1964, 1966
78	The Dilemma		1966	
79	Fate of a Cockroach		1966	1969, Act 1; ?, Acts 2 and 3 at Masrah al Hakim[8]
80	Everything's in its Place		1966	
81	The Anxiety Bank		1967	1970
82	The Moonmen		1969	
83	Harun ar Rashid and Harun ar Rashid		1969	
84	This Comic World		1971	1972

REFERENCES

1 Mandur 1, p 95, 2, pp 159, 161
2 Mandur 2, pp 172-3
3 Shukri, p 388
4 Berque, L'Egypte, Imperialisme et Revolution, Gallimard, Paris, 1967, p 670
5 Mandur 2, p 118
6 Introduction to the Spanish translation of Death Song
7 Implied by Hakim to Farag, p 175
8 Mandur 2, pp 172-3

APPENDIX 3

a Foreign Editions of Al Hakim Plays

Shahrazad
French	1936:	trs. A Khedry and Morik Brin, introduction by Georges Lecomte of the Academie Francaise, Nouvelles Editions Latines, Paris
English	? :	extracts, Pilot, London
"	1944:	Most of Scene One and half of Scene Two, tr. H Howarth and I Shukrallah in Images from the Arab World, London, pp 17-20 and 65-70 (reproduced in James Kritzeck (ed), Anthology of Islamic Literature, Pelican, London, 1964)
"	1945:	extracts (?), Crown, New York
French	1950:	Theatre Arabe: ›Tewfik al-Hakim (trs. A Khedry, N Costandi and A S Sabra), Nouvelles Editions Latines, Paris
Japanese	1970[1]	
English	1977:	Most of Scene One and half of Scene Two, tr. H Howarth and I Shukrallah in Images from the Arab World, Gazelle, London

The Cavemen
French	1940:	tr. A Khedry, introduction by Gaston Wiet
Italian	1941	
French	1945	
Italian	1945:	Rome
Spanish	1946:	Madrid
French	1950:	in Theatre Arabe
English	1955:	Act One, tr. P J Vatikiotis, in The Islamic Literature, Lahore, 7, pp 191-212
Italian	1959:	tr. Robert Rubinacci as Quei della Caverna, Istituto Universitario Orientale, Naples
"	1961:	tr. Umberto Rizzitano as La Gente della Caverna, Centro per le Relazione Italo-Arabe, Rome
French	1961:	extracts from Acts 3 and 4, tr. V Monteil, Anthologie Bilingue de la Litterature Arabe Contemporaine, Imprimerie Catholique, Beirut
Italian	1962:	Milan

The Cavemen (contd)

Spanish	1963:	as La Gente de la Caverna in Federico Corriente Cordoba (ed), Tawfiq al-Hakim: Teatro, Instituto Hispano-Arabe de Cultura, Madrid
Japanese	1970[1]	
English	1971:	Act One, tr. J A Haywood, Modern Arabic Literature, 1800-1970, Lund Humphries, London

First playlet in The Tree of Ruling

Italian	1943:	tr. Rizzitano in OM 23, pp 440-6

The Piper

Hebrew	1945:	tr. M Kapelyuk
French	1950:	in Theatre Arabe

Devant son Guichet

English	1947:	tr. Chaim Rabin in Arabic, Lund Humphries, London

The Anthill

French	1950:	in Theatre Arabe
Italian	1960:	tr. Virginia Vacca as La Casa delle Formiche in Levante 8, iv, pp 3-17
Spanish	1963:	as La Casa de las Hormigas in Tawfiq al-Hakim: Teatro

Death Wish[2]

French	1950:	in Theatre Arabe
Italian	1962:	tr. Vacca as Sapeva come Sarebbe Morto in Levante 9, iii-iv, pp 7-24

King Oedipus

French	1950:	in Theatre Arabe

Pigmalyun

French	"	"

The Producer

French	"	"

The River of Madness[2]

French	1950:	"

Solomon the Wise

French	1950:	"

I Want to Kill
    French   1954:   in Theatre Multicolore (trs. Khedry and Costandi), Nouvelles Editions Latines, Paris

A Day's Work
    French   1954:   "
    Spanish   1963:   as De la Noche a la Manana in Tawfiq al-Hakim: Teatro

Death Song
    French   1954:   in Theatre Multicolore
    Spanish   1963:   as El Canto de la Muerte in Tawfiq al-Hakim: Teatro
    Italian   1964:   tr. B Volpi as Il Canto della Morte in Annali Istituto Orientale de Napoli NS 14, pp 817-36
    English   1972:   tr. C W R Long in New Middle East, June, pp 24-30
    "   1973:   as The Song of Death in Denys Johnson-Davies (tr.), Fate of a Cockroach and Other Plays, Heinemann Educational Books, London

The Devil in Danger
    French   1954:   in Theatre Multicolore

The Honourable Lady Member
    French   1954:   "

The Clock Strikes[2]
    French   1954:   "

The Peaceful Nest
    French   1954:   "

Praksa
    French   "   "

Rejuvenation
    French   "   "

The Treasure
    French   "   "

Witch
    French   "   "

Foreign Editions

Muhammad
- English   1955:   last scene tr. W R Polk in New Directions 15, pp 277-83

Death Game
- French   1960:   as La Mort et l'Amour, Nouvelles Editions Latines, Paris

Journey into the Future [2]
- French   1960:   "

The Sultan's Dilemma
- French   1960:   "
- Italian   1964:   tr. Vacca, Istituto per l'Oriente, Rome
- English   1973:   in Fate of a Cockroach and Other Plays

Platonic Love
- Italian   1964:   tr. Vacca as L'Amore Ideale in Annali Istituto Orientale de Napoli NS 14, pp 799-816

The Tree Climber
- English   1965:   tr. Johnson-Davies, OUP

Everything's in its Place
- English   1973:   as Not a Thing out of Place in Fate of a Cockroach and Other Plays

Fate of a Cockroach
- English   1973:   "

Shams an Nahar
- Italian   1974:   tr. Vincenzo Strika, Rome: Istituto per l'Oriente; Palermo: Universita. Collana di letteratura araba contemporanea

REFERENCES

1   Adib, December 1970, p 59
2   Unpublished translations exist in English, as of A Train Journey.

216   Tawfiq al Hakim

b Productions outside the Arab World [*]

Pigmalyun	Salzburg, December 1953
	Cambridge, June 1961
Death Song	Athens, 1954
	Madrid, ?
Shahrazad	BBC, March 1955
	Paris, November 1955
Death Wish	Paris, November 1955
The Cavemen	Palermo, ? (1950s)
The Anthill	Madrid, March 1963
Soft Hands	West Jerusalem, 1964
The Sultan's Dilemma	BBC World Service, 6 (twice), 7 and 9 November 1973
The Tree Climber	Canada, 1969
Fate of a Cockroach	BBC World Service (announced for late 1978)

---

[*] Hakim plays have been staged in Copenhagen and Stockholm, but which ones and when remain obscure. It will be observed that the scripts used in the performances listed above have not necessarily been published.

Further Reading

a Books and Articles

Abd al-Malek, Anouar	– Anthologie de la Litterature Arabe Contemporaine: les Essais, Editions du Seuil, Paris, 1965
Abd as Subur, Salah	– Madha yibqa min hum li't tarikh?, Dar al Katib al Arabi, Cairo, 1968 (Subur 1)*
	– Wa tibqa al kalima, Dar al Adab, Beirut, 1970 (Subur 2)
Abd el Jalil, J M	– Histoire de la Litterature Arabe, Maisonneuve, Paris, 1960
Abdel Wahab, Farouk	– Modern Egyptian Drama: an Anthology, Bibliotheca Islamica Inc., Minneapolis, 1974?
Adham, Dr Isma^{c}il and Nagi, Dr Ibrahim	– Tawfiq al Hakim, Dar Sa^{c}ad Misr, Cairo, 1945 (Adham)
Awad, Luwis	– Al masrah al misri, Dar Izis, Cairo, 1954
	– Maqalatun fi'n nuqd wa'l adab, Maktabat al Anglu al Misriyya, Cairo, 1964
	– Dirasatun arabiyya wa gharbiyya, Dar al Ma^{c}arif, Cairo, 1965 (Awad 2)
	– Ath thawra wa'l adab, Dar al Katib al Arabi, Cairo, 1967
	– Awdat ar Ruh, in Al Ahram, 23 October 1970 (Awad 1)
Awad, Dr Ramsis	– Tawfiq al Hakim alladhi la ta^{c}rafuhu, Cairo, 1974
Brockelmann, C	– Geschichte der Arabischen Litteratur, Supplement 3, Brill, Leiden, 1942
Cachia, P J E	– Taha Husayn: his Place in the Egyptian Literary Renaissance, Luzac, London, 1956 (Cachia)

---

* In the References the abbreviations given in parentheses indicate these most-quoted works. The titles by Hakim included in this list are those which have been regularly cited.

Dardiri, Dr Ibrahim	- Al qassas ad dini fi masrah al Hakim, Mu'assasat Dar ash Sha^{c}ab, Cairo, 1975
Dawara, Fu'ad	- Fi'n nuqd al masrahi, Al-Mu'assasa al Misriyya al Ama, Cairo, 1963 (?) (Dawara 1)
	- Asharatu udaba yatahaddathun, Kitab al Hilal, Cairo, 1965 (Dawara 2)
Dolinina and Zand	- Tawfiq al Hakim, a Bibliographical Guide (in Russian), Kniga Press, Moscow, 1968
Farag, Alfrid	- Dalil al mutafarrig az zaki ila'l masrah, Kitab al Hilal, Cairo, 1966 (Farag)
Gabrieli, Francesco	- Storia della Letteratura Araba, Casa Editrice, Milan, 1951
Hakim	- Al Hakim's Donkey (AHD)
	- Action and Response (AR)
	- The Documentary Background to Awareness Regained (ARD)
	- Awareness Regained (AW)
	- From the Ivory Tower (FTIT)
	- In the Spotlight of Thought (IST)
	- The Literary Art (LA)
	- Life in Bud (LIB)
	- Literature is Life (LL)
	- Life's Prison (LP)
	- My Donkey Said to Me (MDS)
	- The Sultan of Darkness (SD)
	- Tawfiq al Hakim Says ... (TAY)
	- Tawfiq al Hakim the Artist (TF)
	- Under the Green Lamp (UGL)
Hourani, Albert	- Arabic Thought in the Liberal Age, 1798-1939, OUP, 1970 (Hourani)
Husayn, Taha	- Mustaqbal ath thaqafa fi Misr, Dar al Ma^{c}arif, Cairo, 1944
	- Fusulun fi'l adab wa'n nuqd, Dar al Ma^{c}arif, Cairo, 1945 (Husayn)
Id, Dr Raga	- Dirasatun fi adabi Tawfiq al Hakim, Munsha'at al Ma^{c}arif, Alexandria 1977

Jamal Muhammad Ahmad	- The Intellectual Origins of Egyptian Nationalism, OUP, 1960
Khidr, Abbas	- Ghuram al udaba, Dar al Ma^{C}arif (Iqra 157), Cairo, 1956
Landau, Jacob M	- Etudes sur le Theatre et le Cinema Arabes, Maisonneuve et Larose, Paris, 1965 (Landau)
Makarius, Raoul	- La Crise de l'Intelligentsia Egyptienne, Mouton, The Hague, 1960
	- Anthologie de la Litterature Arabe Contemporaine: le Roman et la Nouvelle, Editions du Seuil, Paris, 1964 (with Laura Makarius)
Mallakh, Kamal	- Al Hakim bakhilan, Al Maktab al Misri al Hadith, Cairo, 1973. Notable for its photographs of Hakim and his family. (Mallakh)
Mandur, Muhammad	- Masrah Tawfiq al Hakim, Dar al Ma^{C}arif, Cairo, 1960
	- Al fann at tamthili, 1: al masrah, Dar al-Ma^{C}arif, Cairo, 1963 (Mandur 1)
	- Masrah Tawfiq al Hakim, Dar Nahdat Misr, Cairo, 1966 (Mandur 2)
Manzalaoui, Mahmoud (ed)	- Arabic Writing Today: the Short Story, Dar al Ma^{C}arif and the American Research Centre in Egypt, Cairo, 1968
Miquel, Andre	- La Litterature Arabe, Presses Universitaires de France (Que Sais-Je?), Paris, 1969
Mohamed, Abdel Moniem Ismail	- Drama and Society in Contemporary Egypt (unpublished SOAS doctoral thesis), 1964
Mosharrafa, MM	- Cultural Survey of Modern Egypt, Longman, London, 1947-8
Muhammad al Hasan Fadl al Mawla	- Lamahatun min an nuqd al adabi al hadith, Dar al-Awda, Beirut, 1969 (Muhammad al Hasan)

Mustafa, Ahmad Abd ar Rahim	- Tawfiq al Hakim: afkaruhu, atharuhu, Al Matba^{c}a an Namuzagiyya, Cairo, 1952
Najm, Muhammad Yusuf	- Al masrahiyya fi'l adab al arabi al hadith, 1847-1917, Dar ath Thaqafa, Beirut, 1967 (Najm)
Naqqash, Raja^c an	- Udaba'un mu^{c}asirun, Kitab al Hilal, Cairo, 1971 (Naqqash)
Ostle, R C (ed)	- Studies in Modern Arabic Literature, Aris and Phillips, Warminster, 1975 (Ostle)
Papadopoulo, A	- Tawfiq al Hakim wa amaluhu al adabi, Appendix to The Sultan's Dilemma, pp 219-47 (Papadopoulo)
Pellat, Charles	- Langue et Litterature Arabes, Armand Colin, Paris, 1952
Qutb, Sayyid	- Kutub wa shakhsiyyat, Dar al Kutub al Arabiyya, Beirut, 1947 (?)
Qutt, Abd al Qadir al	- Fi'l adab al misri al mu^{c}asir, Maktabat Misr, Cairo, nd
Ra^{c}i, Ali ar	- Masrahiyyat Tawfiq al Hakim al fikriyya, Kitab al Hilal, Cairo, 1968 (Ra^{c}i)
	- Tawfiq al Hakim: fanan al furga wa fanan al fikr, Kitab al Hilal, Cairo, 1969
Safran, Nadav	- Egypt in Search of Political Community, Harvard UP, 1961 (Safran)
Salih, Ahmad Rushdi	- Al masrah al arabi, Al Haiya al Misriyya al Ama Li'l Kitab, Cairo, 1972
Sharuni, Yusuf ash	- Dirasatun fi'l adab al arabi al mu^{c}asir, Al Mu'assasa al Misriyya, Cairo, 1965
Shukri, Ghali	- Thawrat al mu^{c}tazil: dirasatun fi adabi Tawfiq al Hakim, Maktabat al Anglu, Cairo, 1966 (Shukri)
Tarabishi, Georges	- Lu^{c}bat al hulm wa'l waqi^c: dirasatun fi adabi Tawfiq al Hakim, Dar at Tali^{c}a, Beirut, 1972 (Tarabishi)

Foreign Editions 221

Tawfiq, Sa^{c}ad ad Din	- Qissat as sinama fi Misr, Kitab al Hilal, Cairo, 1969 (Sa^{c}ad ad Din Tawfiq)
Taymur, Mahmud	- Al adab al arabi al hadith wa ittijahatuhu, Beirut Arab University, 1964 (Taymur)
Tomiche, Nada (ed)	- Le Theatre Arabe, UNESCO, Paris, 1969 (UNESCO)
Tuma, Salih J al	- Maraji^c li'l adab al masrahi al arabi, 1945-65, Matba^{c}at al Ani, Baghdad, 1969
Vatikiotis, P J (ed)	- Egypt since the Revolution, Allen and Unwin, London, 1968 (Vatikiotis)
Vernet, Juan	- Literatura Arabe, Labor SA, Barcelona, nd
Wiet, Gaston	- Introduction a la Litterature Arabe, Maisonneuve et Larose, Paris, 1966
Winder, R Bayly (tr.)	- Bird of the East, Khayyats, Beirut, 1966 (Winder)

b Journals, etc

Acta Orientalia, Budapest
Al Adab, Beirut
Al Adib, Beirut (Adib)
Al Ahram, Cairo
Al Aqlam, Baghdad (AQ)
The Bulletin of the School of Oriental and African Studies
   London (BSOS)
Al Hiwar, Beirut (Hiwar)
The Journal of American Oriental Studies, Boston (JAOS)
Al Kitab, Cairo
Al Katib al Misri, Cairo
Levante, Rome
Magallat al Magalla, Cairo (MAG)
Al Masrah, Cairo (MAS)
The Middle East Journal, Washington (MEJ)
Middle Eastern Studies, London (MES)
The Muslim World, Hartford, Connecticut (MW)
New Outlook, Jerusalem (NO)
Orient, Paris
Oriente Moderno, Rome (OM)
Revue du Caire
Sabah al Khayr, Cairo

INDEX

Abaza, Aziz 2, 20, 32
Abbas Hilmi, Khedive 205
Abbasids 193
Abd al Al, Mahmud Awad 106
Abd al-Malek, Anouar 27
Abd an Nasir, Gamal v, 28, 65
  67, 73, 79, 105, 108, 109,
  111, 112, 113-4, 115, 152,
  153, 154, 155, 156, 157, 160,
  162, 179-80, 182, 183, 189
Abd al Quddus, Ihsan 187 fn
Abd as Subur, Salah 8, 13, 21,
  27, 34, 49
Abd al Wahhab, Muhammad 23,
  115
The Absurd 85, 86, 87, 88, 89, 90,
  92, 94, 104
Abu Hadid, Muhammad Farid 27
Abyad, Georges 7, 9, 110, 205,
  206, 170
Abyssinia 165
"Action and Response" 49-50,
  69, 170
"Al Adab" 62
Adamov, Artur 86
Adham, Isma^{c}il 8, 27, 31, 32,
  36, 182, 188, 206, 207
Adham, Sulayman ('The Anxiety
  Bank') 160-1
Adil ('Fate of a Cockroach') 102,
  103, 104, 133, 169
'The Adventures of a Black Girl'
  105
Aeschylus 13, 106, 188

Ahmad, Jamal Muhammad 58, 89
'Al Ahram' 36, 105, 107, 108, 109,
  110, 111, 114, 169, 195
Akasha Company, The 8
Akasha, Zaki Bey 8, 9, 11, 21
'Al Akhbar' 173
  'Akhbar al Yawm' 57, 61, 66,
  110
Alarcon, P.A. de 68
Albert, Prince 140, 166
Al Alfi, Nabil 69, 90
Algeria 64
'Ali Baba' 7, 8, 9, 15, 16, 24,
  31, 119
'Alladine et Palomides' 189
Alwan ('Death Song') 70
'Amedee' 87
Amin, Qasim 2, 8, 66, 137
'Aminusa' 7, 8
'Amirat al Andalus' 206
'Amphitryon 38' 52
Anan ('Expulsion from Eden')
  55, 135, 139
Andre 17, 18, 20, 21, 180, 181
the angel ('The Angel's Prayer')
  49
'The Angel's Prayer' 49, 62, 73,
  83, 169-70, 174, 197
Anisa ('Her Majesty') 135, 137,
  142, 151, 152
'The Anthill' 61
Antigone 60
'Antigone' 34
Antonio ('Death Game') 77
'Antony and Cleopatra' 77
Antony, Mark 110
Antun, Farah 8, 70, 187, 205
'The Anxiety Bank' 62, 105-6,
  108, 113, 136, 150, 160-

2, 166, 197
Apollo 50, 51, 52, 190
Al Aqqad, Mahmud Abbas 79
'The Arabian Nights', see 'The Thousand and One Nights'
The Arab Socialist Union 112, 114
Araguz 3
Aristophanes 45-6, 83
Aristotle 13, 188, 190
'The Artists' 16, 30
Asakir ('Death Song') 176
'Ash^{c}ab' 42, 181
Ashur, Nu^{c}man 80, 187
Astre, G. A. 188
Aswan Dam 195
Athens 147, 148, 156 fn
Atif, Munir ('The Anxiety Bank') 161
Atiyat, Sitt ('Food for Every Mouth') 90, 91, 92, 93, 136, 175, 176
'L'Avare' 203
Awad, Luwis 25, 28, 62, 65, 69, 84, 89-90, 107 fn, 109
Al Awalim 3, 4, 6, 8, 15
'Al Awalim' 15, 30
'Awareness Regained' 112, 114, 115
'Al Ayyam' 27
Ayyub, Mahfuz 106
Al Azhar 43, 70

Baalbek 198
'Babil al Khati'' 106
Badawi, Hilmi Bahgat 182
Baghdad 72, 133
Bahadur ('The Tree Climber') 87, 88, 89
Bakathir, Ali Ahmad 32, 34

'Al Balagh' 24
balance 49, 69
Baldwin, Stanley 165
Balpirus ('Isis') 67, 83, 156
Barbour, Neville 26
Bayyumi, Dr. Muhammad Lutfi 58
BBC 67, 115
Beach, Sylvia 13
The Beatles 161, 162, 197
Beckett, Samuel 86, 89
Beethoven 14, 17, 24, 188
beret 43
Bernhardt, Sarah 206
Berque, Jacques 61, 202 fn
Bihana ('The Tree Climber') 87, 88, 89, 133, 136
Bilqais, Queen of Sheba ('Solomon the Wise') 53-5, 134
'The Book of the Dead' 36
Brecht, Bertold 68, 86, 89, 94, 188
'The Bridegroom' 7, 8
British 2, 6, 7, 28, 36, 112, 115, 165
British Columbia Bauerhaus Company 116
'Bullet in the Heart, A' 15, 22 fn, 23, 25 fn, 41, 135
'The Burdensome Guest' 6-7, 8, 164-5
Al Bustami, Asma 1, 2, 3, 4, 5, 6, 9, 11, 12, 20, 23, 39, 142
Byblos, King of 67, 68, 155

Cachia, Pierre 134, 196
Cairo Arabic Language Academy 12, 65, 183

Cairo University 7, 11, 12, 13, 43, 107, 161, 180
Calderon de la Barca 13, 68
Cambridge University 83
Camus, Albert 188
Canadian Television Corporation 107
'Candida' 160
'Candide' 27
Carthage 59
'The Cavemen' 3, 14, 16, 21, 22, 23, 24-6, 28, 30, 31, 32, 33-7, 39, 40, 41, 45, 50, 53, 59, 69, 78, 80, 85, 93, 108, 110, 119, 123, 124, 125, 126, 128, 130, 131, 140, 165, 179, 183, 184, 185, 186, 188, 189, 193, 196, 197, 202, 206, 207
'Les Chaises' 89
Chamberlain, Neville 165
Chekhov, Anton 37, 86, 89, 106
the chemist ('The Angel's Prayer') 174
'The Cherry Orchard' 107
'The Chest' 64
Chiantoni 205
China 203
Christianity 17, 35-6, 119, 120, 121, 122, 170, 190, 197
Churchill, Winston 166
the classical language 25 fn, 70, 71, 86, 95, 96
Cleopatra 66, 77, 134, 135
'The Clock Strikes' 73, 124
the cockroach King ('Fate of a Cockroach') 99, 100, 101, 102, 103, 104, 128, 160, 161
the cockroach Queen ('Fate of a Cockroach') 54, 100, 101, 102, 136, 160, 167

Cocteau, Jean 13, 46, 59
the colloquial language 25 fn, 70, 71, 79, 86, 95, 96, 97
La Comedie de Paris 67
La Comedie Francaise 33, 109, 180
'La Comedie Humaine' 61
Cordoba, Federico Corriente 26
Corneille, Pierre 58, 188, 193, 204
'Cosi e (se li vera)' 104
Cowan, David 27, 197
Creon ('King Oedipus') 60

Damanhur 2, 4, 6
D'Arc, Jeanne 66, 72
Darwish, Sayyid 7, 182
Dawara, Fu'ad 80, 82, 125, 188
'The Deal' 65, 69-73, 79, 83, 88, 92, 95, 96, 97, 106, 136, 179
'Death Game' 65, 76-8, 80, 83, 136, 155, 170-1
'Death in Venice' 109
'Death Song' 61, 70, 72, 73, 115, 176, 197
'Death Wish' 67
Decius, Emperor 36, 119, 120, 121
De Musset, Alfred 7, 13
the dervish ('The Tree Climber') 87
'Devant Son Guichet' 15, 16, 41
'The Devil's Pact' 18, 42, 100, 123, 134, 180
'Dialogues with a Planet' 107 fn
Dickens 13, 166
'The Dilemma' 71, 95-7
Diyab, Mahmud 73

the doctor ('Fate of a Cockroach')
103, ('Journey into the
Future') 128-30, 194
'The Documentary Background to
Awareness Regained' 135
the Drama Supporters' Club 23
the Drama Writers' Association 109
'The Dream' 15
  (Strindberg) 109
  'Dr. Faustus' 40
  Dumas pere 204
  Dupont, Suzy 15, 139
  Durand, Emma 15, 16, 18, 22, 142
  Durenmatt, Friedrich 106
  Dusuq 3, 22, 23

'The Ecclesiazusae' 45-6
'L'Ecole des Femmes' 94
  Edward VIII, King 140, 166
  Egypt, Ancient 86, 100, 119, 189, 194, 195
the Egyptian legal corps 33
  revolution of 1919 5, 6, 27, 28, 146, 195, revolution of 1952 34, state prize for literature 73, state prize for merit 73, University - see Cairo University
Einstein 129
'The Enchanted Palace' 40, 134, 185
the engineer ('Journey into the Future') 129, 130, 194
  'Enrico IV' 125
  Euripides 13, 188
  Eve 66, 137, 141, 142
  'Everything's in its Place' 105, 115

'Expulsion from Eden' 15, 22, 36, 41, 55, 94, 135, 139, 140, 142, 146

Fadl al Mawla, Muhammad al Hasan 89, 105, 106
Fahmi, Abd al Aziz 65
Farag, Alfrid 34, 69, 187
Farah, Iskandar 204, 206
Farid, Prince ('Soft Hands') 153-5
Faruq, King 62, 66, 112, 151, 153, 155
'Fate of a Cockroach' 33, 54, 60, 99-105, 107, 115, 116, 160, 162, 166-9, 179
Fatimids 193
'Faust' 123, 134
Fawzi, Dr. Husayn 13, 24, 110, 182
The Fiction Writers' Club 115
the fisherman ('Solomon the Wise') 53, 55
Les Folies Bergeres 14
'Food for Every Mouth' 66, 86, 89, 90-3, 95, 126, 170, 173-6, 179
'Foreign Literature' 84
France, Anatole 57
'From Beyond' 100
'From the Ivory Tower' 49-50, 100, 134, 143, 148-9
Fu'ad, King 155
Fu'ad, King Ahmad 155

Galatia ('Pigmalyun') 50, 51, 52, 125, 126, 139
Garcia Lorca, Federico 61

'Al Garida' 11
The Generation of '98 42
'The Gentle Sex' 41, 142
   Ghalias ('The Cavemen') 120, 121, 122
   Gibb, H.A.R. 206, 207
   Gide, Andre 13, 59, 60
   Gielgud, John 67
   Gilbert, W.S. 82, 83
   Giraudoux, Jean 46
   Gluck 40
   Goethe 17, 40, 49, 188
   Gorki, Maxim 89
   Gorst, Sir Eldon 11
the four Gospels 36
   Greeks 14, 31, 33, 35, 41, 46, 50, 83, 186, 188-94
   Grobmann, Maria 65
   'Gulliver's Travels' 107
   Gum^{C}a, Muhammad Lutfi 8
   'Al Gumhuriyya' 79

Al Haddad, Nagib 204
Al Hakim, Isma^{C}il (father) 1, 2, 3, 4, 5, 6, 7, 9, 11, 12, 20, 23, 39 (son) 58 fn
Al Hakim, Naga 58 fn
Al Hakim, Nura 58 fn
'Al Hakim's Donkey' 48, 137-8, 181, 182
'Al Hakim's Stick' 58, 66, 181
Al Hakim, Zaynab 58 fn
Al Hakim, Zuhayr 2, 5
   Hamdan, Amir ('Shams an Nahar') 158-9
   Hamdi ('Food for Every Mouth') 90, 91, 92, 93, 126, 174, 176 ('Her Majesty') 151
   Hamid ('The Thief') 149, 150

'Hamlet' 7, 18, 100, 107
Al Hammamsi, Galal 79
   Hamuda, Ali ('Soft Hands') 125-6, 154-5
   Haqqi, Yahya 2, 7, 28
   Hardy, Thomas 128
Al Hariri 106
   'Harun ar Rashid wa Harun ar Rashid' 108
   Haykal, Muhammad Hasanayn 108, 110, 114
   Haykal, Muhammad Husayn 11, 12, 16, 27
   Hemingway, Ernest 13
   'Her Majesty' 65, 66, 73, 87, 135, 136, 151-2
   Heyworth-Dunne 27
   Higazi, Shaykh Salama 3, 96, 204, 206, 207
   Higher Council of Arts, Letters and Social Sciences 69, 73, 83
   Hippocrates 156
   Hiroshima, legend 36
   Hirunimus ('Praksa') 45, 126, 147, 148, 156
   Hitler 48, 49, 66, 114, 169
   Hobbs, Carleton 67
   Hofmannsthal, Hugo von 59
   hoopoe ('Solomon the Wise') 53
   Hugo, Victor 204
   'Hunting Trip, A' 66, 93, 94, 125, 153
   Huris ('Isis') 67, 68, 155, 195
   Husayn, Taha 11, 12, 16, 19, 24-5, 27, 31-2, 33, 38, 39-40, 44, 45-6, 49, 64, 65, 89, 109, 148, 181, 182, 183-5, 187, 190, 195, 196, 206

Husni, Dawud 182
Huxley, Aldous 13, 49

Ibn Abd Rabbihi 43
Ibn Abi Silmi, Zuhayr 2
Ibn al Ahnaf, Al Abbas 5
Ibn al Khattab, Umar 43
'Ibnat al Mamluk' 27
Ibqirat ('Praksa') 83, 102, 126, 147, 156
'Ibrahim al Katib' 27
Ibsen 33, 36, 70, 106, 188, 189
Id, Aziz 204, 205, 206
Idris, Yusuf 73, 187
International Theatre Institute 107, 109
'In the Spotlight of Thought' 42, 137, 147, 192, 195
Ionesco, Eugene 41, 86, 87, 89, 188
Iqbal ('The Suicide's Secret') 126, 136, 137
'Al Iqd al Farid' 43
'Irrationalism' 85, 86, 87, 89, 90, 94, 120
Al Isfahani, Abu'l Faraj 106
Isis ('Isis') 67, 68, 134, 135, 137, 150
'Isis' 45, 65, 67-9, 71, 72, 80, 155, 166, 170
Islam 35, 36, 190, 192, 197
Isma^{c}il, Khedive 113, 203
Ismin ('Pigmalyun') 52
Isocrates 156
Ivanovitch ('A Sparrow from the East') 17, 194

Jabra Ibrahim Jabra 89

Al Jahiz 106, 184, 185, 188
Jimenez, Juan Ramon 79
jinni ('Solomon the Wise') 53-5, 58, 170, 176
Jocasta ('King Oedipus') 59, 60
Johnson-Davies, Denys 196
John the Baptist 93
'Journalistic Incident, A' 43, 142
'Journey between two Eras, A' 111
'Journey into the Future' 66, 76, 78-9, 83, 91, 119, 123, 125, 126-7, 128-30, 131, 135, 155, 170, 172-3, 179, 194
'The Journey of Spring and Autumn' 79, 93
Joyce, James 12, 14
June War 105, 108, 110, 113, 160
'Justice and Art' 18, 23, 42, 64, 205 fn

Kafka, Franz 179
'The Kaleidoscope' 80
'Kalila wa Dimna' 94
Kamil, Adil 187
Kapeliuk, Olga 196
Al Kassar, Ali 23, 206
Al Kayyali, Sami 44
Al Khal^{c}i, Kamil 7, 182
Al Khawli, Lutfi 108, 110, 187
Khayriyya ('The Thief') 150
Al Khayyat, Yusuf 204
Kilyubatra 77, 78, 136, 171
'King Lear' 34
King, Martin Luther 107
'King Oedipus' 25, 45, 58-61,

62, 69, 181, 192, 193
'King of the Parasites' 42
Kishkish Bey 23, 206
'Kitab al Aghani' 107
Kritzeck, James 32, 196-7

Lacedaemonians 147, 156
La Fontaine, Jean de 94
Lampson, Sir Miles 83
Landau, Jacob 8, 26, 41, 134, 180, 196
Lawrence, D.H. 58
Layla ('Modern Woman') 54, 136
Lecomte, Georges 32
Leighton, Margaret 67
Lenormand, Henri-René 188
Liberal Constitutional Party 43
'Life in Bud' 12, 15, 17, 21, 52, 57, 109, 180
'Life is Wrecked, A' 23, 41, 135
'Life's Prison' 1, 3, 16, 93, 140
'The Literary Art' 1, 3, 61, 64, 78, 170, 173, 193
'Literature is Life' 50, 78, 79, 100, 169, 170
lizard ('The Tree Climber') 87, 88
Lloyd George 165
London 109 fn, 189
Lope de Vega 13, 188
Louvre 15, 50
Lugne-Poë 32, 35, 189

Macedonians 156
Madrid 61
Maeterlinck, Maurice 13, 24, 26, 188, 189
'Magallati' 15, 41

Al Mahalla al Kubra 108
Mahfuz, Dr. ('The Suicide's Secret') 126
Mahfuz, Nagib 17, 27, 61, 82, 105, 112, 138, 160, 182-3, 187
Mahmud, Muhammad 43
Al Mallakh, Kamal 28, 58
Mamluks 80, 157
Mandur, Muhammad 7, 8, 12, 21, 26, 27, 32, 34, 36, 42, 45, 52, 53, 58, 59-60, 61, 62, 65-6, 68-9, 72-3, 75, 80, 82, 89, 90, 92, 93, 125, 141, 148, 159, 165, 176, 187
Al Manfaluti, Mustafa Lutfi 27
Marlowe, Christopher 188
Marnush ('The Cavemen') 25, 34, 119, 120, 121, 122, 124, 126, 165
'Al Masrah' 111
Masrah al Hakim 89, 94, 110
masriwayya 105
'Master Kanduz's Property' 150
Al Mazini, Ibrahim Abd al Qadir 27, 70, 182
'Me and the Law ..., and Art' 111
'Memories of Law and Art' 64
'The Merchant of Venice' 34
'The Mikado' 82
Miller, Arthur 89
Ministry of Education 33, 43, 183, 185
Ministry of Social Affairs 42, 43-4
Miquel, André 196
Mishilinya ('The Cavemen') 25,

34, 59, 60, 119, 120, 121, 122, 124, 126, 144, 165
'Misr al Gadida wa Misr al Qadima' 205
'Modern Woman' 7, 8, 24, 54, 73, 135, 136, 150, 158
Mohamed, Abdel Moniem Ismail 89
Moliere 13, 106, 107, 188, 203
'Monk Among Women, A' 111
Monteil, Vincent 188
'The Moonmen' 107
Moulin Rouge 14
Mozart 14, 188
mu'azzin ('The Sultan's Dilemma') 81, 82
Mughals 81, 82, 190, 203
'Muhammad' 40
Muhammad, Ahmad as Sawi 15, 23, 182
Muhammad Ali, Khedive 203
Muhammad Ali Secondary School 4, 6
Muhammad Farid Theatre 90
'Muhammad, the Messenger of God' 115
Muhsin 15, 16, 113, 139, 191, 194
Mukhtar ('Expulsion from Eden') 139
'Al Mulhima' 22
Mumtaz, Mustafa 7, 182, 187
Munzir ('Solomon the Wise') 54, 55
Musa, Salama 182
Mussolini 49, 58, 169
Al Mutanabbi, Abu't Tayyib 39, 40
Mutran, Khalil 33, 39-40, 207
'My Donkey Said to Me' 57, 58, 62, 64, 66, 79, 95, 137, 138, 141, 149, 169, 170, 172

Nadia ('Food for Every Mouth') 91, 92, 136
Nadi al Qissa 115, 180
Nagi, Dr. Ibrahim 58, 182
Nagib, Muhammad 112, 154, 155
Nagib, Muhammad 112, 154, 155
An Nahhas, Mustafa 44
nahda 203
Najm, Muhammad Yusuf 32, 205, 207
Napoleon 66, 141, 165, 203
An Naqqash, Marun 203, 204, 206 Raja[c] 27, 49, Salim Khalil 203
Narsis ('Pigmalyun') 51, 52, 141
Nashati, Futuh 82, 159
National Company 33-4, 35, 39, 40, 41, 207
National Library 12, 64, 69
National Movement 27
National Theatre 67, 79, 80, 82, 93, 94, 125
Nicholls, Beverley 66
Nietszche, Friedrich 59, 60, 134
Nile 67, 68, 118
'Nineteen Eighty-Four' 78
Nobel literature prize 181
Nu[c]aima, Mikha[c]il 70, 207

October War 112, 114, 197
Odeon 15
Oedipus 59, 60
'Oedipus Rex' 7, 59
Opera (Cairo) 34, 41, (Paris) 14
Osiris 67, 68, 69, 135, 155, 195

Othello 7, 100
Ottomans 165, 203
'Our Theatre Model' 106-7

Palermo 34
Palestine 61, 98
Papadopoulo, A 196
Paris Drama Festival 67, 204
Pasha ('Expulsion from Eden') 146, ('The Thief') 149-50
Pasternak, Boris 181
'The Peaceful Nest' 61, 62, 135, 139, 142, 181
Pentateuch 53
People's Party 11
'The Philosophy of the Revolution' 65, 182
Pigmalyun 50, 51, 52, 65, 69, 78, 88, 90, 128, 139, 179
'Pigmalyun' 3, 14, 32, 41, 42, 50-2, 59, 83, 88, 89-90, 94, 125, 128, 181, 192
Pinter, Harold 165
'The Piper' 23, 30, 41, 70, 106
Pirandello, Luigi 14, 16, 36, 104 106, 107, 125, 187, 188
'Platero y Yo' 79
'Plays of Social Life' 61-2, 67, 73, 182
'Plays of Tawfiq al Hakim' 41, 73
Plutarch 69
Pocket Theatre 86
'The Poet' 30, 134, 138
'Point Counter Point' 14
'Post Mortem' 22, 41
Praksa 44-5, 59, 126, 137, 138, 147-8, 156
'Praksa' 42, 44-6, 67, 68, 76, 80, 81, 83, 102, 126, 135, 147-8, 155-6, 162, 179
Priest ('Fate of a Cockroach') 101, 102, 160
Priestley, J. B. 130
Prime Minister ('Fate of a Cockroach') 100-1, 102, 160
'La Princesse Maleine' 189
Priska 52, 59, 60, 120, 121, 122, 134, 135, 165
'The Producer' 61
professor ('Death Game') 77, 78, 170-1

Al Qabbani, Ahmad Abu Khalil 7, 204
Qamar ('Shahrazad') 133, 134, 158, 159
Qanbariyya ('The Peaceful Nest') 61, 143
Al Qardahi, Sulayman 204
qiladat al gumhuriyya 9, 79, 180
Qur'an 35, 36, 53, 147
Qutb, Sayyid 52, 143

Racine 188, 193
Ar Ra^{c}i, Ali 22, 23, 34, 52, 61, 62, 68, 71, 73, 82, 88, 89, 104, 107-8, 109, 110, 207 fn
Ramsis II 43
Ramsis Troupe 205
Ramzi, Ibrahim 8, 187, 204, 205
Ar Raqim 35
Ar Rashid, Harun 40

'Reflections on Politics' 66, 149
Reinhardt, Max 40
'Rejuvenation' 61, 62, 79-80,
    110, 119, 121, 123-5, 126,
    128, 130, 136, 176, 179
republican chain, see qiladat
    al gumhuriyya
Ridwan ('Her Majesty') 151-2
Ridwan, Fathi 27, 37, 70, 182,
    187, 188
Ar Rihani, Nagib 21, 33, 34, 73,
    182, 187, 206, 207
Rim ('The Temple Dancer') 15
'Ar Risala' 24, 25, 183, 185
'The River of Madness' 41
Rizzitano, Umberto 8
Romains, Jules 180
Romans 189, 192, 193-4
'Romeo and Juliet' 3, 61
Roosevelt, Franklin D. 169
Roux, Jean 50
Rubinacci, Roberto 26, 196
Ruman, Mikha^{C}il 187
'Rural Deputy's Diary, A' 22 fn,
    23, 41-2, 43, 72
Rushdi, Abd ar Rahman
    Rashad 187 fn

As Sa^{C}adani, Mahmud 187
Sabah 73
'The Sacred Bond' 22 fn, 57-8, 67,
    140, 162
As Sadat, Anwar 111, 112, 114, 115
Sadiq, ('Rejuvenation') 121, 123-
    4, 126
Sadiq, Hatim 108
Sa^{C}id, Dr. 182
Salih, Ahmad Rushdi 79
Salim, Nadir 86

Salzburg Festival 40
    Mozarteum 64
Samira ('Food for Every
    Mouth') 90, 91, 92, 93,
    126, 136, 169, 174, 176
Samiyya ('Fate of a Cockroach')
    102, 103, 104, 133, 136
As Sanhuri, Dr. Abd ar Raziq 43,
    182
Saniyya ('The Soul's Return') 6,
    27, 28, 139, 142
As Santa 1
Sanu^C, Ya^{C}ub b. Rafa^{C}il, 204,
    207
Sartre, Jean-Paul 181
As Sayyid, Ahmad Lutfi 11-12, 17,
    27, 64, 195
Scarron, Paul 188
Schoonover, Kermit 196
Schwarz, Sacha 15, 77, 143, 181
Scientist ('Fate of a Cockroach')
    101, 102, 128, 160
Seneca 58
Seven sleepers 119
Sha^{C}ban ('The Anxiety Bank')
    154, 161, 162
shadow play 203, 204, 207
Shahba ('Solomon the Wise') 54
Shahin ('A Life is Wrecked') 23
Shahrazad 30, 31, 32, 40, 52,
    55, 87, 127, 133-4, 135,
    138, 141
'Shahrazad' 14, 24, 28, 30-3,
    34, 36, 39, 40, 41, 45, 53,
    59, 67, 69, 74, 81, 86, 94-
    5, 119, 127-8, 130, 133-4,
    139, 143, 179, 180, 184,
    185, 188-9, 196
Shahriyar 30, 31, 32, 88, 127,
    128, 133, 134, 135

Shakespeare 13, 82, 106, 188, 194, 204
Shakhla^C, Labiba 3, 4, 30
Shams an Nahar 136, 158, 159
'Shams an Nahar' 93, 94, 110, 158-60, 179
Ash Shanawi, Kamil 79
Ash Sharqawi, Abd ar Rahman 115
Shaw, Bernard 13, 14, 45, 50, 52, 94, 105, 160, 188, 189
Shawqi, Ahmad 2, 14, 134, 206
Shaykh al Balad ('Isis') 67, 68, 150
Sheba 54
Sherif, Nur 105
Sherlock Holmes Hotel 109 fn
'Ships of the Sun' 66 fn
'Show Me Allah' 64-5, 105, 136, 173
Shukri, Ghali 16, 27, 34, 49, 78, 82, 89, 157-8, 182, 187
As Siba^{C}i, Yusuf 79, 114, 198
As Siddiqi, At Tayyib 107 fn
Six Day War 110, 113
slave ('Shahrazad') 30, 32
'Soft Hands' v, 22 fn, 65-6, 67, 71, 72, 73, 80, 83, 93, 125-6, 136, 153-5, 162, 179
Solomon, King ('Solomon the Wise') 53-5
'Solomon's Ring' 7, 8
'Solomon the Wise' 53-6, 68, 69, 100, 170, 176, 179, 181, 188
'The Song of Songs' 48, 53
Sophocles 13, 45, 58, 59, 60, 188, 193
Sorbonne 12
'The Soul's Return' 2, 3, 6, 16, 17, 24, 25 fn, 27-8, 40, 42, 48, 65, 67, 94, 107, 109, 113, 182, 195
Soviet Union 166, 169
Spanish literature 68, 72
'Sparrow from the East, A' 13, 15, 17, 42, 109, 139, 166, 169, 191, 194
Speaker's Corner 166
Stetkevych, Jaroslav 26
Stravinsky, Igor 14, 17, 32, 188
Strindberg, August 34, 109, 134, 142
Sudanese National Theatre 82
Suez affair 76, 112, 166
'The Suicide's Secret' 41, 94, 126, 135, 139, 140, 155
'The Suitor' 7, 8
'Sukkar Murr' 106
Sulayman ('Modern Woman') 54
'The Sultan of Darkness' 31, 48, 134, 155, 169
'The Sultan's Dilemma' 78, 80-3, 113, 115, 136, 156-7, 170, 173, 177, 179
Surur, Nagib 107 fn
Swift, Jonathan 107
Sylvain 61, 197
Synge, J.M. 61, 197

Tagore 17, 66
Tahir, Salah 182
At Tahtawi, Shaykh Rifa^{C}a Badawi Rafi 195, 203
Tal^{C}at, Dr. ('Rejuvenation') 121, 123, 124, 125
'At Tamthil' 9
Tanta 22, 23, 58
Tarabishi, Georges 88, 89, 116
tarbush 43
Tariq ('Food for Every Mouth')

91, 174, 176
Tarsus 26, 36, 119, 121, 122
'Tawfik al Hakim Says' 111
'Tawfik al Hakim the Artist' 10, 9
Taymur, Mahmud 2, 34, 65, 183, 187, 206,
  Mohammad 8, 12, 206, 207
'The Temple Dancer' 15, 16, 48, 139
'Thartharatun Fawqa'n Nil' 105
Le Theatre de l'Oeuvre 35
Theatre of the Absurd 85
Theodorus II, Emperor 36
'The Thief' 61-2, 149-51, 182
'third language' 71, 92, 96
Thiriet, Maurice 98
'This Comic World' 110, 125, 176
'The Thorns of Peace' 65, 76, 78, 80, 110, 136, 170, 171-2, 173
'The Thousand and One Nights' 20, 53, 108, 203
Tifun ('Isis') 67, 68, 155
'The Times' 74, 83, 189
Tiresias ('King Oedipus') 60, 154
Torah 36
Toscanini, Arturo 40
'Train Journey, A' 93, 94, 136, 157-8, 162, 166, 179
'The Tree Climber' 3, 66, 85-9, 90, 94, 106, 107, 136, 153, 179, 188
'The Tree of Ruling' 42, 43, 44, 46, 112, 147, 169
Troilus and Cressida period 99, 110
Tulaymat, Zaki 15, 34
''Twixt Dream and Reality' 42, 50

Tyre 53

UAR 79
UK 83, 95, 114, 165-6, 169
Umm Atiya ('Fate of a Cockroach') 102, 103, 104
UN 173, 181
'Under the Green Lamp' 49, 52, 138, 181
UNESCO 79, 83, 86, 107, 173
USA 166, 169, 176
Uzbakiyya Gardens 8
  Theatre 94

'Variety of Theatre, A' 73, 80, 105, 181
Vautier 86
Venus ('Pigmalyun') 50, 51, 52
Verne, Jules 92
Vernet, Juan 42, 197
Victoria, Queen 141, 166
Vietnam 169
Voltaire 27, 58, 59, 188, 193
Von Grunebaum, G.E. 196

Wafd 12, 24
Wahba, Sa^{c}ad ad Din 187
Wahbi, Yusuf 9, 21, 73, 115, 149, 187, 205, 206, 207
Wanus, Sa^{c}ad Allah 107 fn
'War versus Peace' 135
wazir ('Shahrazad') 30, 32
'The Wedding Night' 22 fn, 105
Wells, H.G. 13, 92
The West 166, 191, 194
'When We Dead Awake' 51
Wiet, Gaston 26

Index   233

Shakespeare 13, 82, 106, 188, 194, 204
Shakhla^C, Labiba 3, 4, 30
Shams an Nahar 136, 158, 159
'Shams an Nahar' 93, 94, 110, 158-60, 179
Ash Shanawi, Kamil 79
Ash Sharqawi, Abd ar Rahman 115
Shaw, Bernard 13, 14, 45, 50, 52, 94, 105, 160, 188, 189
Shawqi, Ahmad 2, 14, 134, 206
Shaykh al Balad ('Isis') 67, 68, 150
Sheba 54
Sherif, Nur 105
Sherlock Holmes Hotel 109 fn
'Ships of the Sun' 66 fn
'Show Me Allah' 64-5, 105, 136, 173
Shukri, Ghali 16, 27, 34, 49, 78, 82, 89, 157-8, 182, 187
As Siba^{C}i, Yusuf 79, 114, 198
As Siddiqi, At Tayyib 107 fn
Six Day War 110, 113
slave ('Shahrazad') 30, 32
'Soft Hands' v, 22 fn, 65-6, 67, 71, 72, 73, 80, 83, 93, 125-6, 136, 153-5, 162, 179
Solomon, King ('Solomon the Wise') 53-5
'Solomon's Ring' 7, 8
'Solomon the Wise' 53-6, 68, 69, 100, 170, 176, 179, 181, 188
'The Song of Songs' 48, 53
Sophocles 13, 45, 58, 59, 60, 188, 193
Sorbonne 12
'The Soul's Return' 2, 3, 6, 16, 17, 24, 25 fn, 27-8, 40, 42, 48, 65, 67, 94, 107, 109, 113, 182, 195
Soviet Union 166, 169
Spanish literature 68, 72
'Sparrow from the East, A' 13, 15, 17, 42, 109, 139, 166, 169, 191, 194
Speaker's Corner 166
Stetkevych, Jaroslav 26
Stravinsky, Igor 14, 17, 32, 188
Strindberg, August 34, 109, 134, 142
Sudanese National Theatre 82
Suez affair 76, 112, 166
'The Suicide's Secret' 41, 94, 126, 135, 139, 140, 155
'The Suitor' 7, 8
'Sukkar Murr' 106
Sulayman ('Modern Woman') 54
'The Sultan of Darkness' 31, 48, 134, 155, 169
'The Sultan's Dilemma' 78, 80-3, 113, 115, 136, 156-7, 170, 173, 177, 179
Surur, Nagib 107 fn
Swift, Jonathan 107
Sylvain 61, 197
Synge, J.M. 61, 197

Tagore 17, 66
Tahir, Salah 182
At Tahtawi, Shaykh Rifa^{C}a Badawi Rafi 195, 203
Tal^{C}at, Dr. ('Rejuvenation') 121, 123, 124, 125
'At Tamthil' 9
Tanta 22, 23, 58
Tarabishi, Georges 88, 89, 116
tarbush 43
Tariq ('Food for Every Mouth')

91, 174, 176
Tarsus 26, 36, 119, 121, 122
'Tawfik al Hakim Says' 111
'Tawfik al Hakim the Artist' 10, 9
Taymur, Mahmud 2, 34, 65, 183, 187, 206,
 Mohammad 8, 12, 206, 207
'The Temple Dancer' 15, 16, 48, 139
'Thartharatun Fawqa'n Nil' 105
Le Theatre de l'Oeuvre 35
Theatre of the Absurd 85
Theodorus II, Emperor 36
'The Thief' 61-2, 149-51, 182
'third language' 71, 92, 96
Thiriet, Maurice 98
'This Comic World' 110, 125, 176
'The Thorns of Peace' 65, 76, 78, 80, 110, 136, 170, 171-2, 173
'The Thousand and One Nights' 20, 53, 108, 203
Tifun ('Isis') 67, 68, 155
'The Times' 74, 83, 189
Tiresias ('King Oedipus') 60, 154
Torah 36
Toscanini, Arturo 40
'Train Journey, A' 93, 94, 136, 157-8, 162, 166, 179
'The Tree Climber' 3, 66, 85-9, 90, 94, 106, 107, 136, 153, 179, 188
'The Tree of Ruling' 42, 43, 44, 46, 112, 147, 169
Troilus and Cressida period 99, 110
Tulaymat, Zaki 15, 34
' 'Twixt Dream and Reality' 42, 50

Tyre 53

UAR 79
UK 83, 95, 114, 165-6, 169
Umm Atiya ('Fate of a Cockroach') 102, 103, 104
UN 173, 181
'Under the Green Lamp' 49, 52, 138, 181
UNESCO 79, 83, 86, 107, 173
USA 166, 169, 176
Uzbakiyya Gardens 8
 Theatre 94

'Variety of Theatre, A' 73, 80, 105, 181
Vautier 86
Venus ('Pigmalyun') 50, 51, 52
Verne, Jules 92
Vernet, Juan 42, 197
Victoria, Queen 141, 166
Vietnam 169
Voltaire 27, 58, 59, 188, 193
Von Grunebaum, G.E. 196

Wafd 12, 24
Wahba, Sa^{c}ad ad Din 187
Wahbi, Yusuf 9, 21, 73, 115, 149, 187, 205, 206, 207
Wanus, Sa^{c}ad Allah 107 fn
'War versus Peace' 135
wazir ('Shahrazad') 30, 32
'The Wedding Night' 22 fn, 105
Wells, H.G. 13, 92
The West 166, 191, 194
'When We Dead Awake' 51
Wiet, Gaston 26

Wigdan ('Her Majesty') 151
Wilde, Oscar 13, 33, 188, 189
Wilson, President Woodrow 169
Women's Union 41, 43

Yamlikha ('The Cavemen') 26,
    34, 119, 120, 121, 122, 124,
    126, 165
Yeats, W. B. 59
Yemeni civil war 112-3
Yokoi, Sergeant 122

Zaghlul, Sa^{c}ad 6, 12, 27, 28,
    195
Zaki, Amal Amin 179
Az Zaman, Badi 106
  'Zaynab' 12, 16, 27
  Ziza ('A Life is Wrecked') 137
  'Zuqaq al Midaqq' 82